IMAGES
of America

Brewing in Delaware

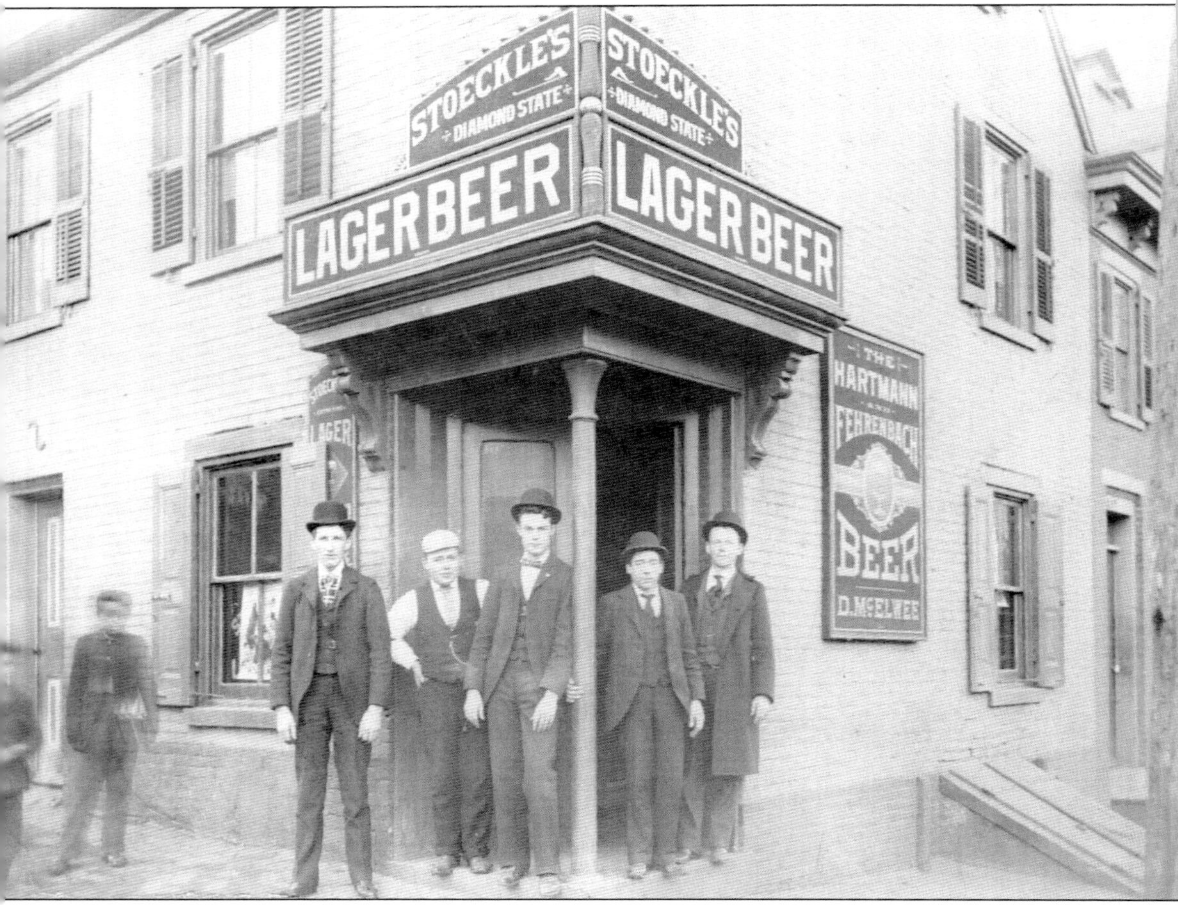

DANIEL McELWEE'S SALOON, C. 1890. From the earliest days, most beer was purchased on draft and consumed at local taverns and saloons. Until the implementation of Prohibition in 1920, taprooms were the very lifeblood of the brewing industry. Pictured here is Daniel McElwee's saloon, located on the northeast corner of Fifth and Tatnall Streets in Wilmington, Delaware. McElwee operated the Emmett House Hotel at this location from just after the Civil War until about 1872 and then reopened the saloon from about 1892 until 1899. (Delaware Historical Society.)

ON THE COVER: DIAMOND STATE BREWERY. This mid- to late-1930s photograph shows workers filling beer kegs in the storeroom of the Diamond State Brewery at Fifth and Adams Streets in Wilmington. The revival of the brewing industry after the repeal of Prohibition resulted in a transition in the way beer was stored and dispensed, as wooden kegs yielded to more reliable, easier to sterilize metal vessels. (Delaware Historical Society.)

IMAGES
of America

BREWING IN DELAWARE

John Medkeff Jr.

ARCADIA
PUBLISHING

ISBN 978-1-4671-2368-6

Published by Arcadia Publishing
Charleston, South Carolina

Printed in the United States of America

Library of Congress Control Number: 2014958849

For all general information, please contact Arcadia Publishing:
Telephone 843-853-2070
Fax 843-853-0044
E-mail sales@arcadiapublishing.com
For customer service and orders:
Toll-Free 1-888-313-2665

Visit us on the Internet at www.arcadiapublishing.com

To my dear late grandfather William B. McGough, who inspired my passion for history and gave me that first sip of warm Ballentine beer.

Contents

ACKNOWLEDGMENTS

This book would not have been possible without the generous cooperation and support of the Delaware Historical Society; Hagley Museum and Library; the Wilmington Library; the Library of Congress; and the Delaware Public Archives. Special thanks to photographer Frank Brevoort III and editor Donna Brown. Others who provided valuable assistance include, in no particular order, Larry Handy and the East Coast Breweriana Association, Dale Van Wieren and the American Breweriana Association, the National Brewery Museum, Trudy Gilgenast and the Delaware Saengerbund and Library Association, the late Ernest Oest, the family of Hulett "Gus" Kincaid Jr., Jacob Kalb, Richard McElwee, Bob Kay Beer Labels, William H. Day, James Prettyman, Larry and Ruby Wood, Edward Sobocinski, Harry Rogerson, Norman Buckalew, Scott Bieber, Joseph R. "Joebob" Jacobs, Robert Fullmer, Jordan Dougherty, Michael Dixon, Standard Distributing Company, Delaware Art Museum, University of Pennsylvania Press, Karen Baumgartner, New Castle Historical Society, Kansas State Historical Society, National Gallery of Art, Doris Dunn and the Beer Institute, Jeffrey Johnson, David Dietz, Stewart's Brewing Company, Dogfish Head Craft Brewery, Iron Hill Brewery, Twin Lakes Brewing Company, Fordham and Dominion Brewing Company, 16 Mile Brewing Company, 3rd Wave Brewing Company, Mispillion River Brewing Company, Argilla Brewing Company, Blue Earl Brewing Company, Pizza by Elizabeths, WDEL 1150AM radio, *Out and About* magazine, Jay Brady, Richard Wachtel, the late Sally MacLeod Stoeckle, Robin and David Doody, Richard Wagner, Susan K. Appel, Jessop's Tavern, Cindy Small, Scott Palmer, and Friends of Historic Riverview Cemetery. Last, but certainly not least, thank you to the loves of my life, my wife, Tina, and my son, Logan, for their sacrifice and constant encouragement.

The images in this volume appear courtesy of the author (Author's collection), Bob Kay Beer Labels (BKBL), Frank Brevoort III (FB), the Delaware Historical Society (DHS), Delaware Public Archives (DPA), Edward Sobocinski (ES), the family of Hulett "Gus" Kincaid Jr. (HK), Hagley Museum and Library (HML), Jacob Kalb (JK), the Library of Congress (LOC), Larry and Ruby Wood (LRW), National Brewery Museum and photographer Ernest Oest (NBM), William H. Day (WHD), Wilmington Public Library (WPL), and institutions and individuals as otherwise noted.

The painting *Johan Printz, First Governor of Delaware* is from *The Dutch and Swedes on the Delaware* by Christopher Ward (Philadelphia: University of Pennsylvania Press, 1930), N.C. Wyeth (1882–1945), watercolor and gouache on illustration board, 13.25 by 11.5 inches, Delaware Art Museum, gift of Marion D. Higgins, 1953, ©University of Pennsylvania Press. (UPP.)

Introduction

What has been is what will be,
and what has been done is what will be done,
and there is nothing new under the sun.
Is there a thing of which it is said,
"See, this is new"?
It has been already
in the ages before us.

—Book of Ecclesiastes 1:9–10

Ecclesiastes reminds us that there is no greater prologue than the past. That is certainly the case with beer and the brewing industry that grew up around it over the centuries.

Today, in Delaware and across the United States, craft beer has become something of a cultural phenomenon, a thriving commercial enterprise, an important economic driver, a source of tourism, and point of local pride. Since the early 2000s, the first state has become increasingly more recognized for its breweries and beer culture. Led by the inventive Dogfish Head Craft Brewery of Milton, breweries in the state continue to garner national and even worldwide attention, regularly winning medals at the Great American Beer Festival and World Beer Cup.

With all of the recent success and well-deserved notoriety experienced by Delaware's breweries, it is easy to believe that much of what is happening now is happening for the first time. While that is certainly true in some respects, in others it has simply been a case of the past repeating itself.

Brewing was one of Delaware's first occupations and among its earliest commercial ventures, having begun with Swedish settlers at Fort Christina in the late 1630s. It would take 250 years, but brewing eventually evolved into one of the most profitable industries in the state. By 1900, brewing and its allied industries accounted for more than $2 million in revenue and hundreds of jobs. Flashing forward to 2012, beer production would contribute nearly $83 million to Delaware's economy. In 2010, the state's tourism office created the Delaware Beer, Wine, and Spirits Trail, as it recognized beer's cultural and economic significance.

Delaware's craft brewers have made reputations for themselves not only by expertly producing traditional ales and lager styles, but also by introducing new flavors to beer using uncommon ingredients. In fact, creativity has been the hallmark of brewers for centuries. The lack of available raw materials often forced the state's 17th-century Swedish and Dutch settlers to improvise by supplementing the ales they made with native fermentables such as persimmons, pumpkins, gourds, and Indian corn. They sometimes spiced their beer with birch, sassafras, spruce, and myrtle when hops were in short supply or could not otherwise be procured. In the mid-19th century, German immigrants to America introduced what were then unique and unusual beer styles, lager and weiss, and the former helped popularize the country's culture and revolutionize its brewing industry.

With the encouragement and input of Sam Calagione of Dogfish Head, Al Stewart of Stewart's Brewing Company, and David Dietz of Brandywine Brewing Company, Delaware passed regulations permitting brewpubs to operate in the state in 1995. While the name was new, the concept of brewing beer for on-site consumption certainly was not. Proprietors of Colonial-era taverns were brewing ale for their patrons in the 17th and 18th centuries. Those that brewed the very best tended to be among the most popular locations for meeting and lodging. From the 1850s through the 1870s, a number of Wilmington's German hotel and saloon keepers began brewing lager beer for their patrons. A few of these more successful entrepreneurs would later graduate to owning and operating large-scale commercial breweries in the city.

Rockford Brewing Company's Marty Haugh worked with state legislators in 1995 to remove repeal-era legal barriers that prevented microbreweries in Delaware. Small-scale production breweries were once the norm rather than the exception in the state. That changed with the emergence of Wilmington's "Big Three"—Hartmann & Fehrenbach, Stoeckle, and Excelsior/Bavarian. These breweries accounted for a significant segment of the beer produced in Delaware from the 1880s until Prohibition in much the same way that Dogfish Head does now. However, when demand has warranted it and regulations have allowed, there have been opportunities both now and then for smaller-scale breweries to successfully operate and thrive within the margins.

The growler, one of the first elements targeted for elimination by early-20th-century temperance groups in the state, has even made its return to Delaware. Customers can once again go to their local brewery, brewpub, retailer, or participating taproom and purchase a jug of fresh locally made beer for home consumption.

Delaware's breweries maintain an esprit de corps not typically found in other industries. In the summer of 2011, they formed the Delaware Brewers Guild as a unifying organization. It is not unusual for Delaware breweries to collaborate on beers, participate together in festivals and charitable community events, and, in a pinch, even assist one another with ingredients. This same level of cooperation and commonality was demonstrated by Wilmington's breweries in the 19th and early 20th centuries, driven largely by their shared heritage. The brewery owners and many of their employees during this era were of German descent, often connected by marriage or membership in church or social groups.

With all of the similarities between beer brewing in the past and present in Delaware, there remains one very clear distinction regarding the location of where it was being produced. The history of the brewing industry in Delaware is largely focused on Wilmington for good reason. With the arrival of waves of European immigrants in the mid- to late 19th century, the city had become the population center of the state. In the days before refrigeration and advanced transportation methods, beer was still very much a locally produced, locally consumed product. Naturally, breweries sprung up around the population center that could sustain them. Absent the technological and travel constraints of the past, beer now can be produced statewide in Delaware. In fact, Sussex and Kent Counties have become the centers for commercial brewing in the state, with New Castle County and the city of Wilmington trailing behind.

In Delaware, much of the state's brewing history prior to 1990 has been forgotten, lost, or otherwise obscured by the histories of more prominent and prolific brewing cultures of nearby cities and states. The First State's beer history was not particularly well documented over time, and no one ever took up the challenge of compiling it. Alas, those associated with the industry prior to 1955 are now gone and their knowledge of the past is forever lost. Hopefully, this book will inspire more scholarly research on the topic and lend a greater appreciation for those Delawareans in the brewing and allied industries who plied their trade in more challenging times.

One

Early Ale Brewing 1638–1849

Swedish, Dutch, and English settlers established the first small commercial breweries in the area that would become the state of Delaware. Still, in the 17th and early 18th century, a significant amount of brewing was being done in homes and taverns throughout the countryside. Brewing, like baking, washing, and other duties, was very much part of women's typical household routines. Larger commercial brewing operations would not be feasible until sufficient centers of population began developing in the 1730s.

Two notable breweries were established in the growing city of Wilmington in the mid- to late 18th century, both of which were also involved in the malting business. The Shipley and Sheward breweries supplied taverns and citizens in Wilmington and the surrounding countryside with casked ale, small beer, and porter. Their malt houses also provided malted barley to brewers and tavern keepers as far away as Philadelphia, Pennsylvania. Others who were employed as professional brewers and malsters during the 18th century included Francis Way of Brandywine Village in Wilmington, Thomas and William Morrison of Christiana Hundred, Samuel Corry of Millcreek Hundred, Ezekiel Boggs of New Castle, Thomas and Benjamin Noxon of Noxontown, and Thomas Parry of Smyrna.

While ale remained vitally important to residents through the post–Revolutionary War period, brewing in Delaware had yet to develop into anything resembling the industry that it would later become. The perishable nature of the product and lack of refrigeration meant that beer had to be consumed fairly quickly and close to sources where it was being brewed. Given Delaware's small population and slow growth through the early 1800s, the need to add breweries simply did not exist. The inconsistent, if not poor, quality of the ale being produced and the seemingly endless availability of cheap cider and mead and more spirituous drinks, like rum, brandy, and whiskey, also tempered the demand for breweries through the first half of the 19th century.

Improvements in transportation, the development of brewing science, and large influxes of immigrant populations to Wilmington in the ensuing decades would dramatically impact brewing and transform a once humble pursuit into a bona fide industry.

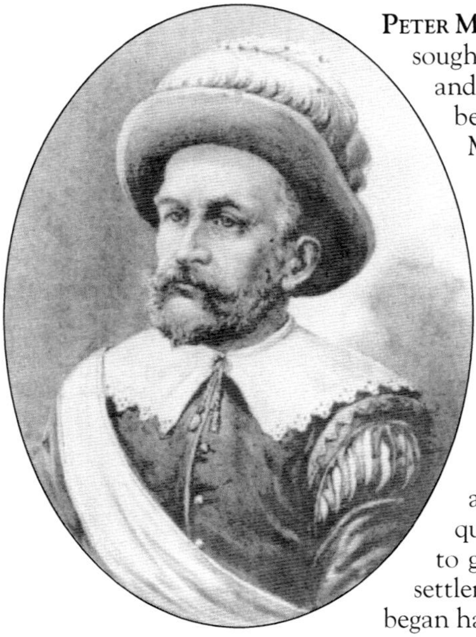

PETER MINUIT. In 1637, emerging world military power Sweden sought to expand its economic reach to the New World and employed Peter Minuit to lead the effort. Minuit is best known for having orchestrated the purchase of Manhattan from the Lenape tribe on behalf of the Dutch West India Company. During his administration as director of New Netherland, construction of the first public brewery in America began at New Amsterdam. (LOC.)

PETER LINDESTRÖM'S MAP OF FORT CHRISTINA, 1655. In March 1638, Minuit and a group of settlers landed at the Rocks in present-day Wilmington, Delaware, and established Fort Christina, named after the Swedish queen. The settlers immediately began planting seed to grow grain for baking and beer brewing. Once the settlement had procured the necessary ingredients, brewing began happening in a very small way at the fort. (DHS.)

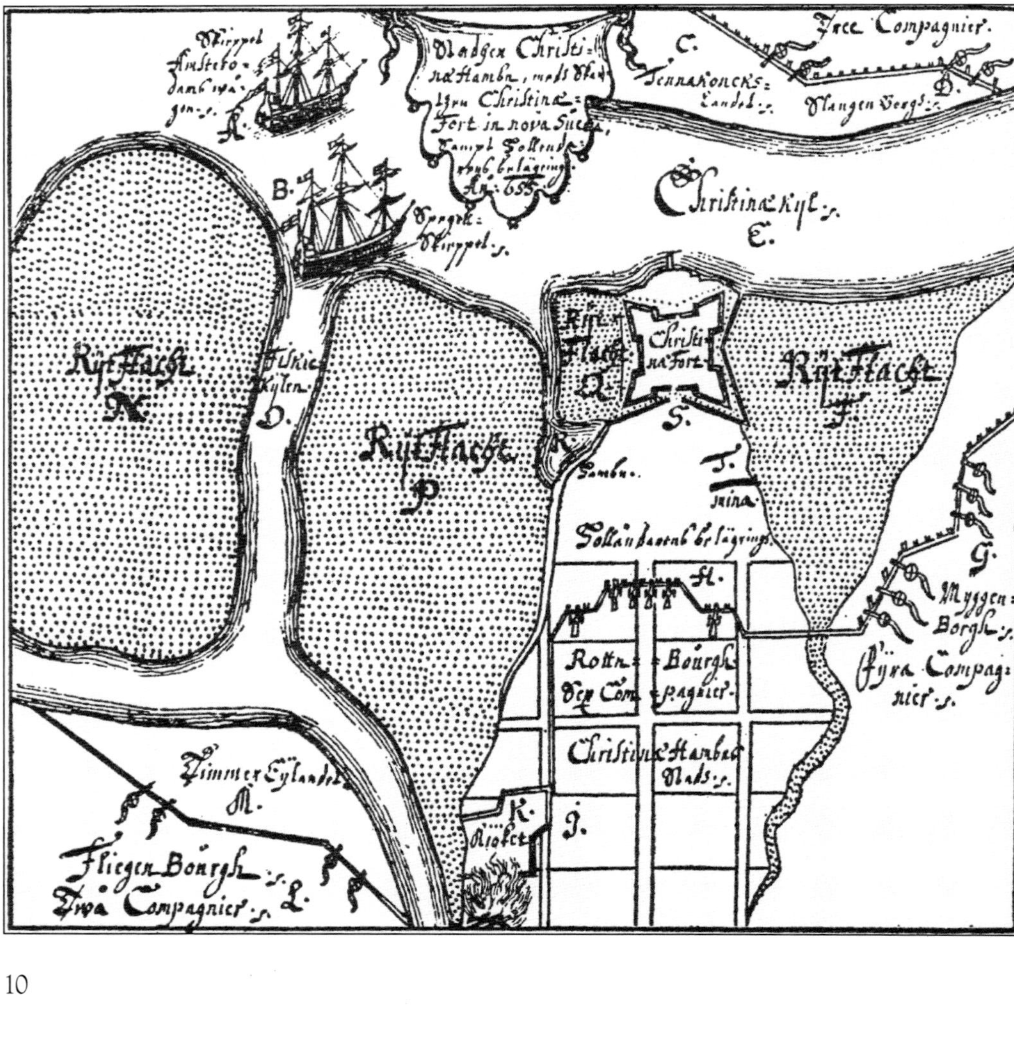

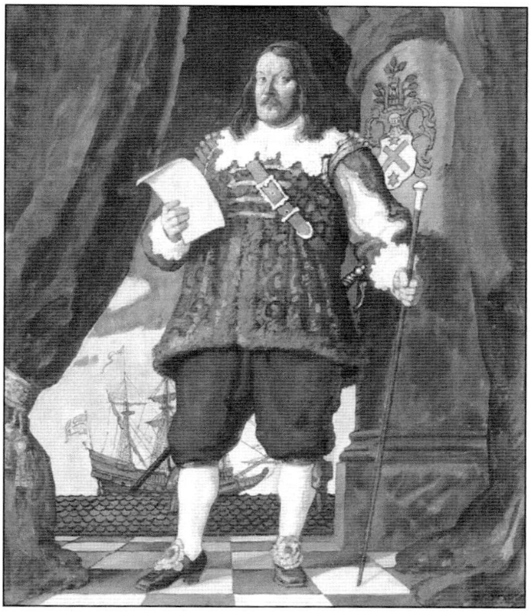

Johan Printz, Governor Of New Sweden by N.C. Wyeth. With the installment of Johan Printz as governor of the Swedish settlement in 1643, the crown's intent shifted from trade to colonization. Printz soon moved New Sweden's command post from Fort Christina upstream to Tinicum Island, where he had Fort New Gothenburg, the manor home Printzhof, and an ale house constructed. In 1648, a large brewing kettle arrived at Fort Christina, and the colony's first dedicated brewery was established there. (UPP.)

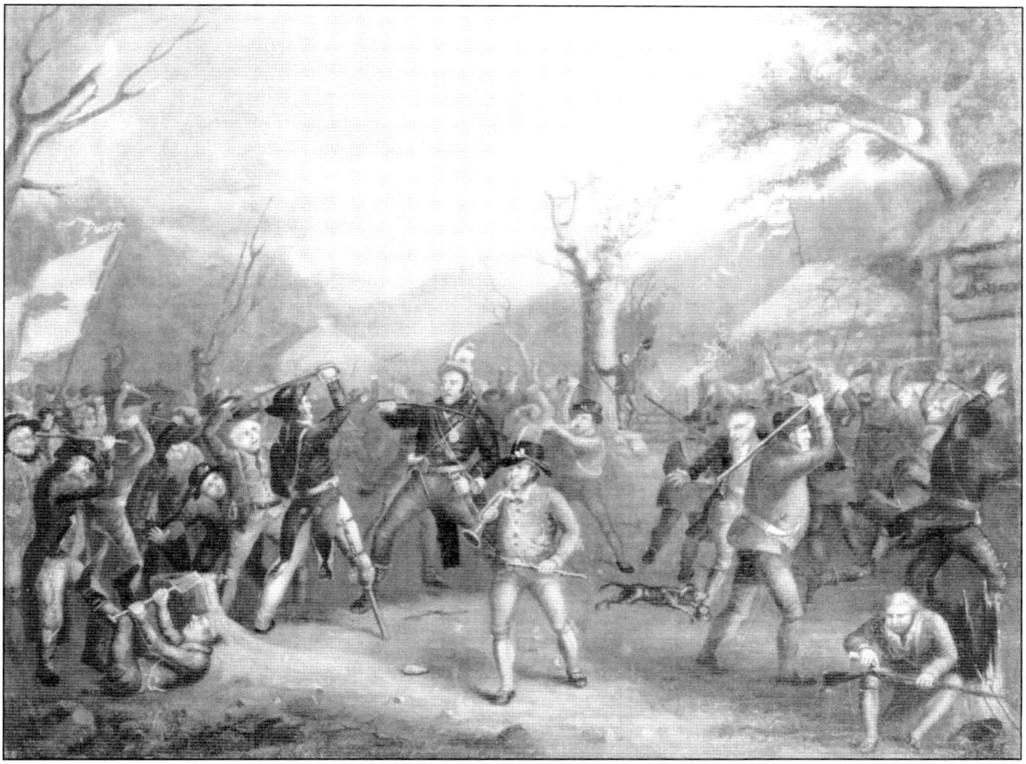

Dutch Invasion of Fort Christina, Artist Unidentified. Johan Risingh arrived as New Sweden's governor in 1654. That year, a special beer was brewed for the Christmas celebration. Risingh had proposed developing hop growing, malting, and brewing into industries of trade for the colony, but those plans would not come to fruition. Peter Stuyvesant's invading Dutch forces captured Fort Christina in 1655. Before surrendering, Risingh vowed to defend the fort until the last barrel of beer was consumed. (DHS.)

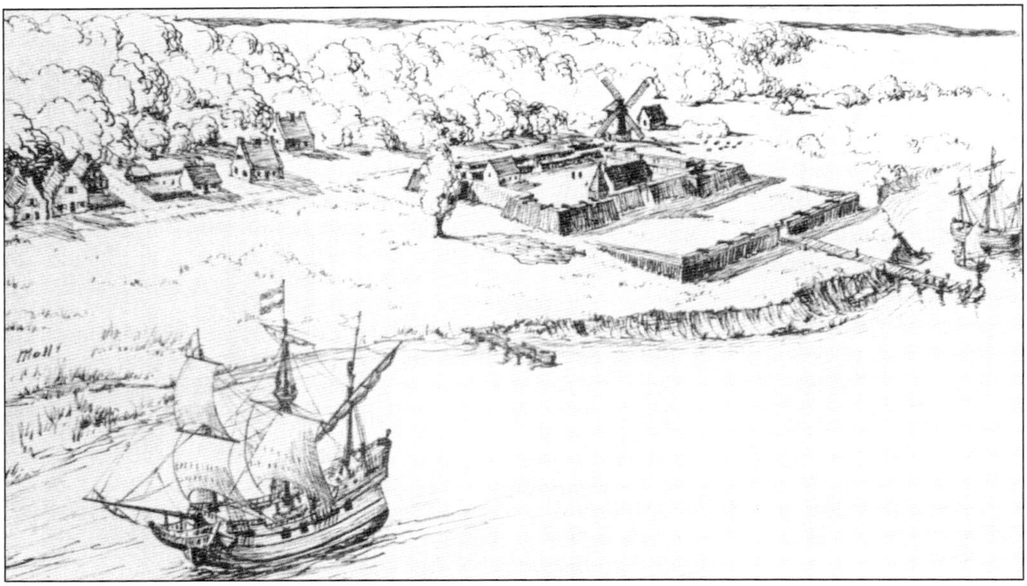

FORT CASIMIR AND NEW AMSTEL, 1655. As part of their conquest of Swedish holdings along the Delaware River, the Dutch reclaimed Fort Casimir at present-day New Castle, which they had surrendered to the Swedes less than a year earlier. Stuyvesant then laid out the village of New Amstel around the fort. The brewing kettle confiscated from the Swedes at Fort Christina was installed in a new brewery at Fort Casimir. (DHS.)

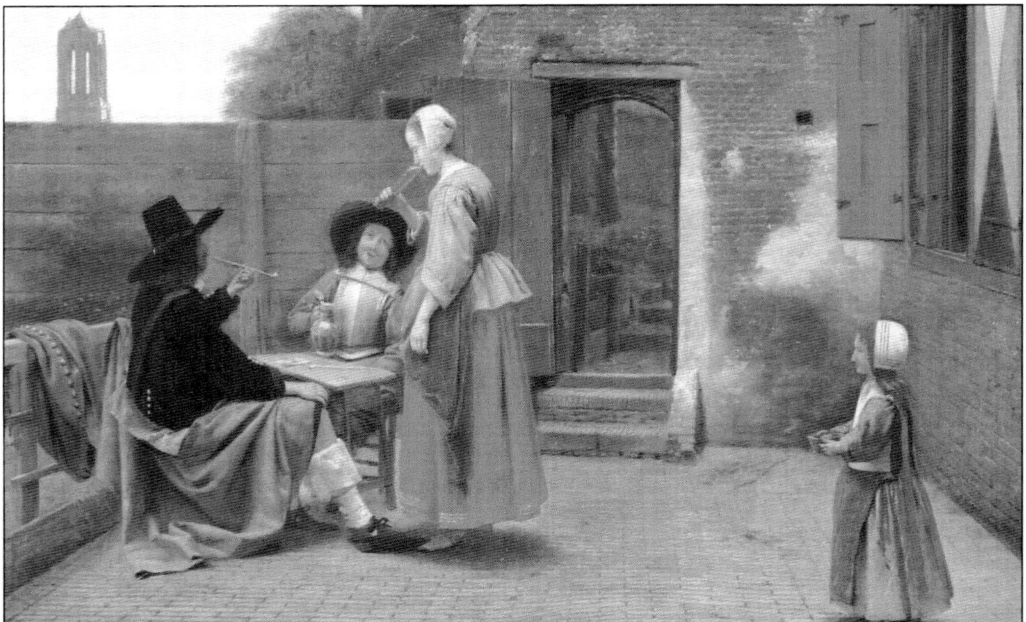

A *DUTCH COURTYARD* BY PIETER DE HOOCH, 1658–1660. The Dutch operated as many as three breweries in New Amstel during their reign from 1655 until 1664. Andries Hudde, Harman Jansen, Hendrick Kip, and Reynier Reynertsen Vandercooley were associated with brewing during their residencies at New Amstel. In addition to supplying the town's residents and village taverns (or ordinaries), the Dutch also traded their ale for tobacco with the English in Maryland, as there were no brewers in that colony. (National Gallery of Art.)

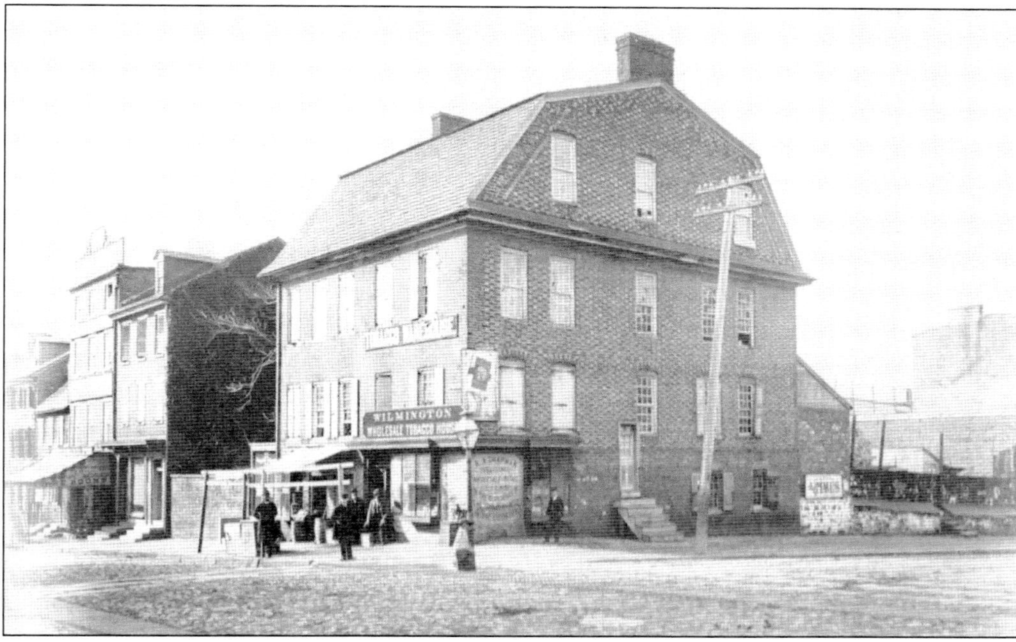

WILLIAM SHIPLEY HOUSE, WILMINGTON, C. 1880. The virtual founder of Wilmington, Quaker William Shipley was among the first to recognize the tiny village of Willingtown's great potential. He relocated from Darby, Pennsylvania, in 1735 to a home he built on the southwest corner of High (Fourth) and Shipley Streets. Shipley not only helped secure the new town of Wilmington's charter, he also served as its first chief burgess (mayor) and was engaged in numerous business enterprises. (DHS.)

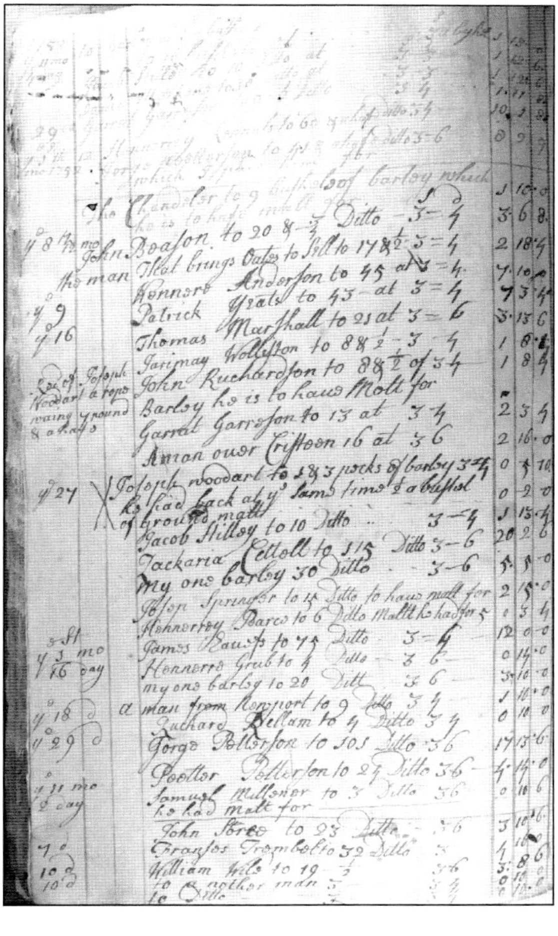

WILLIAM SHIPLEY'S LOG OF MALT SALES, 1752. One of Shipley's chief businesses was a malt house and brewery, which he had strategically constructed on the northwest corner of High and Tatnall Streets to take advantage of a freshwater spring located on the site. Four generations of Shipleys conducted the business, including William Jr., his son Samuel, and grandson Joseph Boone Shipley. A series of proprietors followed them, but the brewery finally closed in the 1830s. (DHS.)

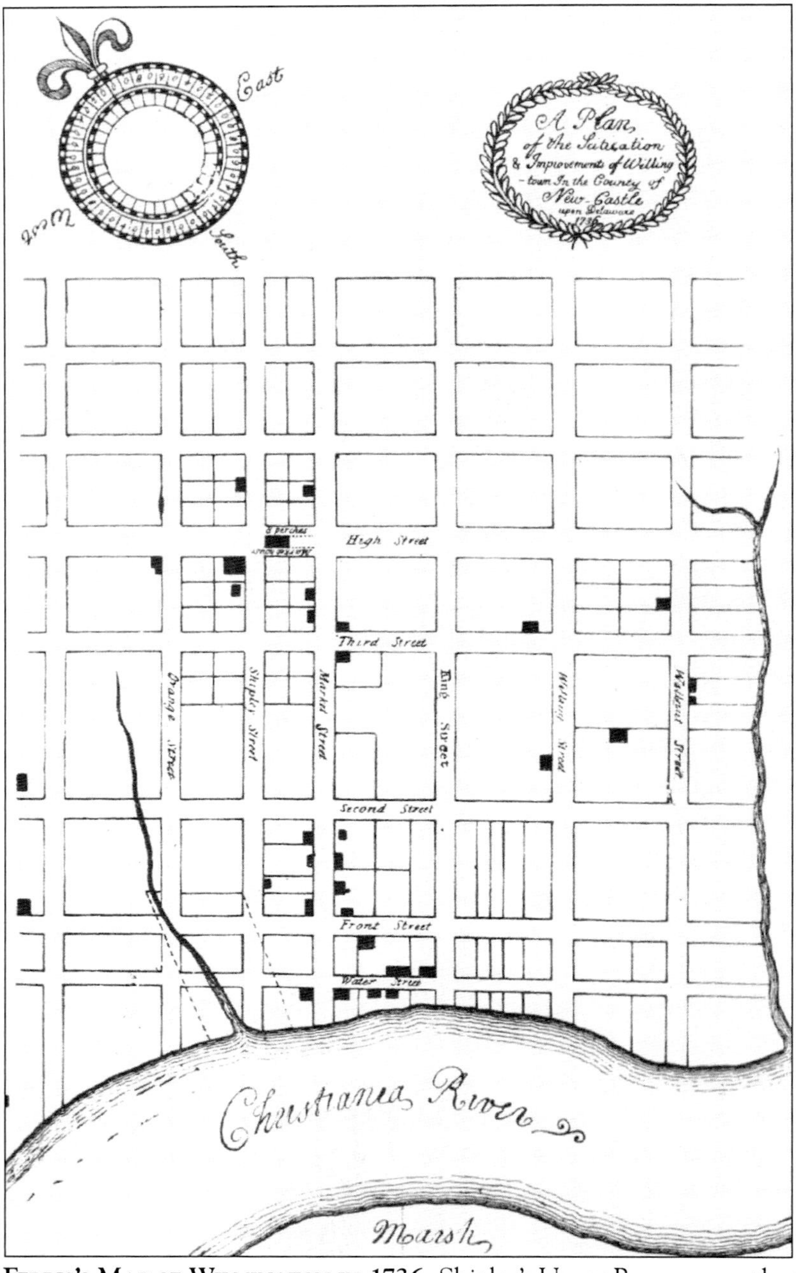

Benjamin Ferris's Map of Wilmington in 1736. Shipley's Upper Brewery was the first, but it would not be the only brewery in Wilmington for long. In the early 1770s, Caleb Sheward built a malt house and brewery on the north side of Second Street, between Orange and Tatnall Streets, two blocks southeast of the Shipley brewery. Sheward likely selected the location due to its proximity to the freshwater source from Shipley's Run, which ran through the property. Sheward's stone brewery was 90 feet long by 50 feet wide. The complex included a stable, stalls, a carriage house, and four small tenements. Upon his death in 1785, Sheward's wife, Hannah, assumed control of the business and turned it over to their son Caleb Jr. in 1805. He was succeeded in the business by his son William, who operated the brewery until closing it for good in 1843, when it was sold to the Plunkett Distillery. (DHS.)

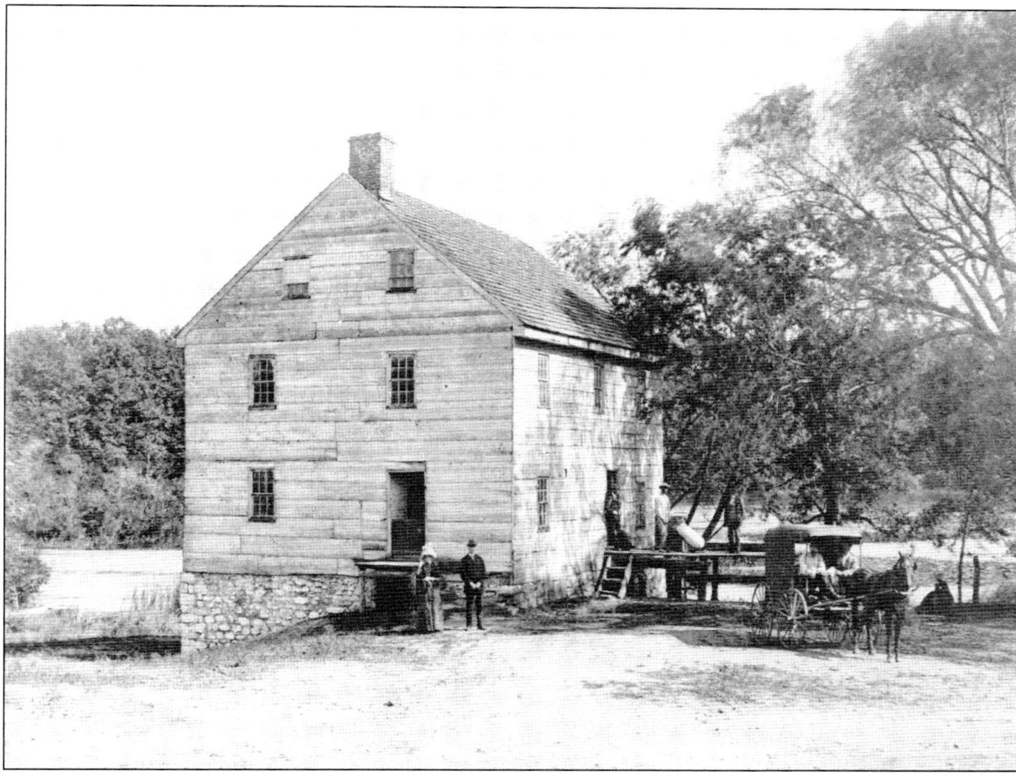

NOXON MILL, MIDDLETOWN, C. 1890. In 1740, Thomas Noxon built a trading and milling center at the head of the Appoquinimink River, near present-day Middletown. A community called Noxontown grew up around the complex, which contained Noxons' dwelling and a gristmill, hotel, bake house, malt house, and brewery. After Noxon's death in 1743, his son Benjamin inherited his estate. He appears to have sold off the brewery and malt house in 1757 or 1758. (LOC.)

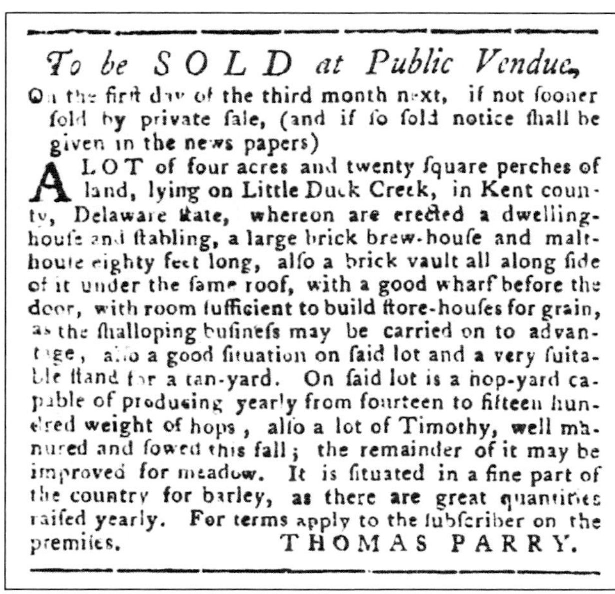

To be SOLD *at Public Vendue,*

On the first day of the third month next, if not ſooner ſold by private ſale, (and if ſo ſold notice ſhall be given in the news papers)

A LOT of four acres and twenty ſquare perches of land, lying on Little Duck Creek, in Kent county, Delaware ſtate, whereon are erected a dwelling-houſe and ſtabling, a large brick brew-houſe and malt-houſe eighty feet long, alſo a brick vault all along ſide of it under the ſame roof, with a good wharf before the door, with room ſufficient to build ſtore-houſes for grain, as the ſhalloping buſineſs may be carried on to advantage, alſo a good ſituation on ſaid lot and a very ſuitable ſtand for a tan-yard. On ſaid lot is a hop-yard capable of producing yearly from fourteen to fifteen hundred weight of hops, alſo a lot of Timothy, well manured and ſowed this fall; the remainder of it may be improved for meadow. It is ſituated in a fine part of the country for barley, as there are great quantities raiſed yearly. For terms apply to the ſubſcriber on the premiſes. THOMAS PARRY.

PENNSYLVANIA PACKET ADVERTISEMENT, DECEMBER 19, 1778. In the 1770s, Thomas Parry had a brick malt house and brewery located along Little Duck Creek, near present-day Smyrna. He produced a sufficient supply of hops and barley on his farm adjacent to the brewery. It is not known what happened to the brewery after Parry sold the property around 1779. (Author's collection.)

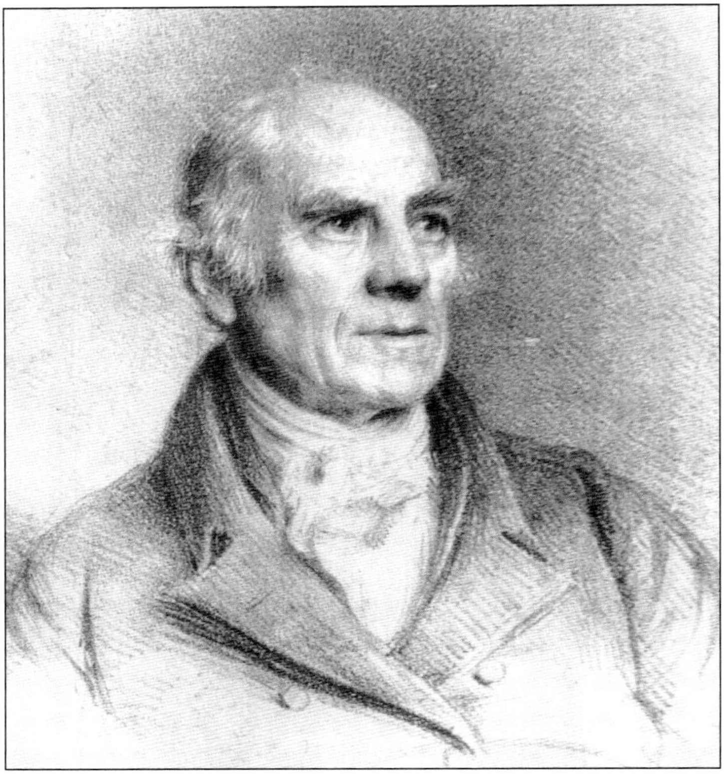

Archibald Hamilton Rowan. Rowan was an Irish firebrand who risked his fortune in support of political causes to unite Ireland. His radical political views ultimately led to imprisonment in 1794. Rowan soon escaped and sought exile in the United States, eventually finding his way to Wilmington. After his calico-printing plant along the Brandywine failed, Rowan resorted to hauling grain and flour for local millers using his wheelbarrow. (DHS.)

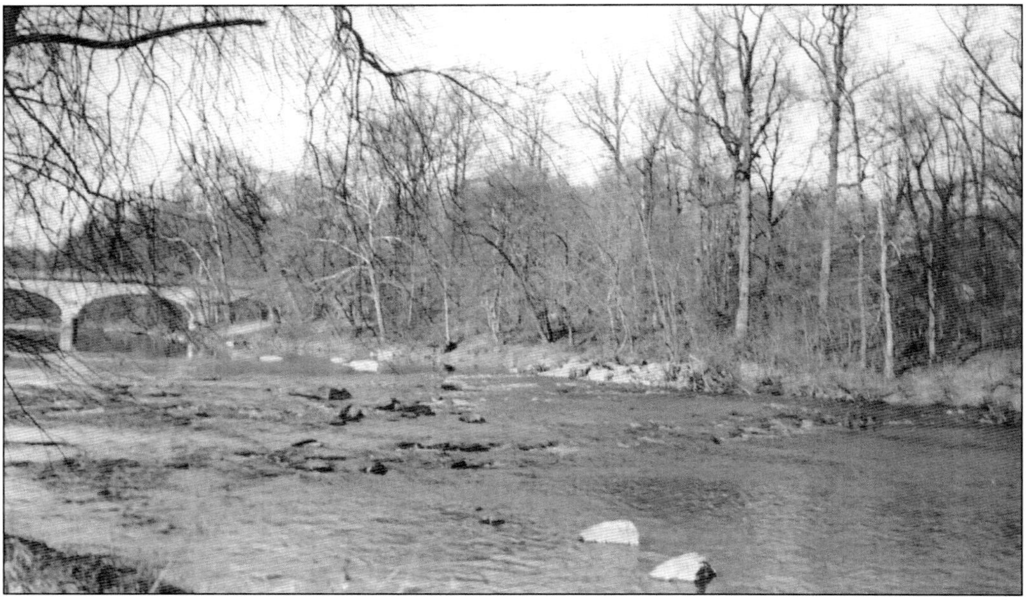

Site of the Old Barley Mill along Brandywine Creek, 1940. Rowan took to brewing spruce beer in a single copper kettle at his home next to the Old Barley Mill to supplement his meager income. He used his trusty wheelbarrow as a beer-delivery wagon, hawking his product through the streets of Wilmington. Rowan's wife eventually secured his departure to Europe in 1799. In 1806, Rowan's passage back to Ireland was cleared, and he returned to his wife and a hero's welcome. (HML.)

Two

Golden Age of Brewing 1850–1919

Social, religious, and economic changes occurring throughout the German states, particularly during the Revolutions of 1848, resulted in a flood of immigration to America. Hundreds of Germans came to the burgeoning city of Wilmington seeking work in the shipyards, carriage-building shops, and tanneries. Lager beer, a beloved drink back in the fatherland, was introduced in Delaware in 1850. Lager's effervescent and thirst-quenching qualities made it an immensely popular drink with Wilmington's working class, German and non-German alike.

Once they had the available means, Wilmington's enterprising Germans began opening saloons, hotels, and restaurants to take advantage of lager's popularity. A few of these men would learn the art of brewing and begin making their own lager and porter for patrons. Among this group, the Nebeker brothers, John Fehrenbach, and Joseph Stoeckle would eventually graduate to running the state's first large-scale commercial breweries in the years preceding and immediately following the Civil War.

The introduction of artificial refrigeration in the 1870s allowed lager beer to be brewed year-round and become more than just a seasonal alternative to porter and other ales. Improvements to rail transport; advances in brewing science, particularly the pasteurization process in the 1880s; and the emergence of advertising would soon transform brewing into a bona fide industry. By 1900, brewing was Wilmington's sixth most valuable industry.

The Hartmann & Fehrenbach, Stoeckle, and Bavarian Breweries dominated the Delaware industry from 1881 until 1919. Several other smaller firms operated as well during this period, both in and outside of Wilmington, though none could compete for long.

Since regulations did not prohibit it, Wilmington's Big Three breweries controlled the distribution of their products and often had direct stakes in hotels, saloons, bottling houses, and liquor retailer stores. The brewers failed to recognize the serious negative social impacts their products were having until it was too late. By the first decade of the 1900s, the temperance movement had gained political strength in Delaware and nationally. The "drys" swayed public opinion in their favor and won important battles along the way, ultimately leading to the implementation of Prohibition nationwide in 1920.

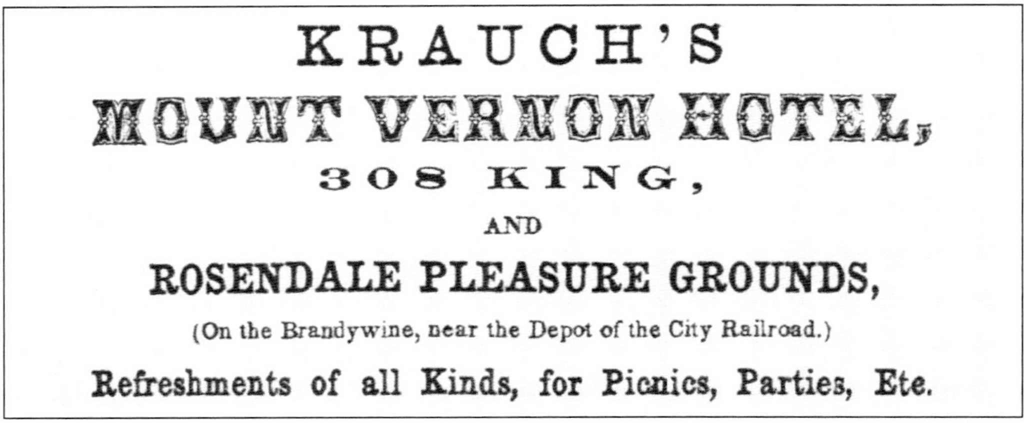

WILMINGTON CITY DIRECTORY ADVERTISEMENT, 1865. Christian Krauch arrived in Philadelphia from Germany in 1834 and began brewing beer at his tavern. By 1850, he made his way south to the burgeoning city of Wilmington and opened the first lager beer saloon in the state at 70 King Street. In 1857, Krauch, affectionately dubbed the "Father of Lager Beer" in Wilmington, moved his saloon and brewery to a more commodious location at 308 King Street. (WPL.)

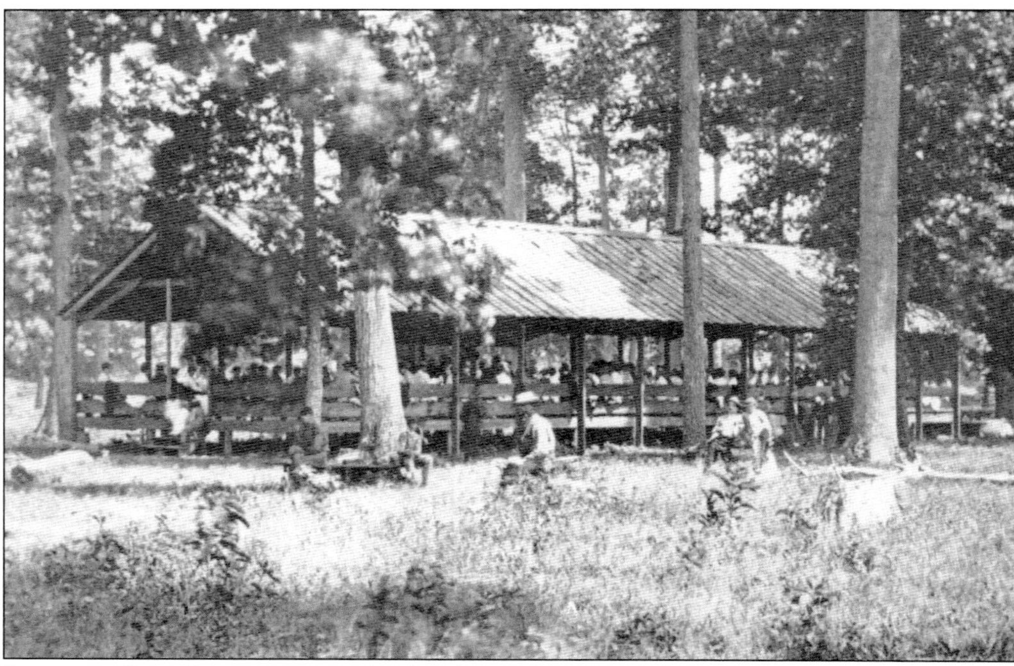

ROSENDALE PARK PAVILION, C. 1880. After the Civil War, Krauch moved his business to the western edge of the city and began operating the Manitoex Saloon at Rosendale Pleasure Grounds, just south of the Brandywine River and Rattlesnake Run, near DuPont Street and Lovering Avenue. The park hosted weekend entertainment, picnics, and other special events. Christian Krauch remained at Rosendale Park until just before his death in November 1870. (DHS.)

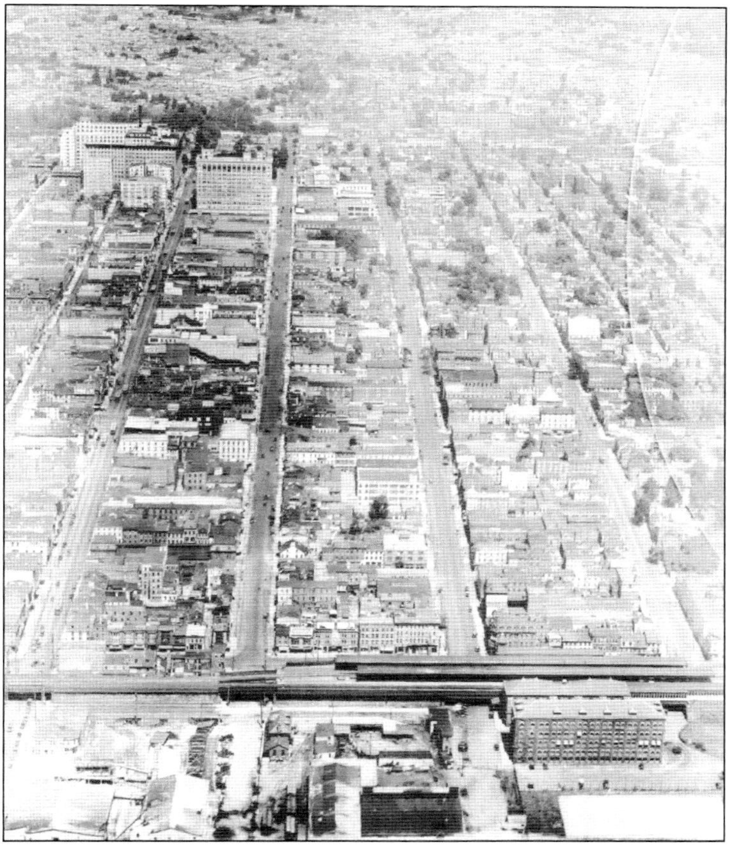

Aerial View from the Christina River, 1925. King and French Streets, featured in the center of this photograph, were the centers of German life and culture in Wilmington during the 1850s through the early 1900s. Not only were dozens of lager-beer saloons and other German-owned businesses located in this area, it was also the location of German meeting halls, social clubs, and a Lutheran church. (HML.)

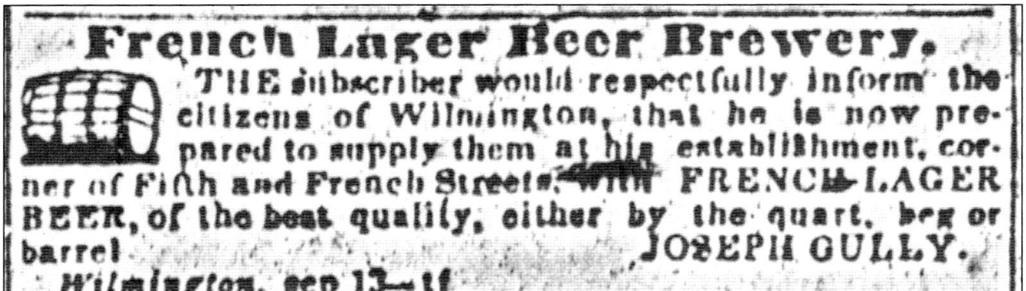

French Lager Beer Brewery.

THE subscriber would respectfully inform the citizens of Wilmington, that he is now prepared to supply them at his establishment, corner of Fifth and French Streets, with FRENCH LAGER BEER, of the best quality, either by the quart, keg or barrel. JOSEPH GULLY.

Wilmington, sep 13—tf

***Blue Hen's Chicken* Advertisement, January 17, 1851.** A native of Alsace, France, brewer Joseph Gully arrived in Wilmington in 1851, proceeding Krauch by about a year. He opened his French Lager Beer Brewery and Saloon at the corner of Fifth and French Streets, which he operated until he removed to Wisconsin in 1856. Before leaving, Gully married Crescentia Stoeckle, the relative of a man whose name would eventually become synonymous with Delaware beer. (WPL.)

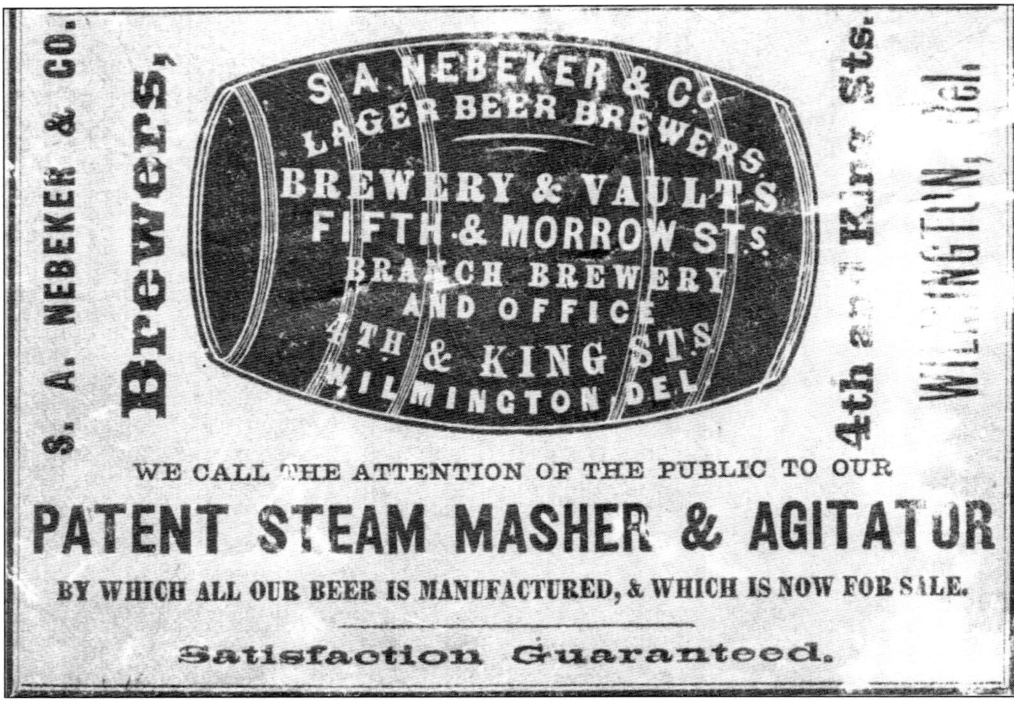

Wilmington City Directory Advertisement, 1866. The first lager brewery in Wilmington was started in 1859 by the Nebeker brothers, Aquilla, George, and Samuel, at the corner of Fifth and Morrow Streets. S.A. Nebeker and Company also maintained a saloon and branch brewery at Fourth and King Streets. Grain rationing, federal taxes, and licensing fees imposed during the Civil War put a strain on the business. By 1871, the Nebekers left brewing to pursue other interests. (WPL.)

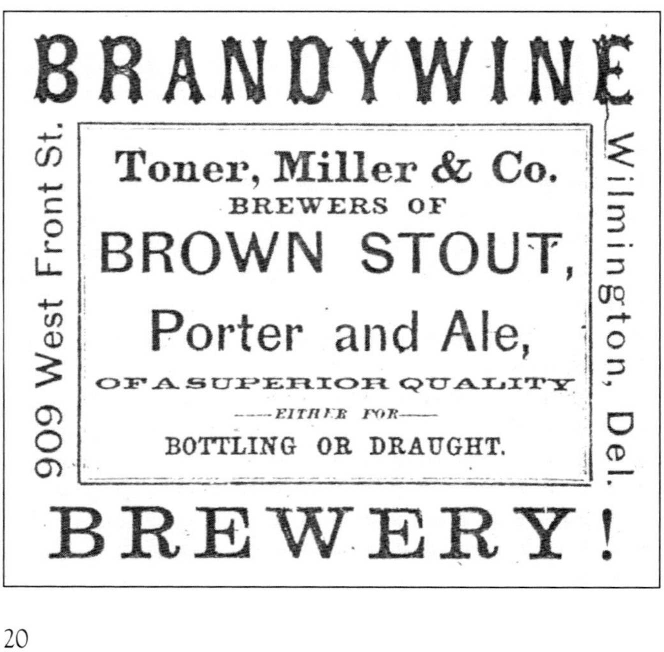

Wilmington City Directory Advertisement, 1868. Although lager was gaining in popularity during the post–Civil War era, there was still a market for quality porter and ale. In 1868, Robert McCabe, John F. Miller, and John J. Toner retooled their vinegar factory at 900 West Front Street and began brewing beer. The brewery operated as DeWitt M. Ogden and Company and later became McCabe and Company, before permanently closing in 1871. (WPL.)

Joel Bryant Bottle. In 1848, Cheshire, New Hampshire, native Joel B. Bryant began his bottling plant and brewery in Wilmington in the basement of the Black Horse Hotel on the southeast corner of Front and Justison Streets. Bryant bottled mineral water and soft drinks and brewed his own brand of mead, porter, ale, and spruce and ginger beers. He moved operations to 609 West Front Street in 1858, retiring in 1883. (JK.)

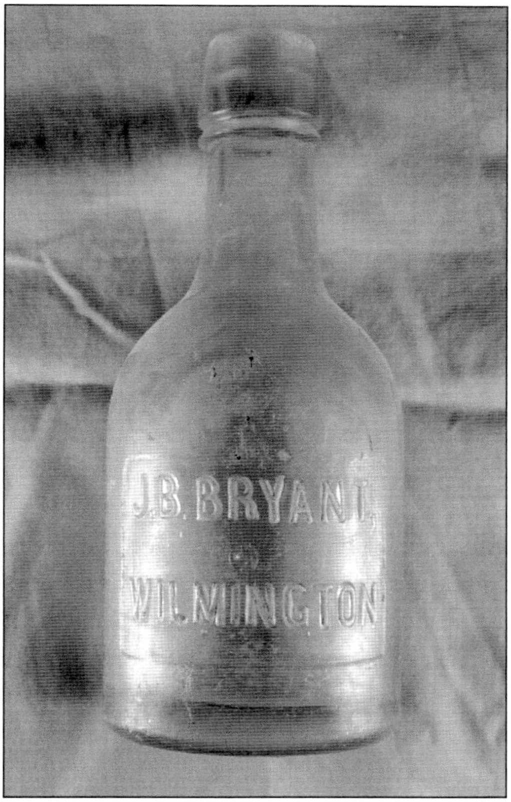

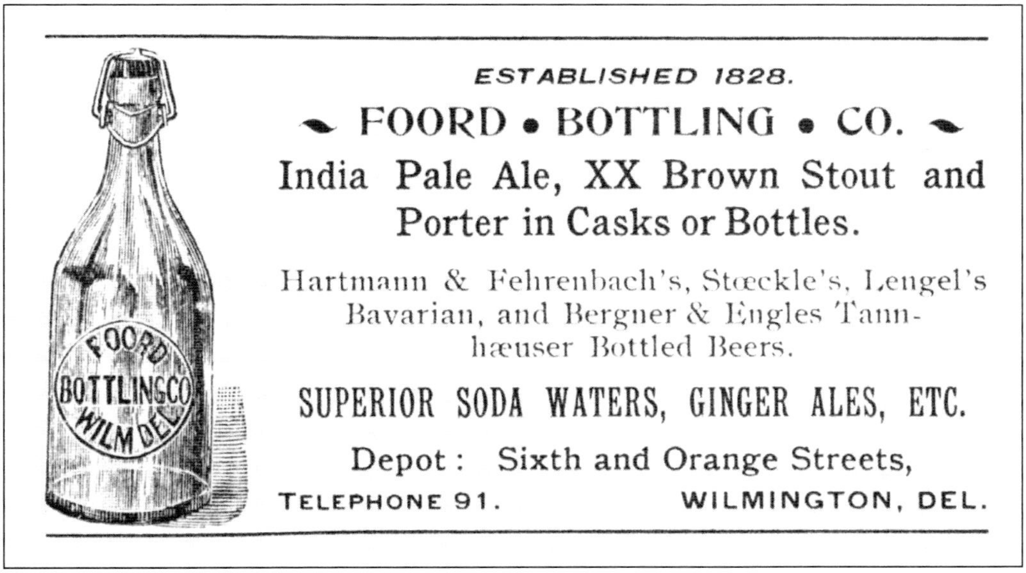

Wilmington City Directory Advertisement, 1893. William Foord founded his bottling works and malt house in Wilmington in 1828 and operated at a few locations along Orange Street until settling at 521 Orange Street about 1858. His son William C. took over in 1870 and grandson William M. succeeded him about 1897, when the business moved to 211–213 West Sixth Street. Though not a brewery, the Foord Bottling Works packaged beer for brewers near and far until it closing during Prohibition. (WPL.)

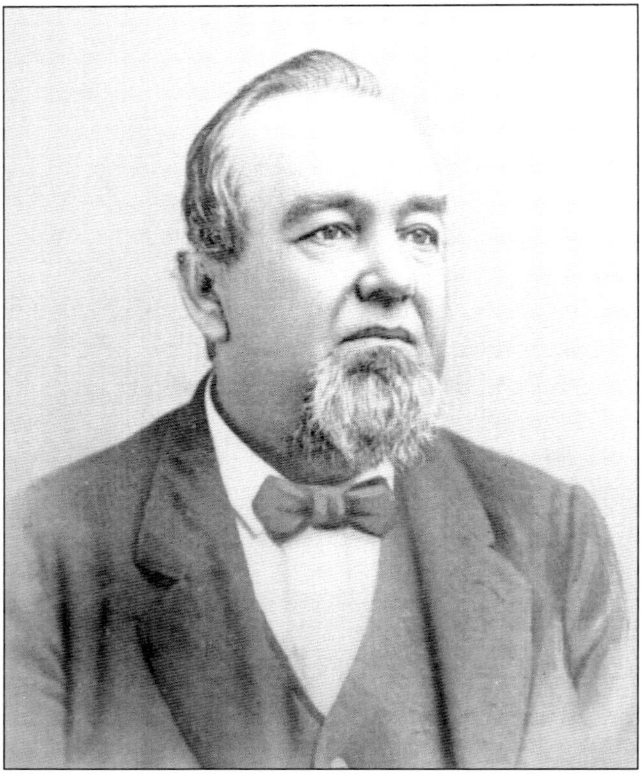

John Fehrenbach. In 1849, eighteen-year-old John Fehrenbach immigrated from Ettenheim, Baden, to Philadelphia and learned the art of brewing while working for Lewis Raab. Fehrenbach moved to Wilmington in 1852 and was employed as a bartender in the lager beer saloons of William Strimple and later Christian Krauch. He returned to Philadelphia in 1854 to open his own lager saloon but not before helping to found a singing club that would become known as the Delaware Saengerbund. (Author's collection.)

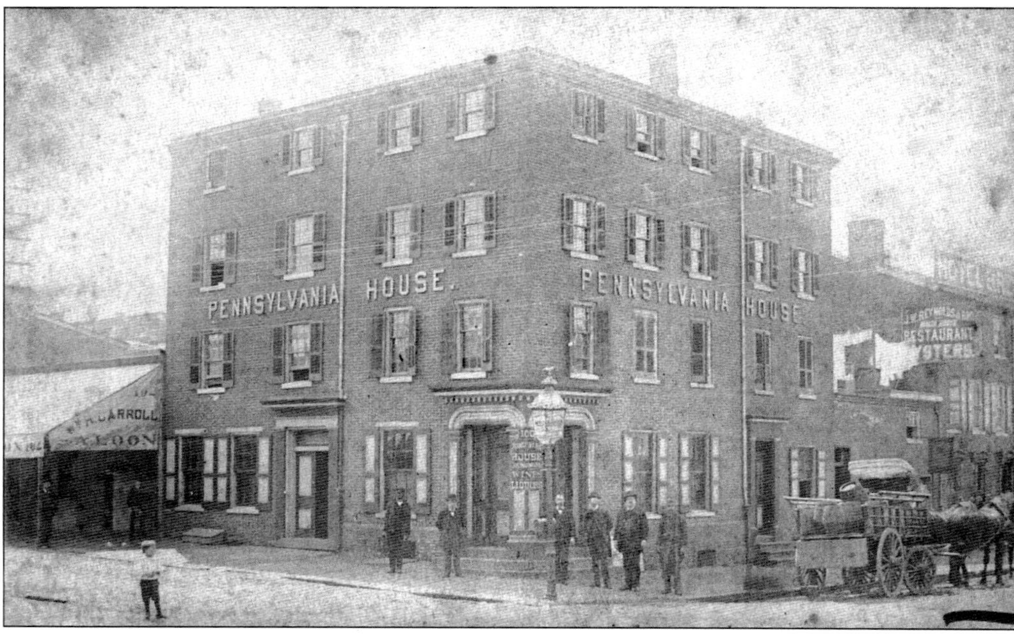

Pennsylvania House Hotel, c. 1885. In this photograph, a brewery dray delivers kegs to the Pennsylvania House, a hotel and saloon located at the southeast corner of Front and King Streets. Proprietor Joseph A. Baumann owned this establishment from 1881 until his retirement in 1893. William Strimple operated one of Delaware's first lager beer saloons at this location in the early 1850s and employed the young Fehrenbach. (DHS.)

John Hartmann. Born in Heidelsheim, Baden, in 1821, John Hartmann arrived in Philadelphia in 1847. He was employed in various capacities for about eight years before starting his tavern. Hartmann made the acquaintance of Theresa Fehrenbach in 1849, soon after her arrival from Germany, and the two married that same year. (Author's collection.)

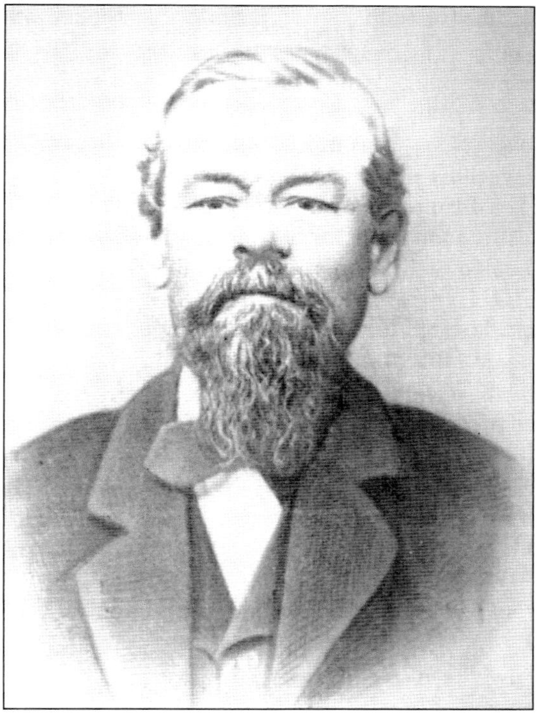

Hartmann & Fehrenbach Brewing Company Sign. Fehrenbach returned to Wilmington in 1860 and began a successful run as proprietor of the Franklin House hotel and saloon at 117 East Fourth Street. Three years later, he built a larger establishment on the northwest corner of Fourth and French Streets, where he began brewing lager beer. In 1865, Fehrenbach enticed his brother-in-law Hartmann to relocate to Wilmington to form a business partnership. (HK.)

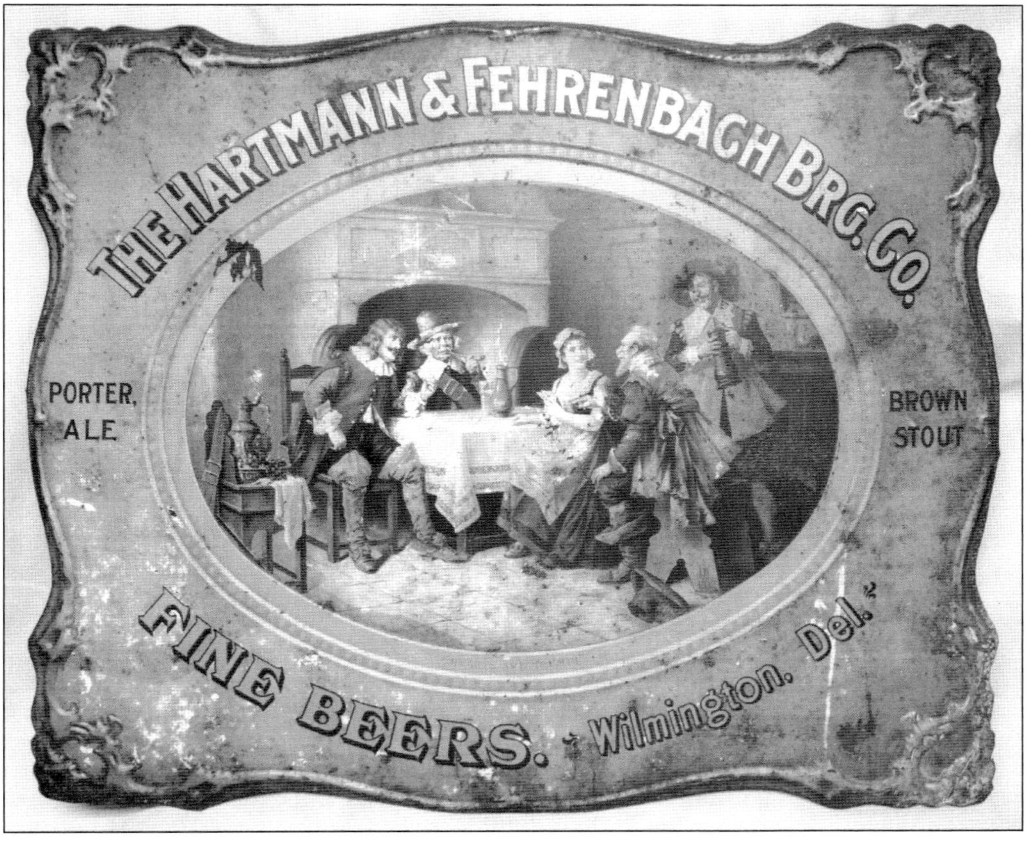

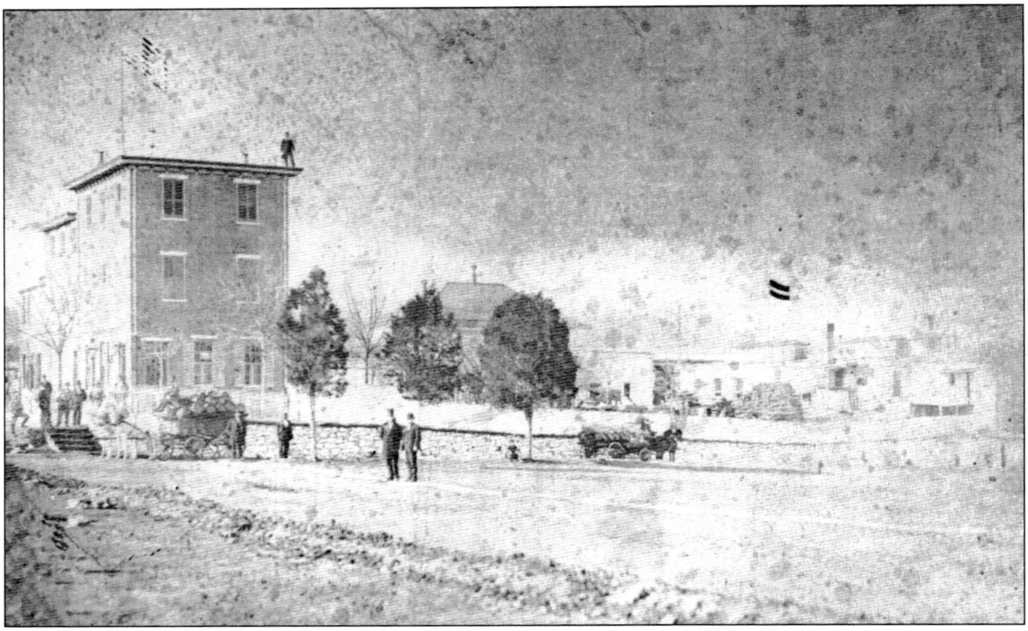

Hartmann & Fehrenbach Brewery, c. 1870. In 1865, Fehrenbach purchased an acre of land at Lovering Avenue and Riddle's Road at Wilmington's western edge for the purpose of constructing a hotel and saloon, which was run by Hartmann. The next year, Hartmann & Fehrenbach constructed its Brandywine Lager Beer Brewery complex behind the hotel at a cost of $60,000. (Author's collection.)

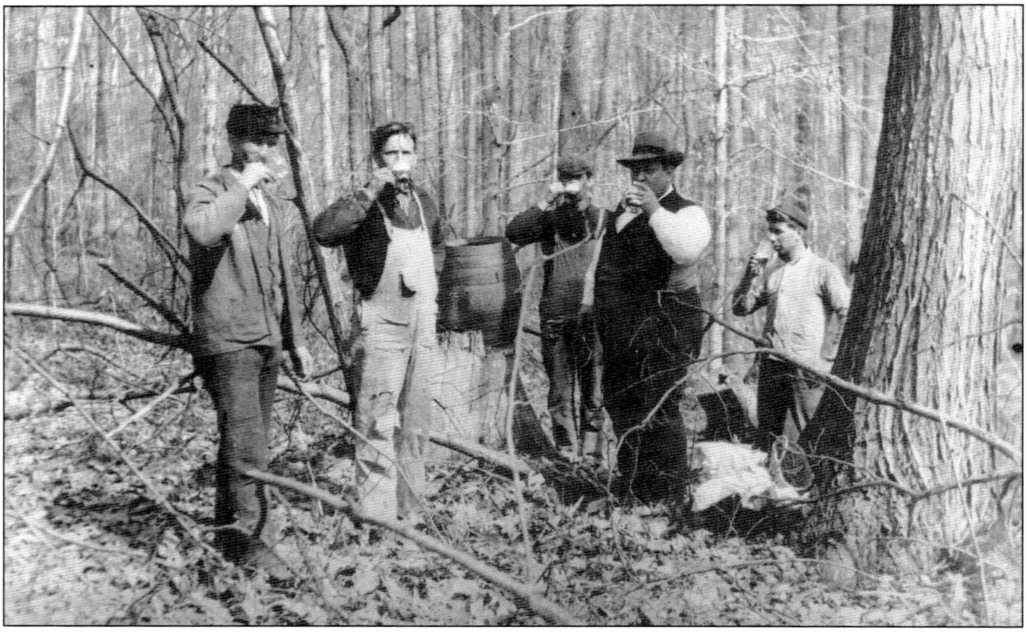

Dupont Powdermen Drinking Beer along the Brandywine, c. 1900. The H&F brewery's location along the Brandywine afforded the company an unlimited supply of water for cleaning and washing. An artesian well 1,100 feet beneath the complex was tapped as a freshwater source for brewing. The brewery, which featured two underground stone storage vaults quarried from Brandywine granite, had an annual production capacity of 3,000 barrels. (HML.)

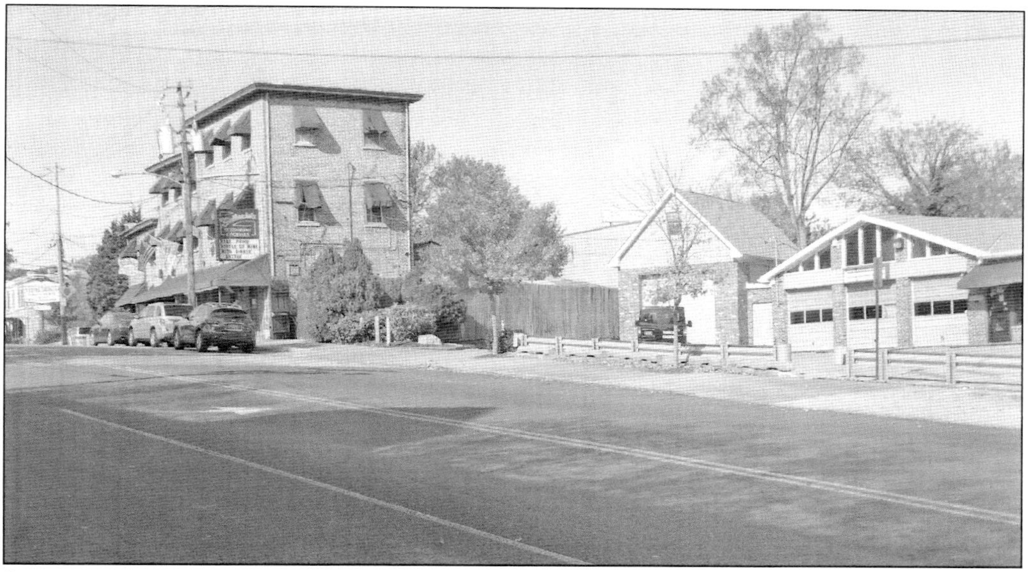

SITE OF THE FORMER HARTMANN & FEHRENBACH BREWERY, 2012. Though all of the original brewery structures have long since been removed, the original hotel and saloon operated by John Hartmann still remains on the north side of Lovering Avenue, near Scott Street. Gallucio's Pub and Restaurant has occupied the historic building since 1972. (Author's collection.)

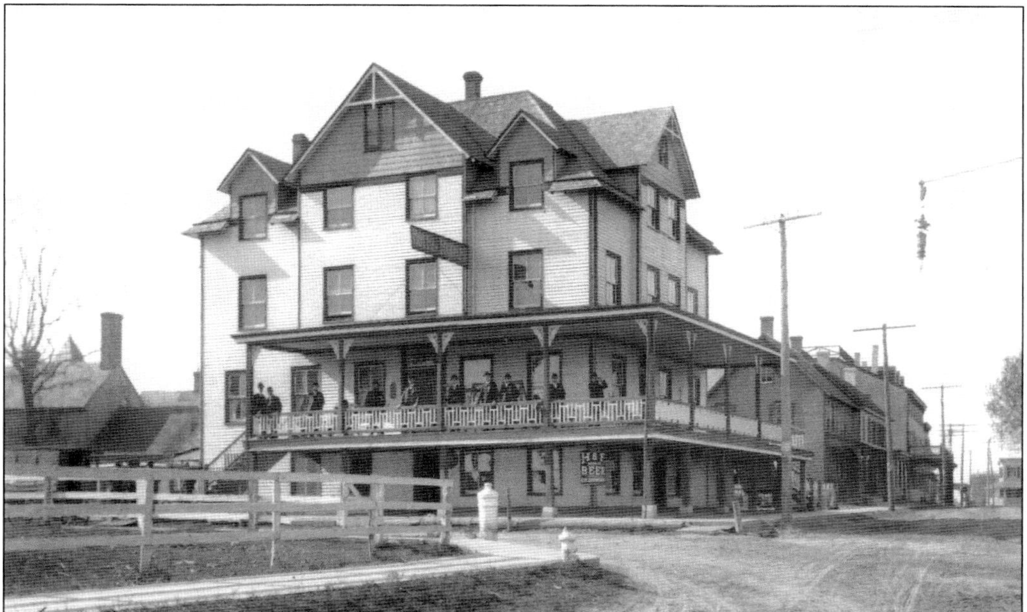

HOTEL RODNEY, LEWES, C. 1900. The Hotel Rodney stood at the corner of Front and South Streets from 1890 until it was destroyed by fire in 1925. As the sign indicates, the Rodney's saloon sold H&F Beer, as did many of their late 18th-century counterparts up and down the Delmarva Peninsula. From its earliest days, Hartmann & Fehrenbach shipped its lager, porter, and brown ale to customers beyond Wilmington. (DHS.)

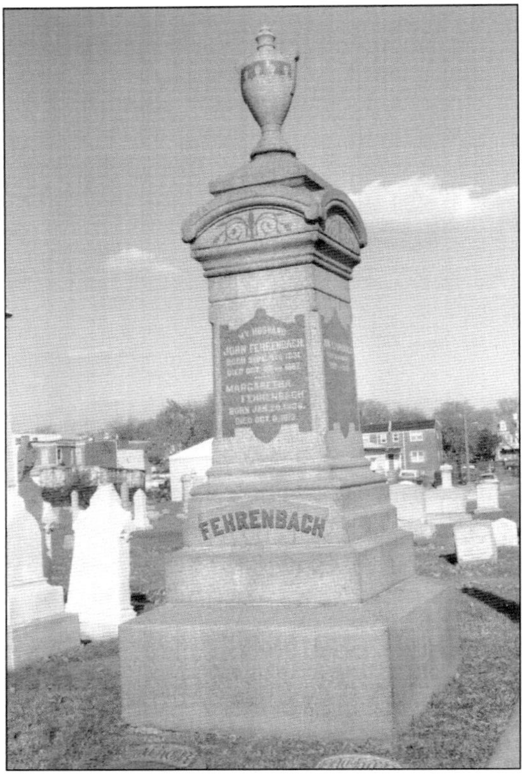

JOHN FEHRENBACH'S MONUMENT, RIVERVIEW CEMETERY, WILMINGTON, 1997. Hartmann & Fehrenbach's brewery, the largest in Delaware at the time, continued to flourish through the 1870s and into the 1880s. By 1885, H&F's annual production had grown to 35,000 barrels. The company made constant capital improvements to meet the rising demand for its products. Its first setback occurred in October 1887 with the death of founder John Fehrenbach. (Author's collection.)

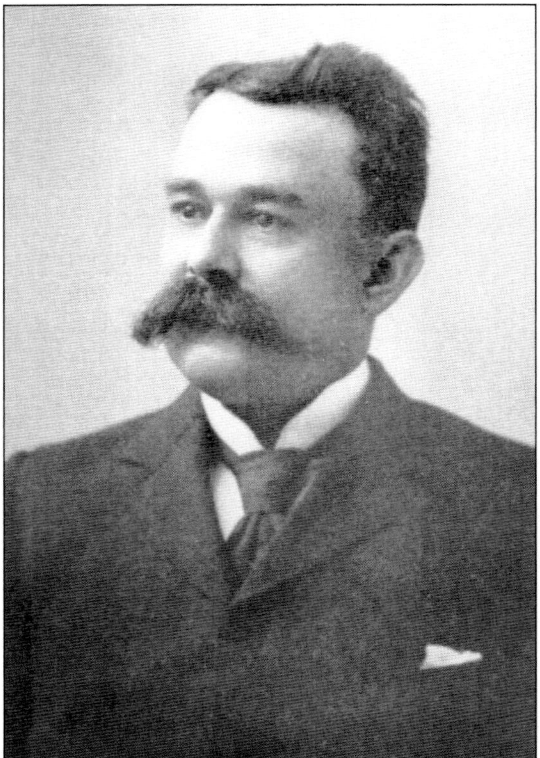

JOHN G. HARTMANN. In 1885, the firm officially incorporated as the Hartmann & Fehrenbach Brewing Company, Inc., with founder Hartmann as president, founder Fehrenbach as vice president and treasurer, and Hartmann's son John G. Hartmann as secretary. The latter also assumed the role of vice president upon founder Fehrenbach's death. (Author's collection.)

J. George Fehrenbach. In 1881, George Fehrenbach entered his father's business as a clerk, and upon his father's death, he became the brewery's treasurer. Fehrenbach later served a stint as H&F's vice president (1890–1893) before settling in as the secretary-treasurer beginning in 1895. He would remain in those roles until his retirement in 1921. For a brief period in the early 1890s, Fehrenbach also conducted a saloon at 203 West Seventh, between Orange and Tatnall Streets. (Author's collection.)

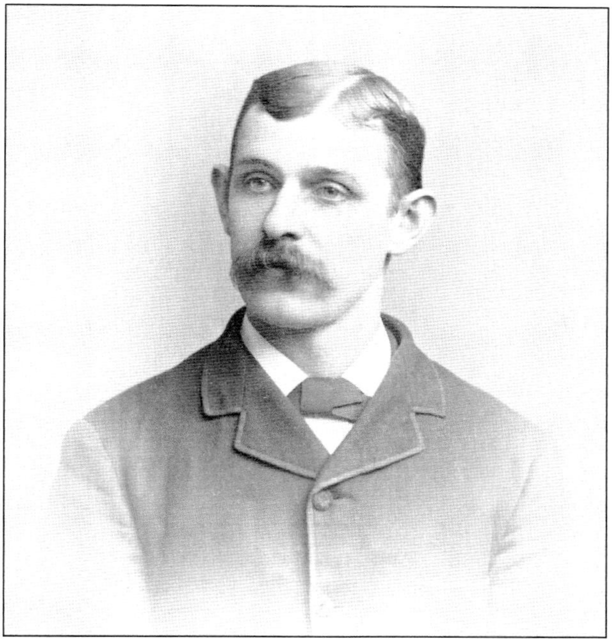

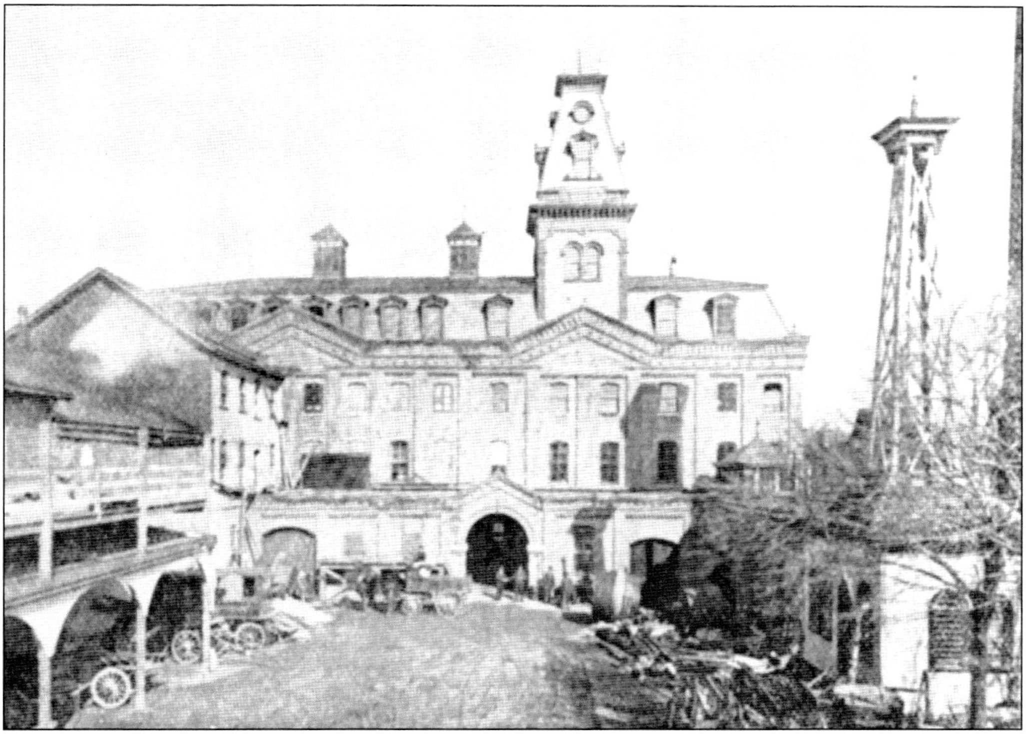

Hartmann & Fehrenbach Brewery, c. 1890. H&F undertook its most significant capital upgrades ever in 1888 when they added a 125-foot-long four-story structure, housing a new brewhouse and cold-storage facility. In addition, the old lagering vaults were retrofitted with a refrigeration machine. The Frederick Wunder–designed building increased the brewery's annual capacity to 75,000 barrels, which, at that time, made it the largest and best-outfitted brewery between Philadelphia and Baltimore, Maryland. (DHS.)

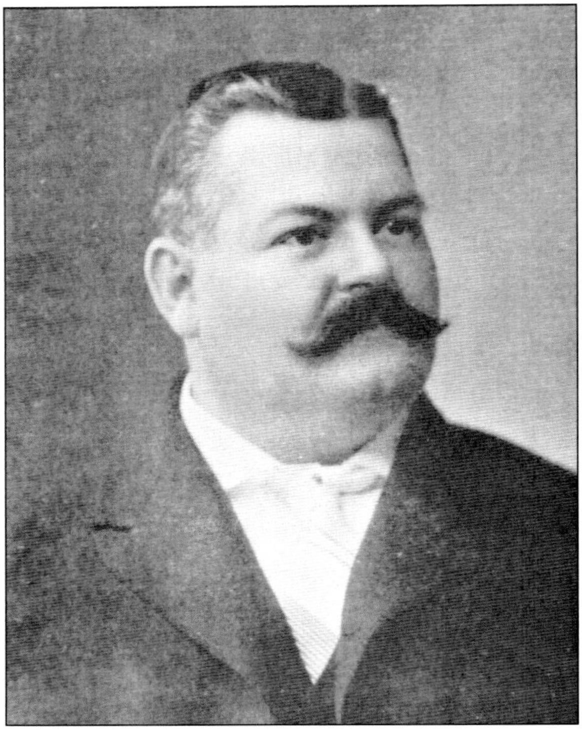

Charles Fehrenbach. The youngest surviving son of brewery founder John Fehrenbach, Charles earned a business degree and began working as a clerk and collector for the family brewery in 1885. He became treasurer of the company in 1888 and, two years later, also took over the family's French Street saloon. In 1893, Charles was nominated as H&F's vice president, a position he held until his death in 1925. (Author's collection.)

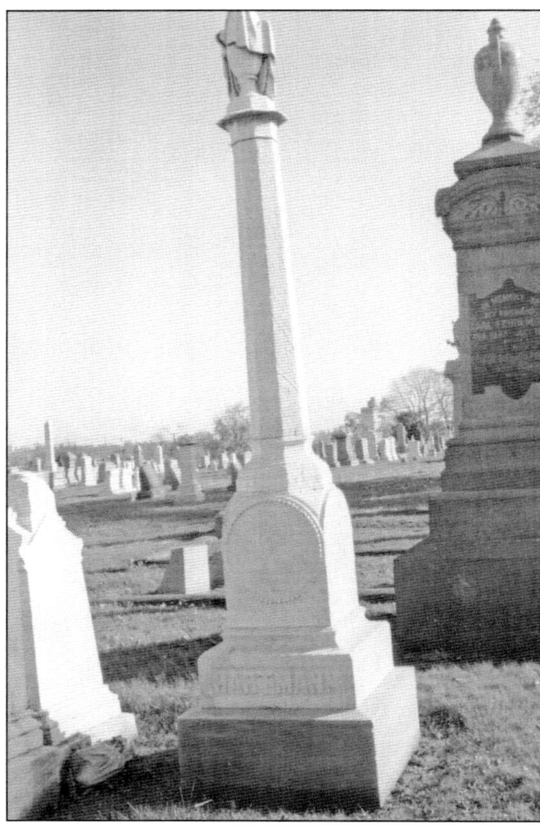

John Hartmann's Monument, Riverview Cemetery, 1997. While he maintained the title of president, illness had forced founder John Hartmann to cede control of the brewery to his heir. Hartmann's son John G. took over as company president upon his father's death in 1890 and six years later also assumed the role of general manager. He would prove a capable leader, guiding the brewery through its final three tumultuous decades. (Author's collection.)

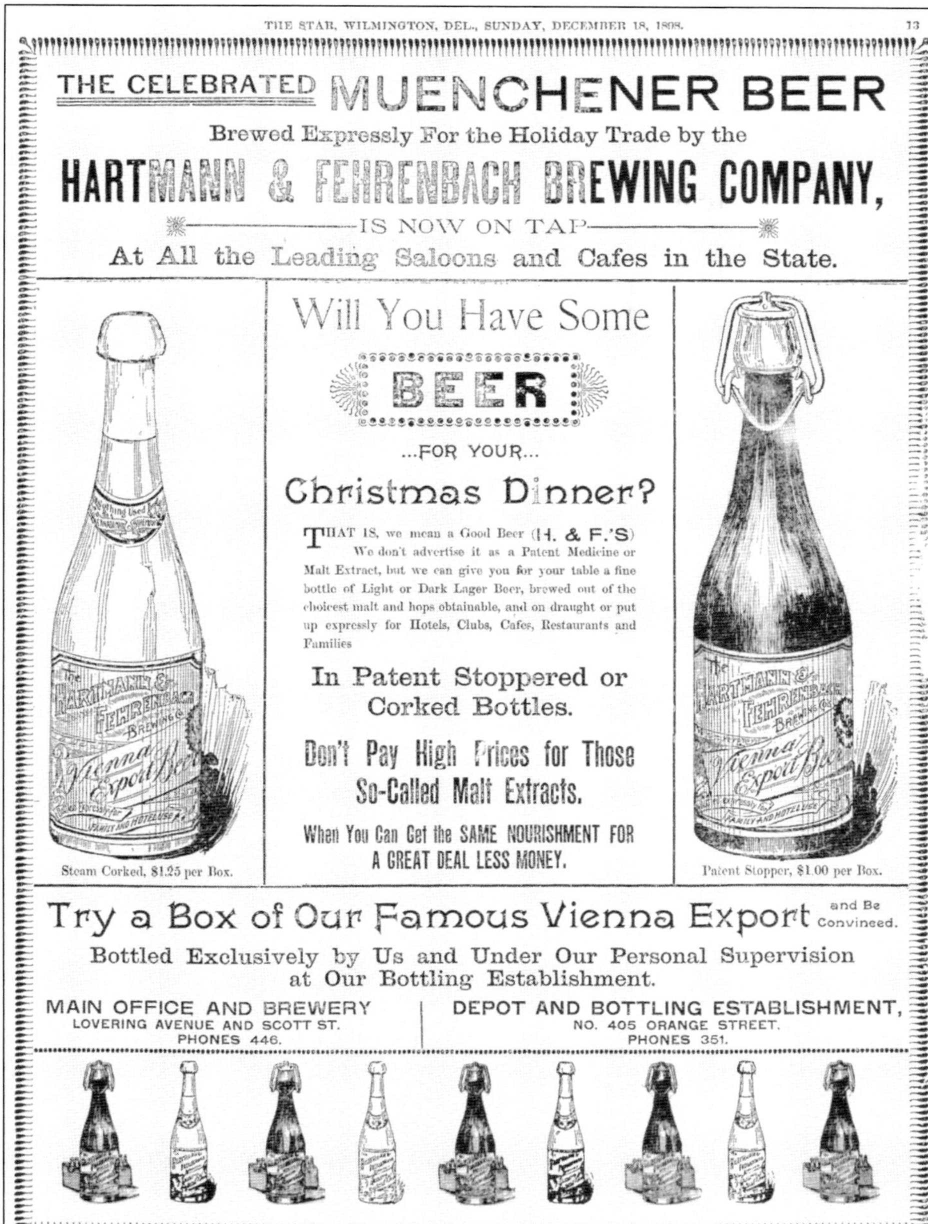

WILMINGTON SUNDAY STAR ADVERTISEMENT, DECEMBER 18, 1898. H&F began bottling its own beer when they constructed a bottling house and depot across town at 405 Orange Street in 1890. Seven years later, the company purchased a pasteurizing machine, which improved the shelf life of its bottled products. In time, the popularity of H&F's bottled beer made it necessary to expand operations. In the spring of 1899, the firm moved its bottling operations closer to the brewery when it added a 40-by-65-foot two-story bottling plant. The new $12,000 structure was built on Wawaset Street next to the existing brewery complex. The new plant had the capacity to turn out 24,000 bottles per day. This volume of H&F's bottled beer produced was in addition to the product kegged in the brewery. That fall, H&F's beer was awarded a silver medal at the National Export Exposition in Philadelphia, attesting to its superior quality. (Author's collection.)

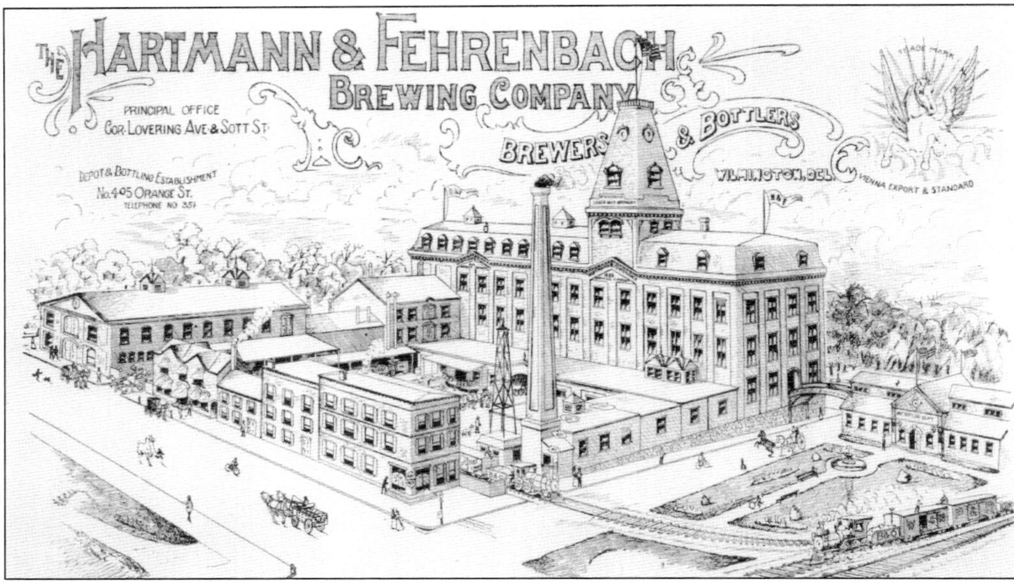

H&F Brewing Company Print, c. 1900. This print shows the H&F brewery at its peak, with the new bottling plant located on the far right. To the far left is the refurbished stable house. A track was extended to go inside of the H&F complex, where railcars could be loaded with cases of beer for delivery to accounts throughout the Delmarva Peninsula, southeastern Pennsylvania, and northern Maryland. (HML.)

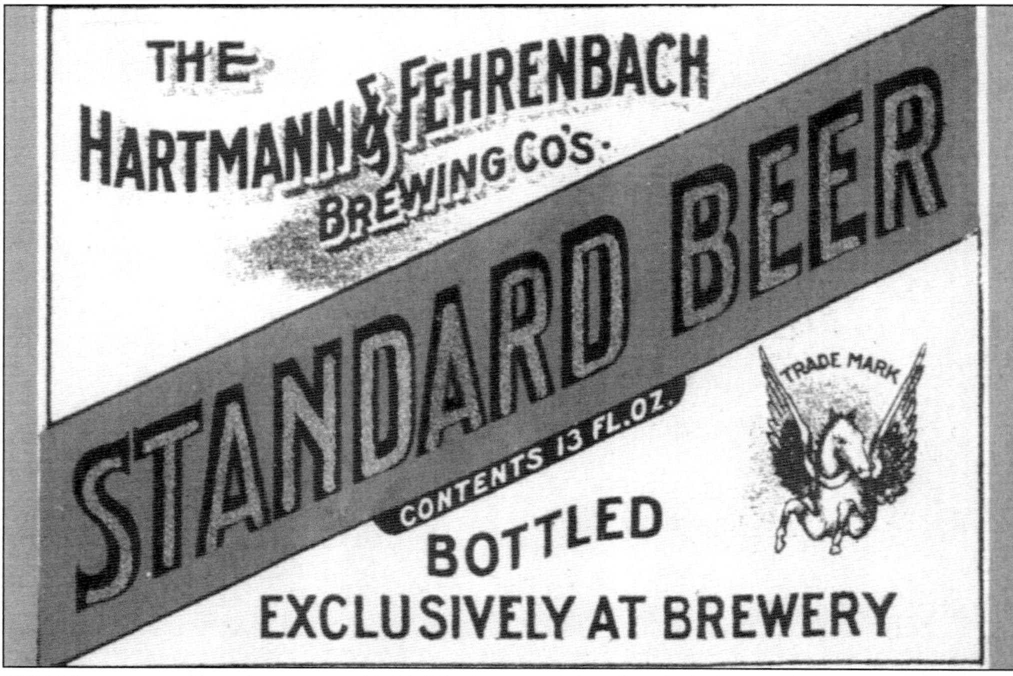

H&F Standard Beer Label, c. 1905. The brewery's bottle labels featured the H&F trademark, the Greek mythological figure of Pegasus. H&F bottles were also embossed with the same image of Pegasus among the clouds. In addition to its standard beer, H&F also produced its lager, ale, brown stout, XXX porter, Wurzburger, the nonalcoholic pure-malt tonic Vienna export, and two seasonal brews, bock in the spring and Christmas pilsner. (BKBL.)

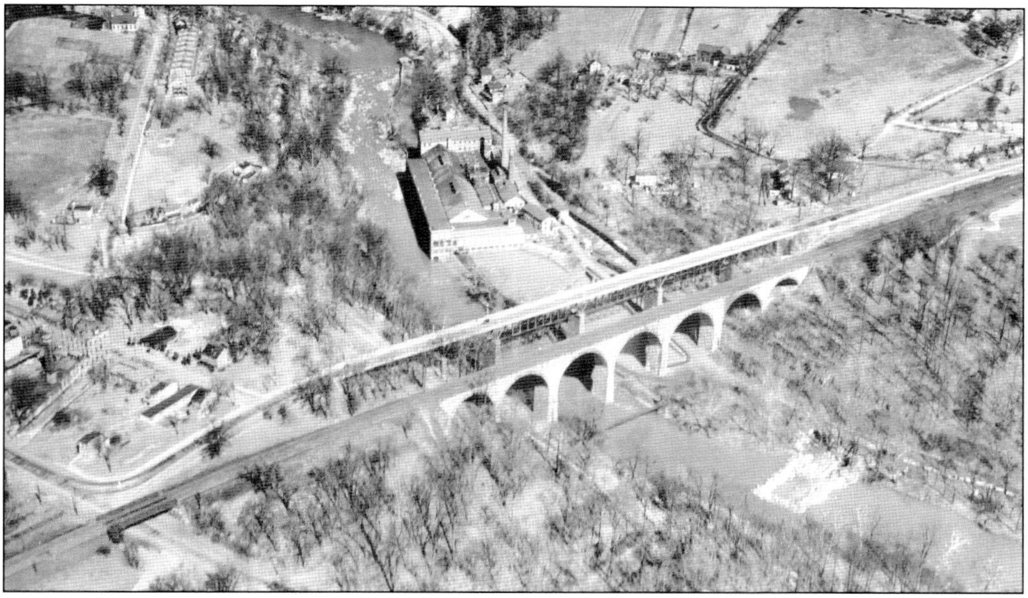

Railroad Bridge over the Brandywine, 1931. This aerial image features the H&F brewery at the far bottom left of the photograph. Just out of view in the foreground was the site of the pleasure grounds at Rosendale Park. The brewery sold the amusement grounds at Rosendale in the 1880s, and the land was eventually incorporated into Brandywine Park. (HML.)

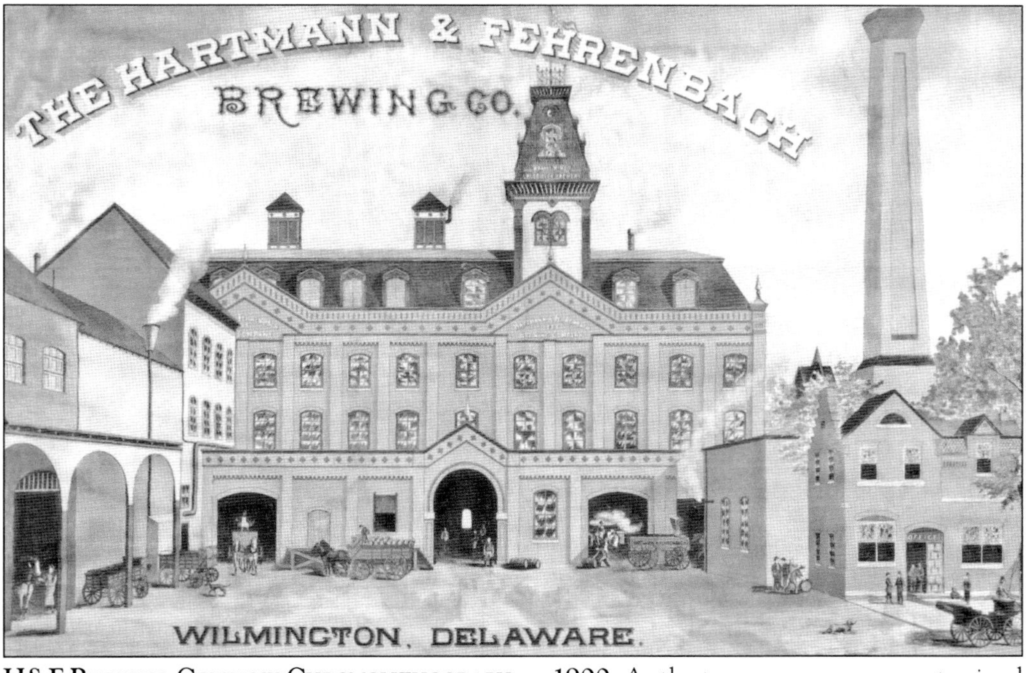

H&F Brewing Company Chromolithograph, c. 1900. As the temperance movement gained strength in the early 1900s, John G. Hartmann emerged as a leader of the "wet" forces in Delaware. The eventual passage of the 18th Amendment left the brewery little choice but to reorganize as the H&F Products Company. Its near-beer product, Good Cheer, proved unpopular, and the company was unable to sustain itself by bottling soft drinks. H&F ceased operations on August 25, 1920. (HML.)

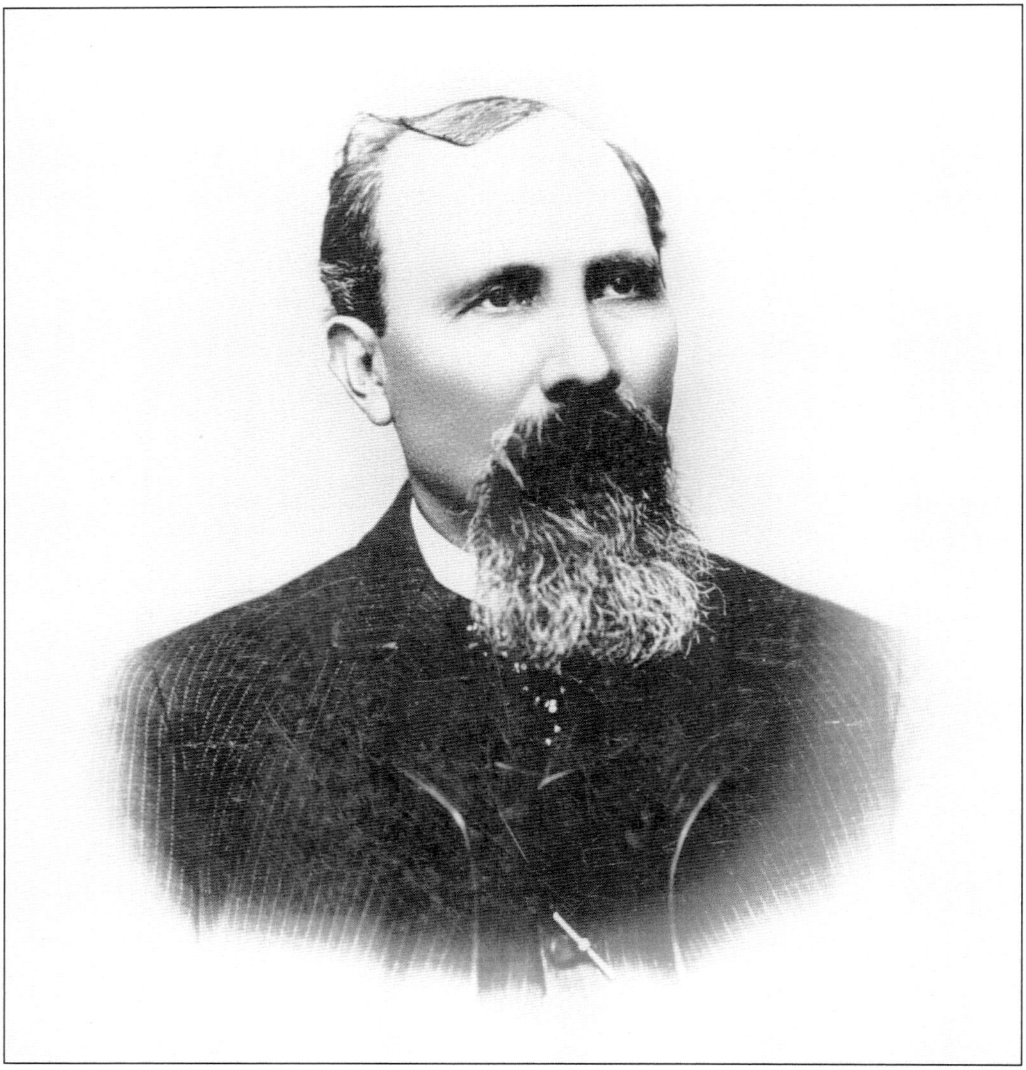

Joseph Stoeckle. A native of Buchau, Württemberg, Stoeckle arrived in Wilmington in 1854 and married Johanna Gropp two years later. He worked as a cabinetmaker during the day while his wife attended to their saloon at 202 Tatnall Street. In 1858, the Stoeckles moved their business to larger quarters at 225 King Street. The following year, Joseph's brother-in-law Gebhard Mutschler taught him how to brew and the two began brewing for customers in back of Stoeckle's saloon. The business prospered, and the Stoeckles soon acquired an adjoining property at 223 King Street, where they constructed a brick building housing a hotel, saloon, and summer garden. Named Mechanics Hall, it was said to have been a perfect facsimile of a German biergarten and became a popular retreat for Wilmington's German community. In 1871, Joseph also began operating a saloon at Schuetzen Park entertainment grounds at Wilmington's western edge, along the Kennett Pike. (Author's collection.)

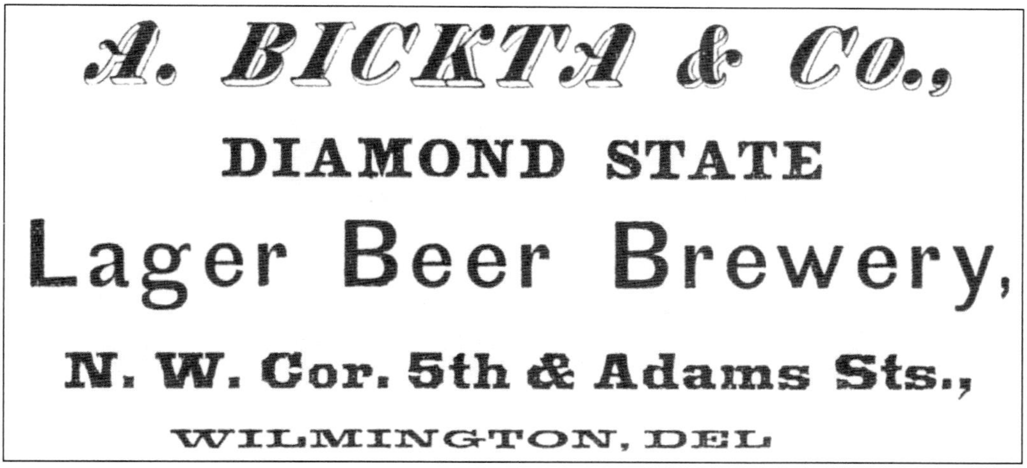

Wilmington City Directory Advertisement, 1874. During his 18-month tenure at Schuetzen Park, Stoeckle was instrumental in organizing a new brewing company in Wilmington. He, along with brother-in-law Francis Bickta, Augustus Bickta, James Clark, Edward J. McManus, and James Murphy, formed A. Bickta and Company in 1872 and purchased the old Nebeker brewery at Fifth and Adams Streets. Stoeckle, the only partner with any practical brewing experience, was appointed general manager of the firm. (WPL.)

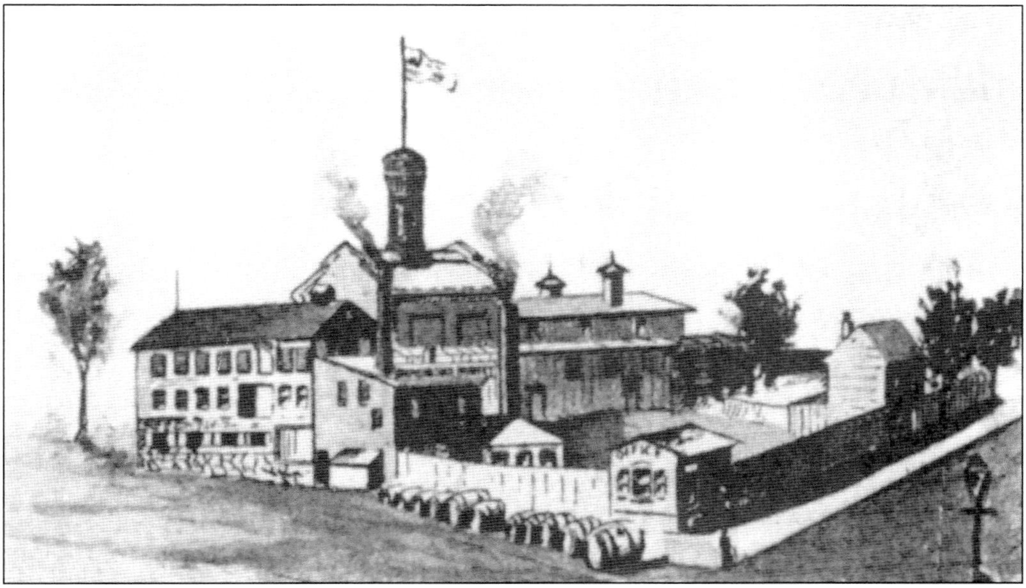

Bickta Brewery, 1872. The new brewing company improved upon and expanded the former Nebeker brewery, renaming it the Diamond State Lager Brewery. In September 1874, Augustus Bickta withdrew from the partnership, and the remaining investors reorganized as Bickta and Company. Upon the death of Francis Bickta in 1875, Stoeckle purchased the business outright. The brewery struggled through the 1870s and by 1879 had an annual production of only 4,555 barrels. (Author's collection.)

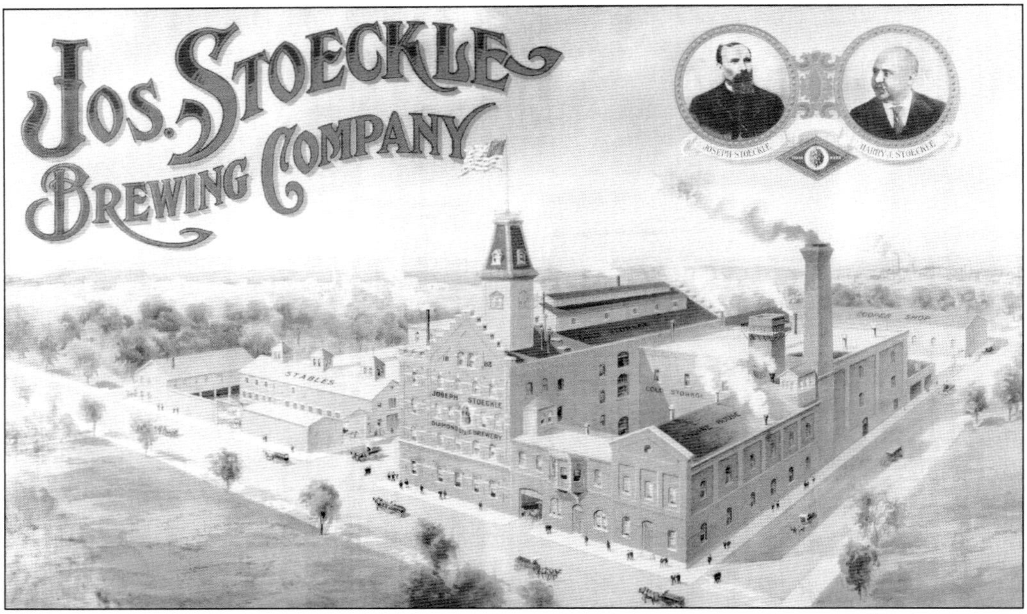

Joseph Stoeckle Brewing Company's Diamond State Brewery, c. 1915. Tragically, the original Diamond State complex, framed mostly of wood, burned to the ground in October 1881. Stoeckle recouped the fire insurance money and within nine months opened a much larger, more complete brewery at the same location. This image, taken from a metal advertising tray, shows many of the buildings that were added as part of the 1881–1882 renovation. (HML.)

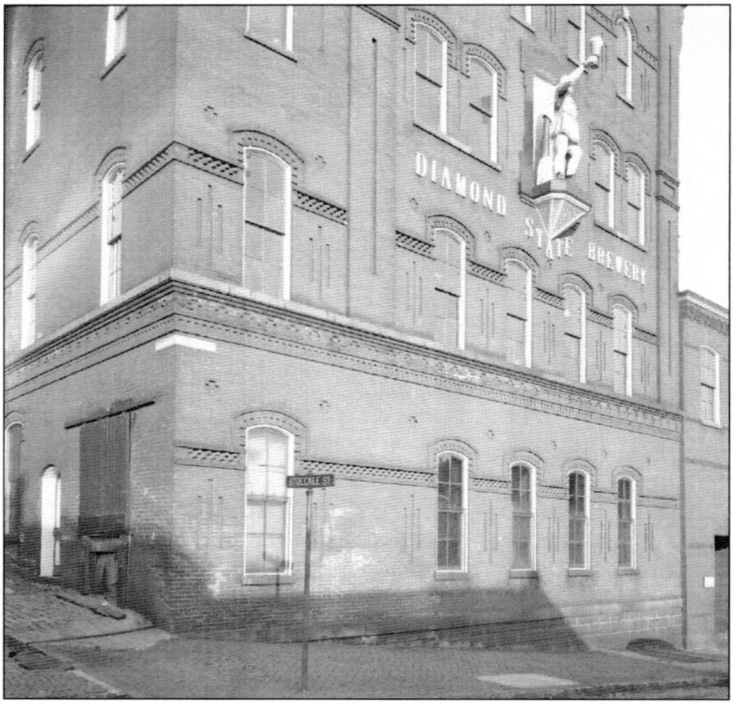

Diamond State Brewhouse, November 1943. The new buildings included a brewhouse, an engine house, several cold-storage houses, a cooper shop, and horse stables. Stoeckle's other addition included an 11-foot zinc statue of Gambrinus, the legendary icon of the brewing trade, which was placed in an alcove above the second story of the brewhouse. In time, the statue would become a veritable symbol of the Diamond State Brewery. (DHS.)

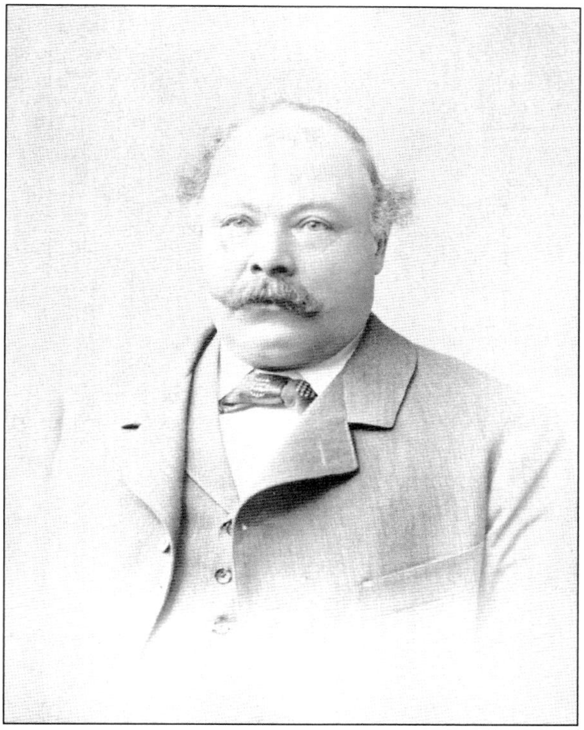

David Dangel Sr. A native of Winterbach, Württemberg, Dangel arrived in Wilmington in 1881 and began working as a carpenter. By 1890, he had enough capital to begin his own construction business, and his sons later became partners in the business. Dangel befriended Joseph Stoeckle and was hired by him to perform renovations to his brewery. When Stoeckle's business was eventually incorporated, Dangel served on its board of directors. (WHD.)

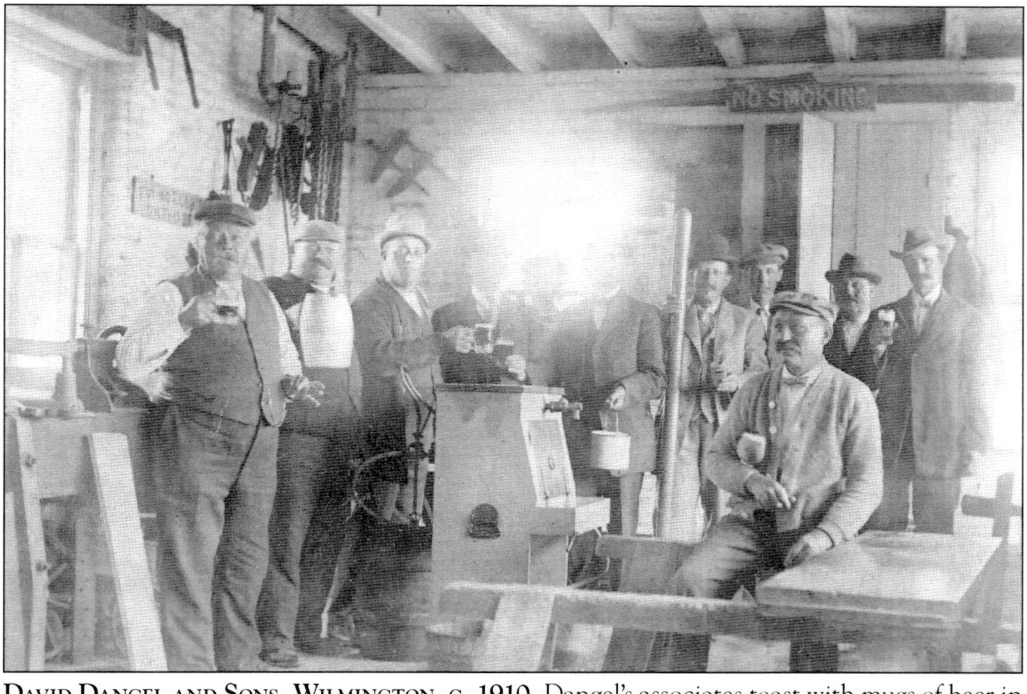

David Dangel and Sons, Wilmington, c. 1910. Dangel's associates toast with mugs of beer in the company workshop at 506–508 North Van Buren Street. The men identified here are, from left to right, David Dangel and his sons David Jr. and Adolph. In addition to work on the city's three large breweries, the Dangels also built several notable Wilmington structures, including Zion Lutheran Church, the Garrick Theatre, and numerous homes on the city's west side. (WHD.)

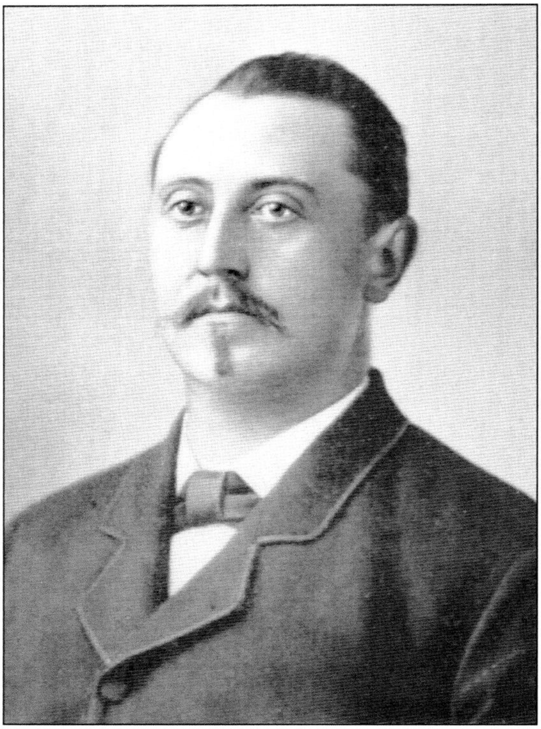

Hermann Erb. Trained as a brewer by his father in his native Weidersheim, Germany, Erb arrived in the United States in 1857. He worked as a brewer in Newark, New Jersey; Philadelphia; and Portsmouth, New Hampshire, before being hired by Joseph Stoeckle as brewmaster of the Diamond State Brewery in 1884. Erb's expertise contributed greatly to Stoeckle's success, as brewery sales increased from 4,000 barrels per year to 75,000 barrels during Erb's 33-year tenure. (WPL.)

The Brick Hotel, Georgetown, c. 1890. As evidenced by the sign on the Brick Hotel, Stoeckle's beer was widely distributed to outlets in southern Delaware. The Brick Hotel opened at Green and West Market Streets in 1836 and was operated by a series of proprietors over the decades, including brothers James A. and Joseph H. Manlove in the late 1800s. (DPA.)

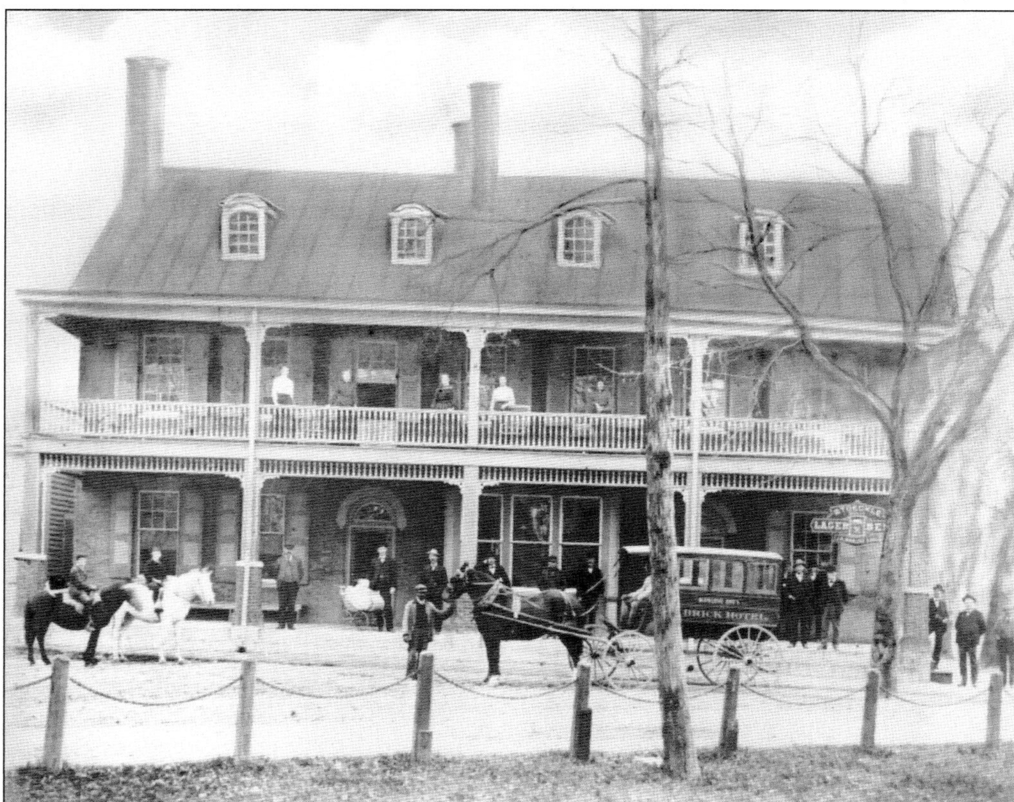

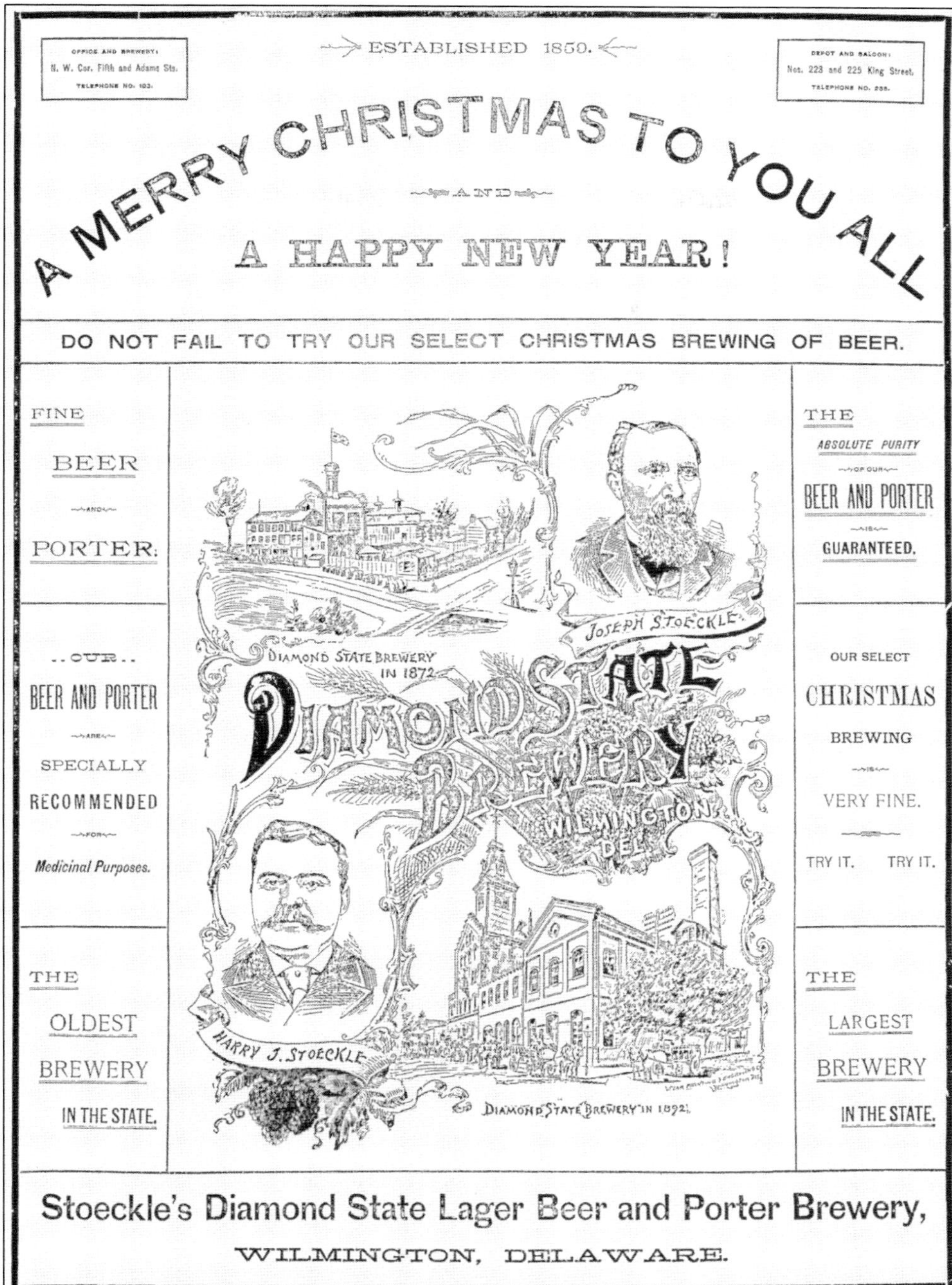

WILMINGTON SUNDAY STAR ADVERTISEMENT, DECEMBER 25, 1892. Trained in the business from an early age, Stoeckle's only son, Harry J., was promoted to general manager of the brewery in 1886. That same year, Benjamin Gam, Stoeckle's son-in-law, took over the family's King Street saloon. Sales grew steadily through the 1880s, resulting from additional brewery expansion, advancements in technology and production, and the exceptional quality of Stoeckle's extra-fine lager and porter. In 1893, the Diamond State Brewery employed 35 men and sold about 30,000 barrels of beer to saloons, hotels, and homes throughout the Delmarva Peninsula and into Pennsylvania and New Jersey. (Author's collection.)

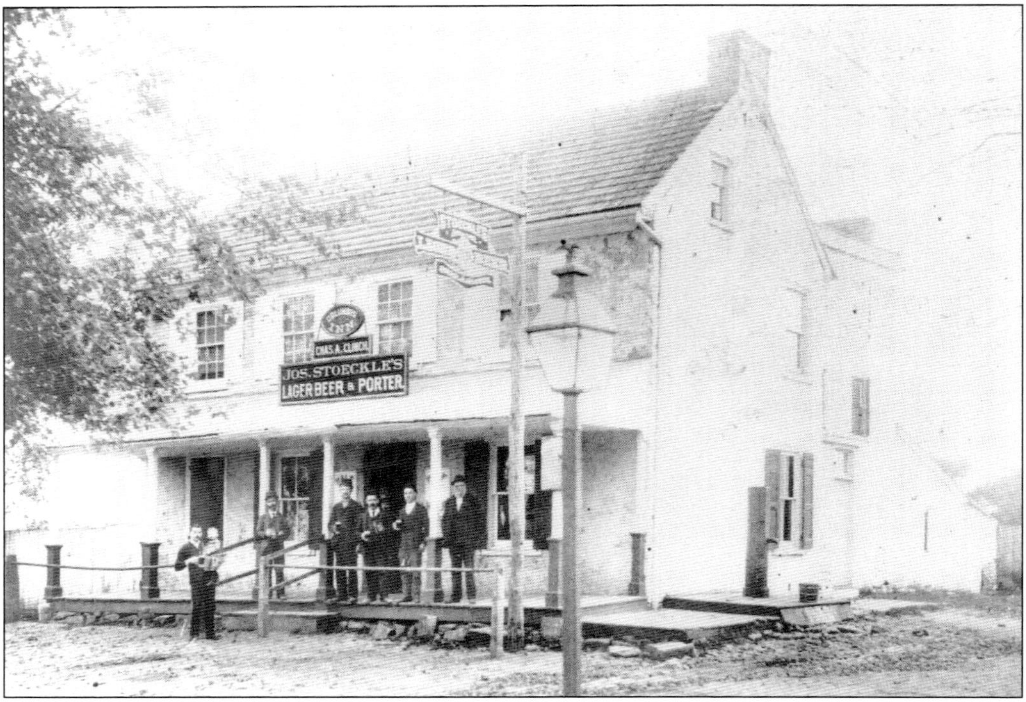

Columbus Inn, c. 1885. The Columbus Inn at Pennsylvania and Woodlawn Avenues remains one of Wilmington's oldest continuously operated businesses. The Schmaltz family operated a bakery on the site in the late 1790s and as early as 1812 had converted it to a tavern. In the mid-1880s, Charles A. Clinch's Columbus Inn and the adjacent Schuetzen Park fairgrounds were centers of activity along the Kennett Pike. Both served as outlets for Stoeckle's beer. (HML.)

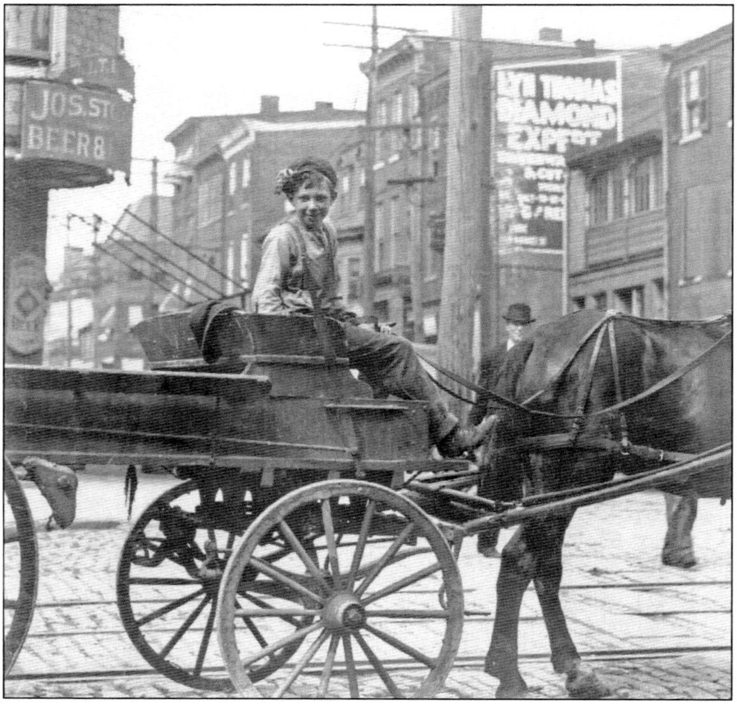

Empty Brewery Dray, May 1910. Paperboy Robert Reynolds sits atop a brewery dray carriage in front of another Stoeckle outlet, James T. Laws's saloon at the northwest corner of Fourth and Shipley Streets. In the days before motorized trucks, breweries employed teams of draft horses to make daily deliveries of their kegged and bottled products. An integral element of their business, these horses represented significant investments for brewing companies. (LOC.)

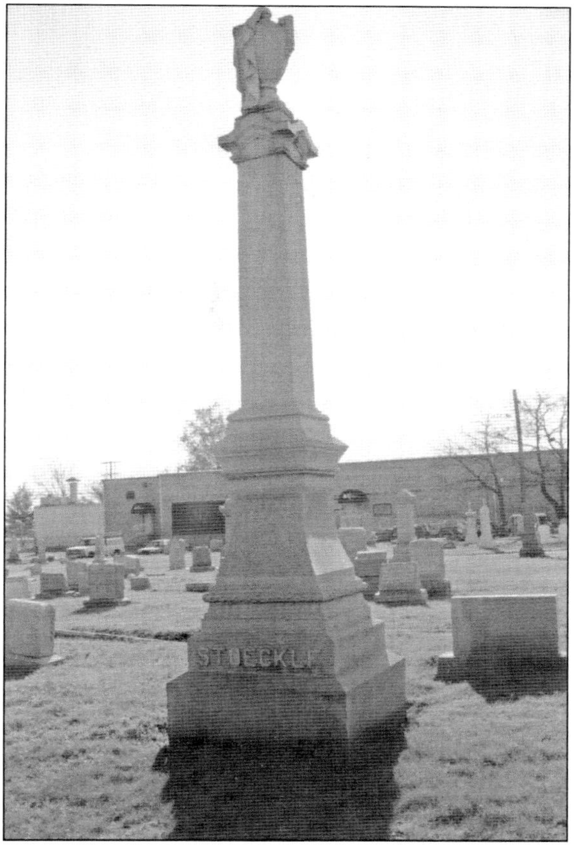

ORIGINAL STOECKLE MONUMENT, RIVERVIEW CEMETERY, 1997. Although the Diamond State Brewery would survive for many more years, sadly, its founder would not. Joseph Stoeckle, whose health was never robust, contracted tuberculosis in 1891. He never recovered, and the disease eventually took his life in December 1893. (Author's collection.)

DIAMOND STATE BREWERY CARRIAGE STONE, OCTOBER 1955. Stoeckle was a generous and beloved citizen, and his funeral was said to have been one of the largest ever witnessed in Delaware. The enormous procession from the Stoeckle home to Riverview Cemetery included hundreds of mourners. The City of Wilmington changed the name of Morrow Street to Stoeckle Street in 1898 to honor Joseph's memory. (DHS.)

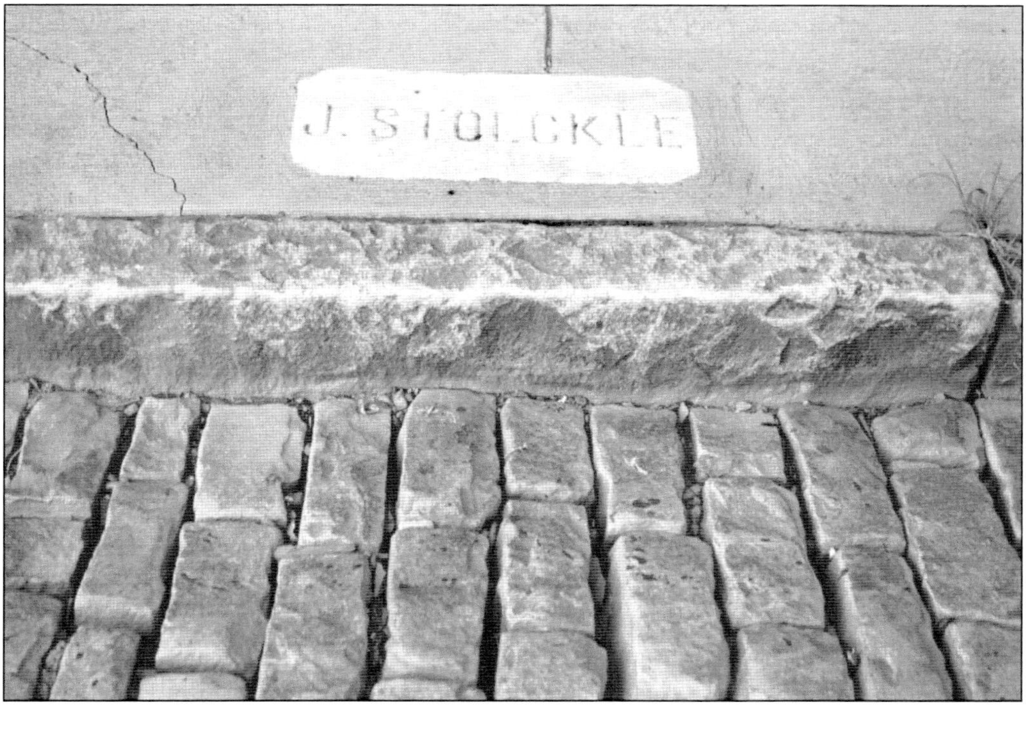

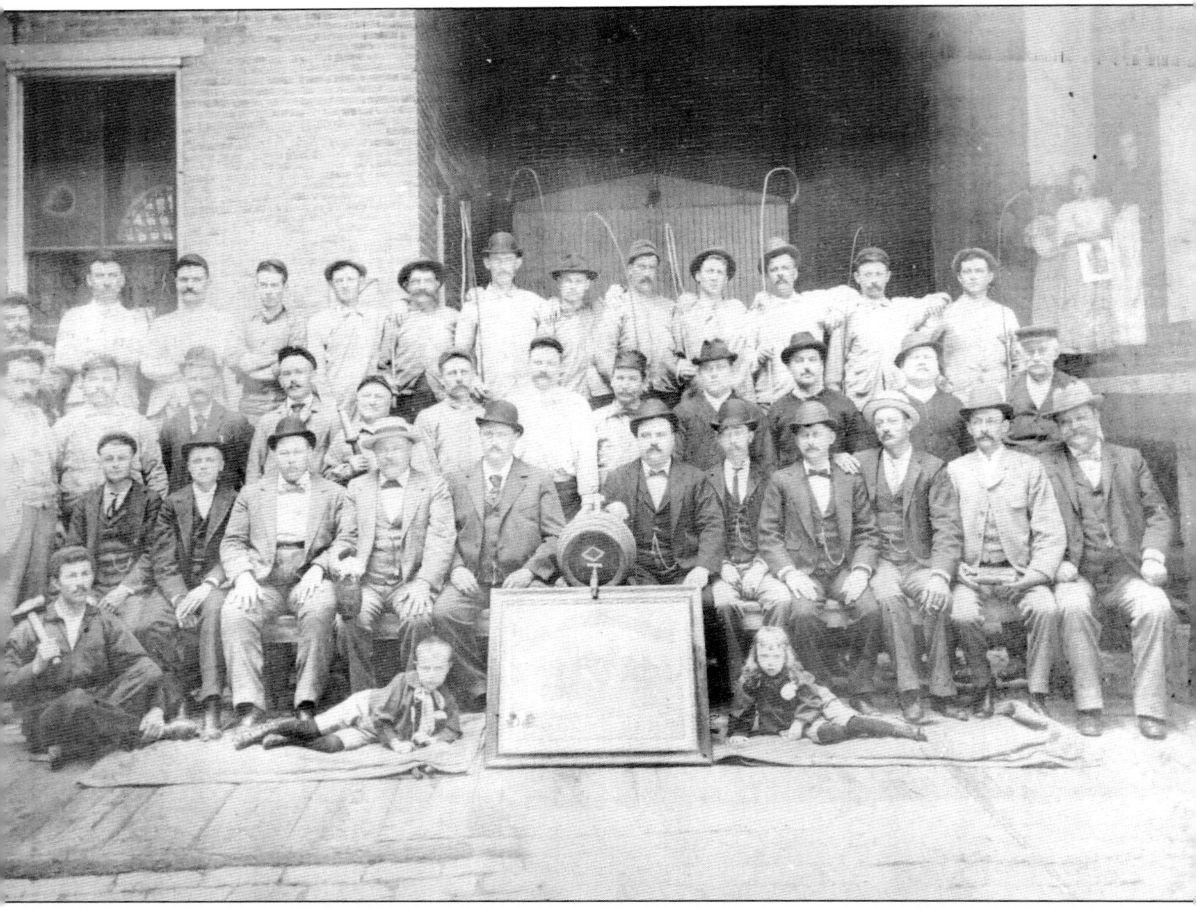

DIAMOND STATE BREWERY STAFF, C. 1898. Workers, associates, and Stoeckle family members pose for a photograph in the brewery courtyard. The following have been identified and are seated in the first row: Harry S. Neher, bookkeeper (third from the left); David Dangel Sr., board of directors (fourth from the left); Hermann Erb, brewmaster (fifth from the left); Harry J. Stoeckle, general manager (sixth from the left); and Morris Grubb, collector and solicitor (seventh from the left). Seated on the ground are Victor E. Ullmann, cooper (far left), and Leila Stoeckle, daughter of Harry S. Stoeckle (far right). (WHD.)

JOHANNA S. (GROPP) STOECKLE. Following the death of her husband, Joseph, in 1893, Johanna Stoeckle assumed control of the Diamond State Brewery. She had long been a driving force in the family's success and great fortune, and the brewery business continued to grow in the next eight years under her ownership. Son Harry Stoeckle continued to run the brewery's day-to-day operations as general manager. (Author's collection.)

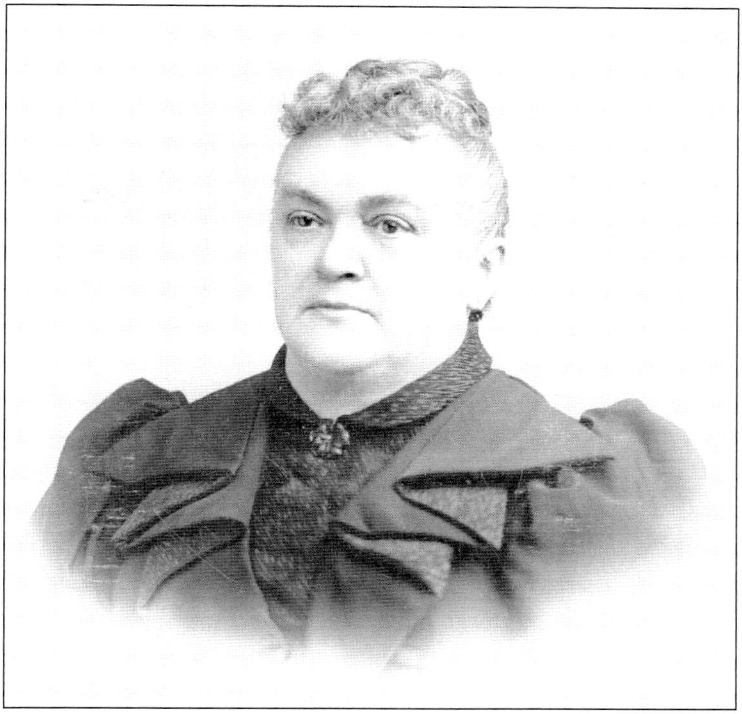

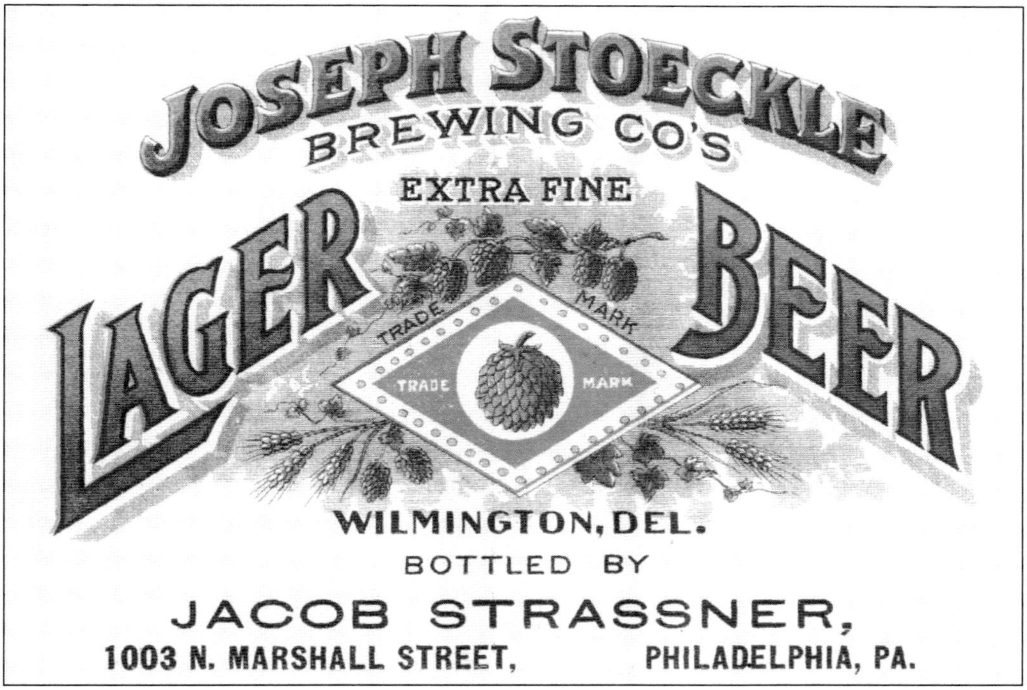

JOSEPH STOECKLE BREWING COMPANY BOTTLE LABEL, c. 1910. Ownership of the Diamond State Brewery passed into the hands of the five surviving Stoeckle children when their mother died in 1902. They incorporated the business as the Joseph Stoeckle Brewing Company, honoring their father's memory. The brewery had not yet invested in its own bottling plant and continued contracting with bottlers near and far, such as Jacob Strassner of Philadelphia. (BKBL.)

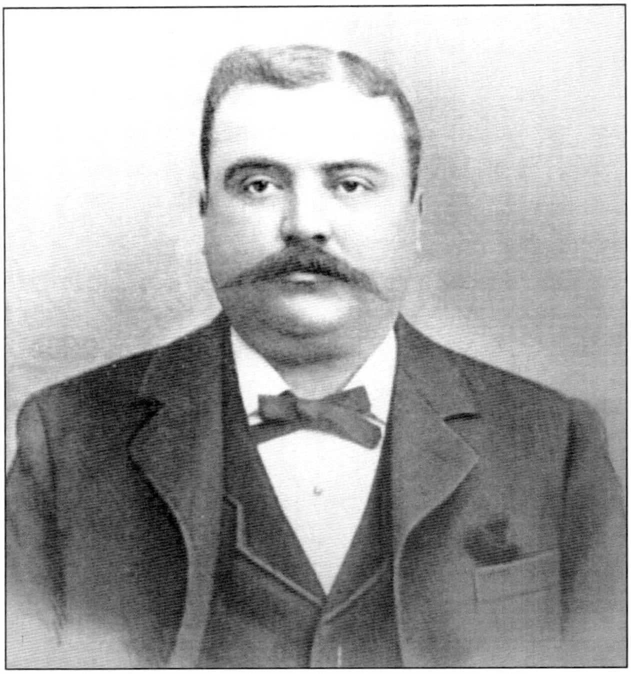

Harry J. Stoeckle. Raised in the family's brewing business, Harry received additional training at the Huber Brewery in Brooklyn and the Pabst Brewery in Milwaukee, Wisconsin. His superior management of the Stoeckle business for more than 15 years led to his selection as president of the company following the death of his mother. He would serve in that role, navigating the brewery through its most challenging period, until his death in 1925. (Author's collection.)

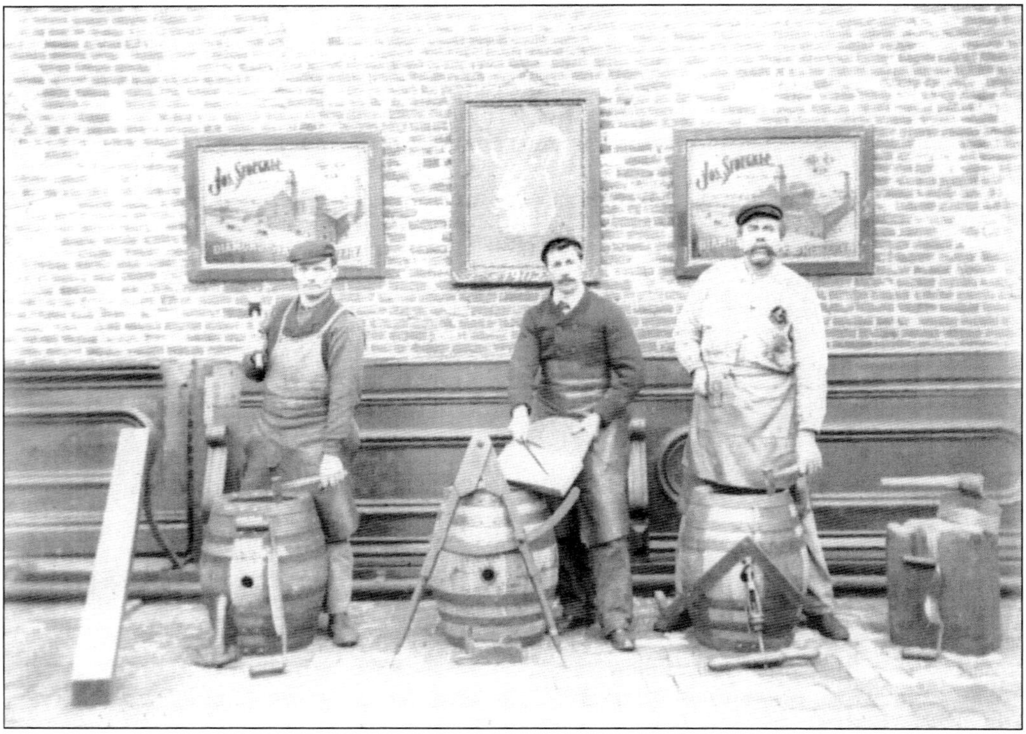

Diamond State Brewery Coopers, c. 1902. Many pre-Prohibition breweries found it cost effective to maintain their own cooper shops, including all three of Wilmington's large breweries. Kegs were in high demand. Absent a bottling plant, all of beer that left Stoeckle's brewery had to be kegged. Identified in this photograph are Victor Ullmann at center and a Mr. Rothschild on the right. (Author's collection.)

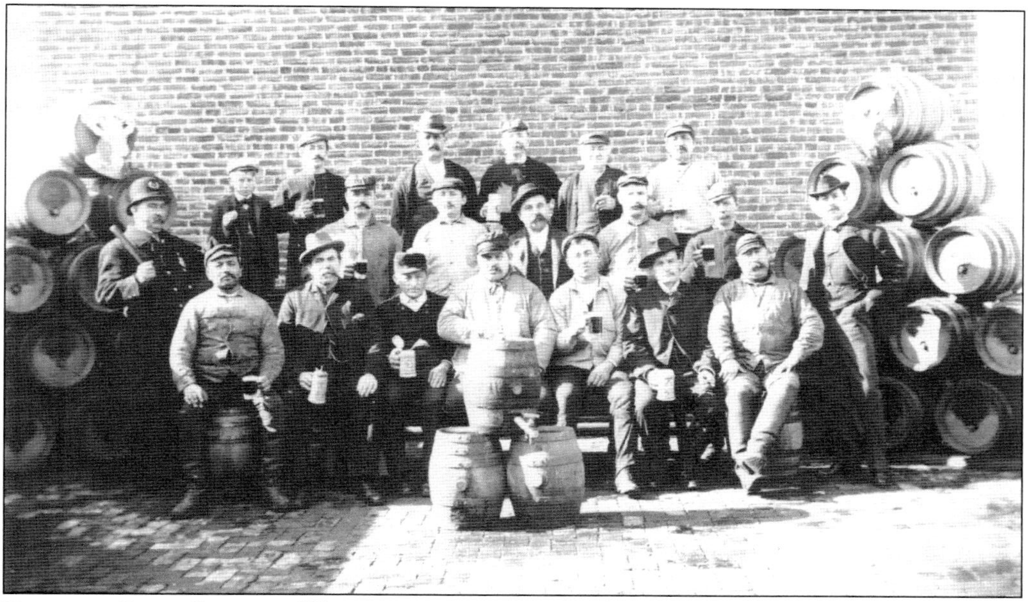

Diamond State Brewery Workers, c. 1900. Pictured here are, from left to right, (first row) Anton Buckenhue (brewer), a Mr. Rothschild, Jacob H. Schnepf, Tony Romanoff, Henry Ernst, unidentified, and Dave Conner (brewer); (second row) Frank Kane (patrolman), William Mitchell (chief engineer), William Bodenstedt, unidentified, a Mr. Wendell, Charles H. Mack (brewer), and Victor Ullmann (chief cooper); (third row) Joseph Stoeckle Mammele, unidentified, Gottlieb Hess (night watchman), Antone Feulie, Christian Leuckel (brewer), and Franz Fuchs. (DHS.)

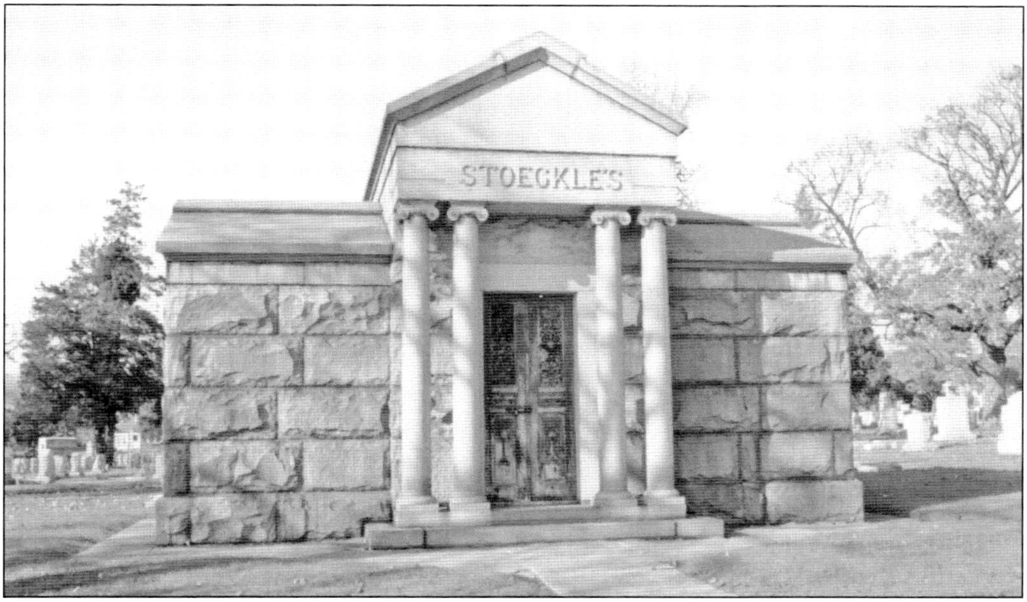

Stoeckle Mausoleum, Riverview Cemetery, 1997. This mausoleum, built by Harry Stoeckle in July 1907, is the largest gravesite in Riverview. It is the final resting place of many members of the Stoeckle family, including Joseph and Johanna, who were reinterred there. The mausoleum was vandalized in 2002 and has been permanently sealed. The Friends of Historic Riverview Cemetery have since taken control of the grounds and greatly improved the condition of the cemetery. (Author's collection.)

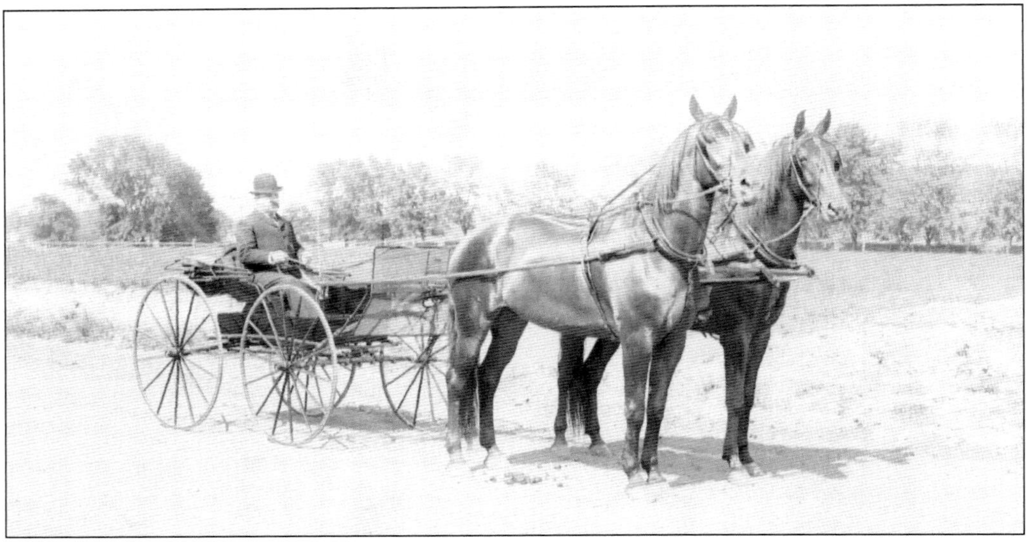

HARRY STOECKLE AT WAWASET DRIVING PARK, WILMINGTON, 1897. Among Stoeckle's passions and prized possessions were his horses. In this photograph, he is seen driving his carriage at Wawaset Driving Park. Stoeckle's father operated a tavern at the park when it was known as Scheutzen Park. Over the years, the park hosted picnics, festivals, shooting competitions, horse racing, baseball games, and auto racing. The Wawaset Park residential community was built on the site in the 1920s and 1930s. (DHS.)

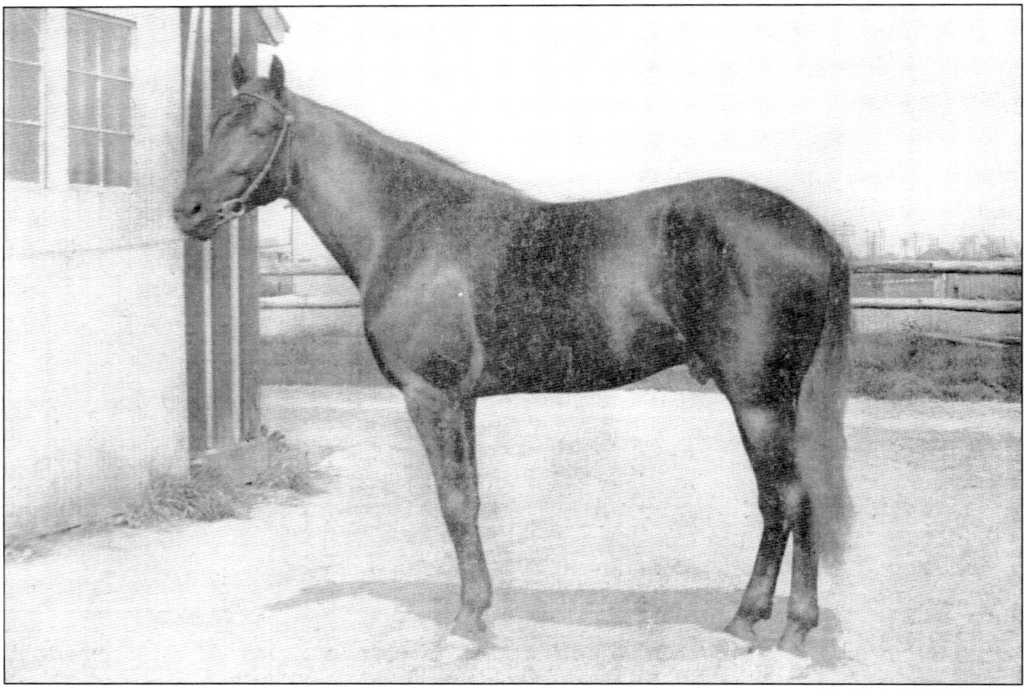

HARRY J.S., C. 1915. Harry Stoeckle owned several racehorses, but none were as beloved as his namesake. Harry J.S. was said to have been so intensely black that he sparkled as he trotted, and indeed he shined on the track as well. Harry J.S. set numerous world records in his 11-year career, including one at Wawaset Park. He was retired in 1920 as the greatest half-mile trotter ever. (Author's collection.)

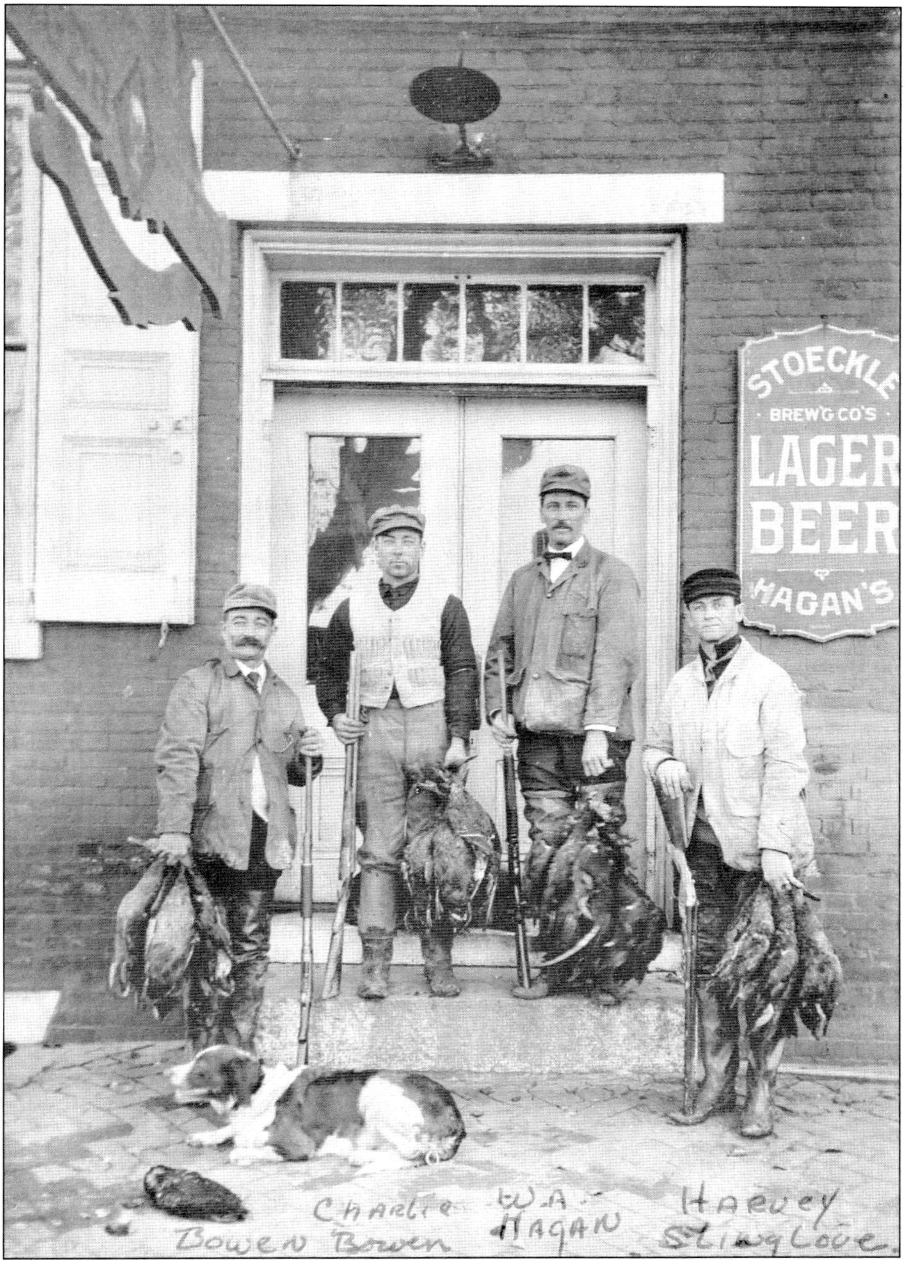

CENTRAL HOTEL, DELAWARE CITY, c. 1910. From left to right, Delaware City resident James Bowen, his son Charles H. Bowen, hotel owner William A. Hagan, and Harvey Slinglove display the results of their successful hunting venture in front of the Central Hotel on the east corner of Clinton and Canal Streets. The tavern sign indicates that Hagan's establishment sold Stoeckle's lager. In 1903, Hagan opened a hotel and restaurant on the site and named it the Central Hotel. Coincidentally, he sold the business 10 years later to the Joseph Stoeckle Brewing Company, who renamed it the Stoeckle Hotel. The struggling brewing company sold the hotel in 1926. After repeal in 1933, George and Theresa Sterling opened a tavern and inn at the location bearing their name. Sterling's Tavern stood at the site for several decades. The complex was renovated in 2014 and currently functions as the headquarters for the American Birding Association. (JK.)

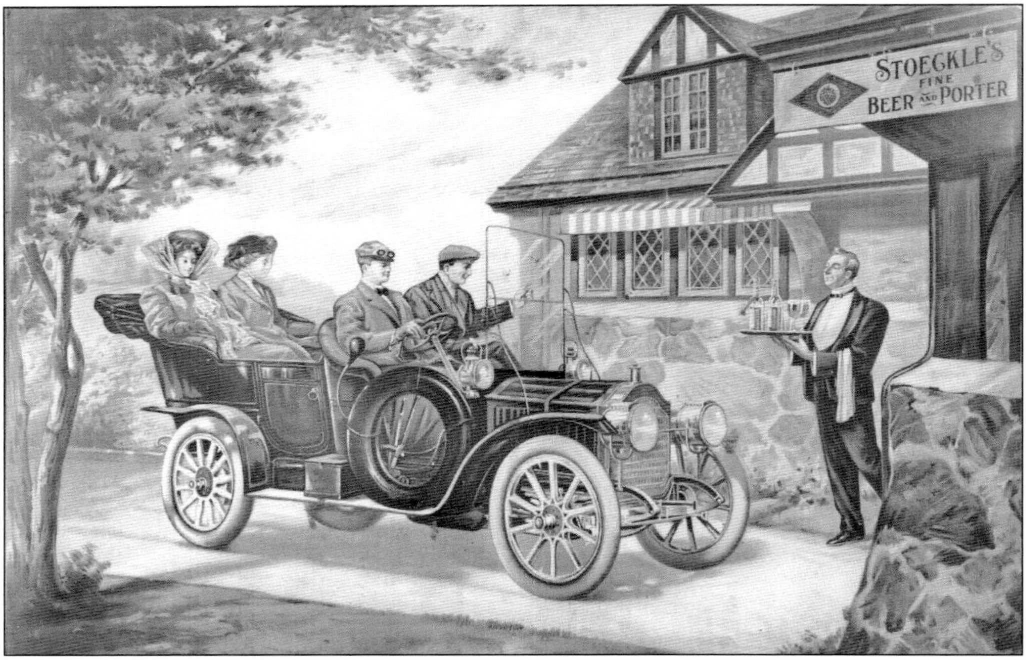

Joseph Stoeckle Brewing Company Promotional Sign, c. 1910. Stoeckle continued to make capital improvements at the Diamond State Brewery throughout the 1910s, despite the fact that Delaware's two lower counties had gone dry, and the industry became subject to stricter regulations. Sales of Stoeckle's lager, porter, and specialty beers remained brisk in Wilmington and rural New Castle County. (HML.)

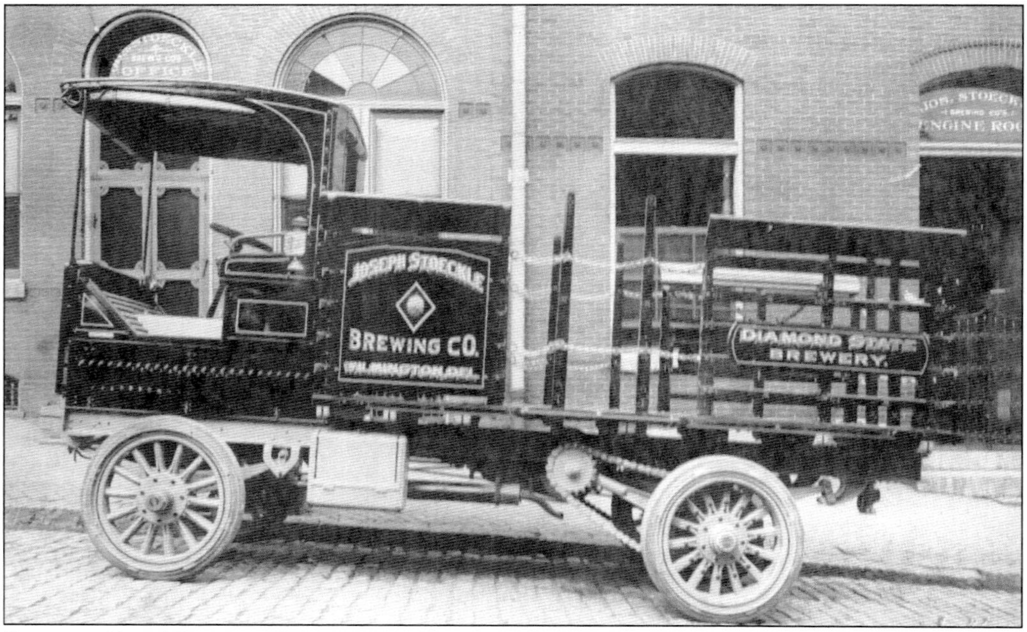

Stoeckle Beer Truck in Front of the Brewery Office, c. 1912. In 1911, Stoeckle had the largest brew kettle in the city installed in the brewery. About the same time, the company purchased this gasoline engine delivery truck with a chain drive. While horses were still employed for local deliveries, this truck was capable of making long-distance hauls in quick time. (Author's collection.)

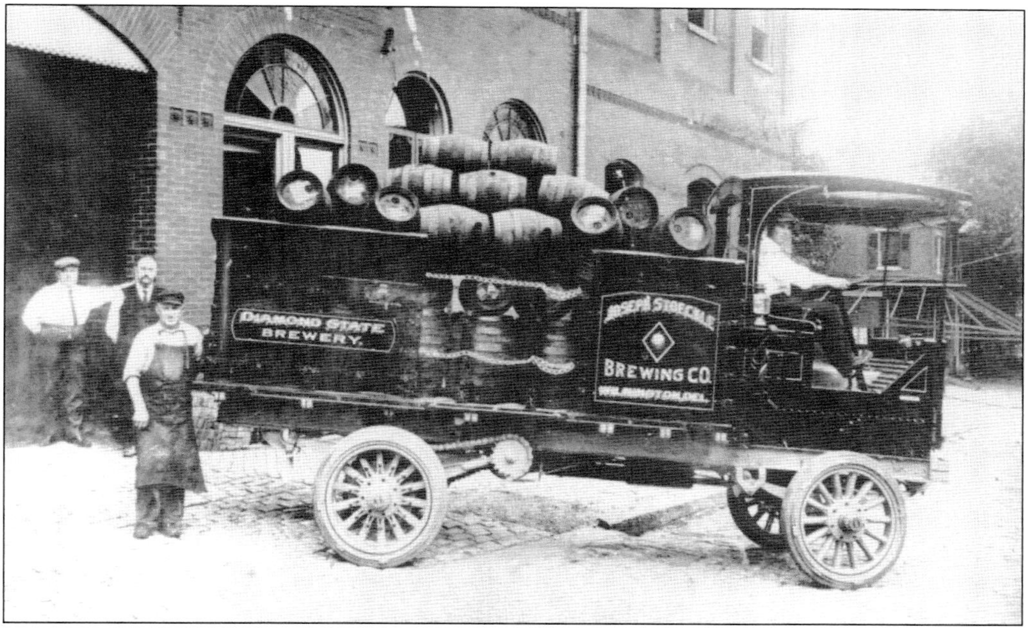

Stoeckle Beer Truck, c. 1912. Brewmaster Hermann Erb, in the back center of this photograph, looks on as a truck loaded with kegs departs the brewery. In May 1917, Stoeckle opened its new power plant and boiler house, which was constructed on the south side of Fifth Street, opposite the brewery. In November of that year, rural New Castle County opted to go dry. Prohibition in Wilmington was inevitable. (Richard McElwee.)

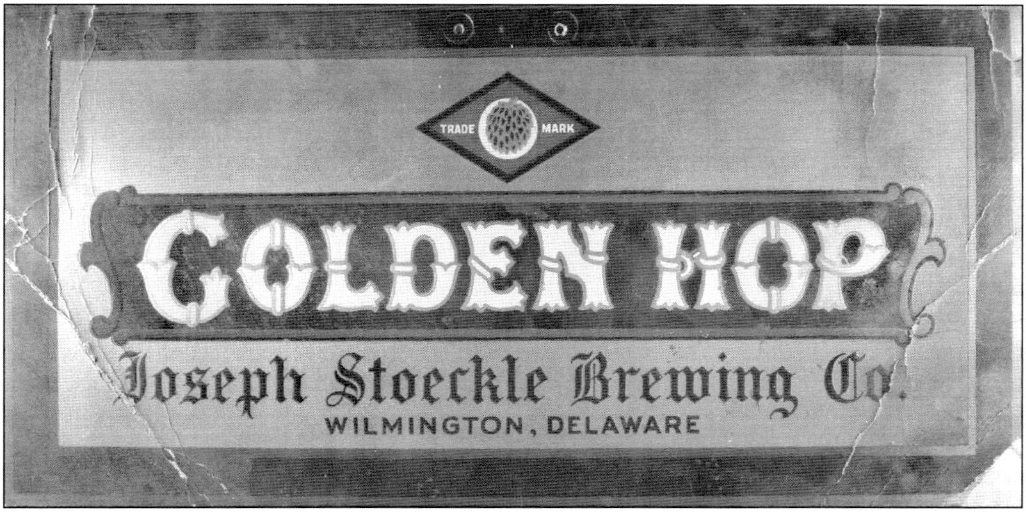

Stoeckle Golden Hop Sign, c. 1920. With the passage of the 18th Amendment, Stoeckle added a bottling plant so that they could continue manufacturing beverages. They began producing near-beer products, Dublin XX and Golden Hop, light and dark, and also bottled and distributed soft drinks. The company went out of business when Harry Stoeckle retired in late 1924. He died in January 1925. (JK.)

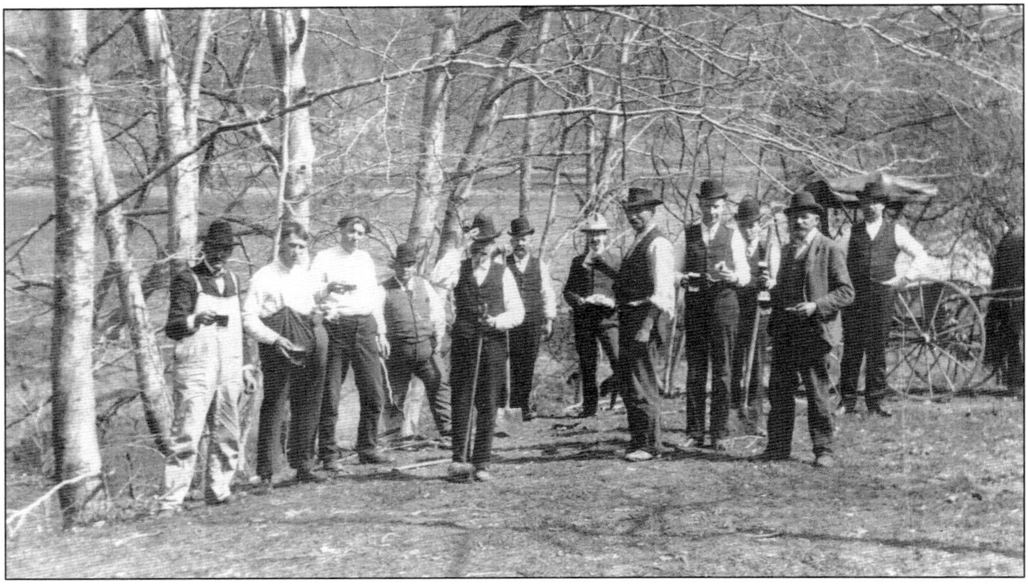

DuPont Powder Mill Workers, Wilmington, c. 1900. Lager beer was culturally important to the wave of German immigrants that began arriving in Wilmington and the surrounding area in the late 1840s. Its effervescent, thirst-quenching qualities proved to be perfectly suited to America's climate and tastes. Indeed, lager soon became the preferred beverage of non-Germans, particularly among those in the burgeoning working class. (HML.)

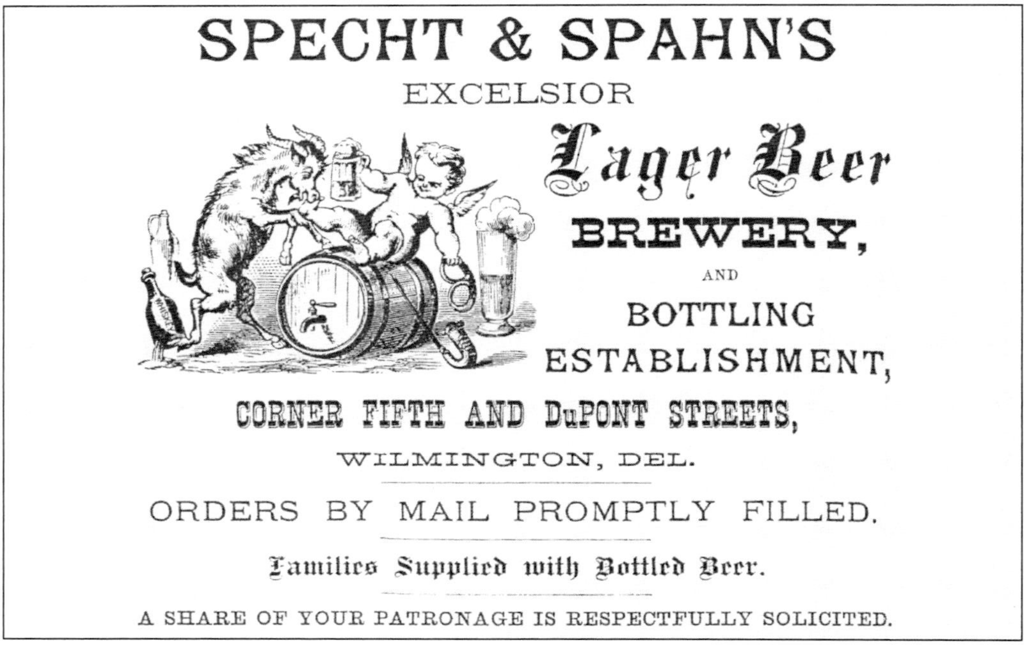

Wilmington City Directory Advertisement, 1881. Carl Specht, a native of Saxony, immigrated in 1848 and worked as a brewer in Baltimore and Havre de Grace, Maryland, and Philadelphia, Pennsylvania. In 1878, he began operating a saloon and brewery in Wilmington on the southwest corner of Fifth and DuPont Streets. Specht and his son-in-law Adam Spahn purchased the property on the northeast corner and opened the Excelsior Lager Beer Brewery and bottling establishment in 1880. (WPL.)

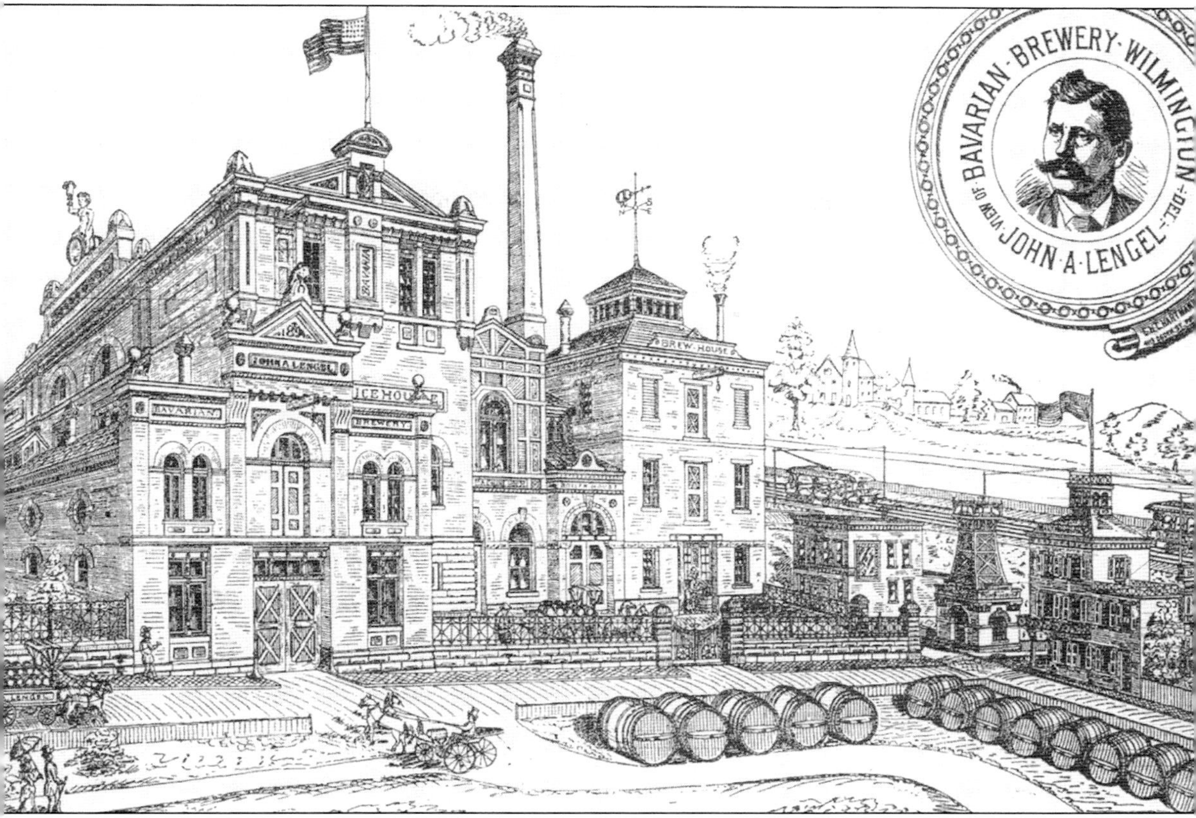

Bavarian Brewery, c. 1896. Although lager beer remained in high demand, Specht and Spahn were unable to compete with Stoeckle and Hartmann & Fehrenbach, two better-established breweries. In 1886, Specht and Spahn sold out to a firm called the Excelsior Brewing Company, headed by Evan Rice, president, and secretary/treasurer B. Frank Townsend. Despite the ownership change, the business languished and went out of business by 1889. The brewery sat idle until 1890, when it was purchased by John A. Lengel, who renamed it the Bavarian Brewery. (Author's collection.)

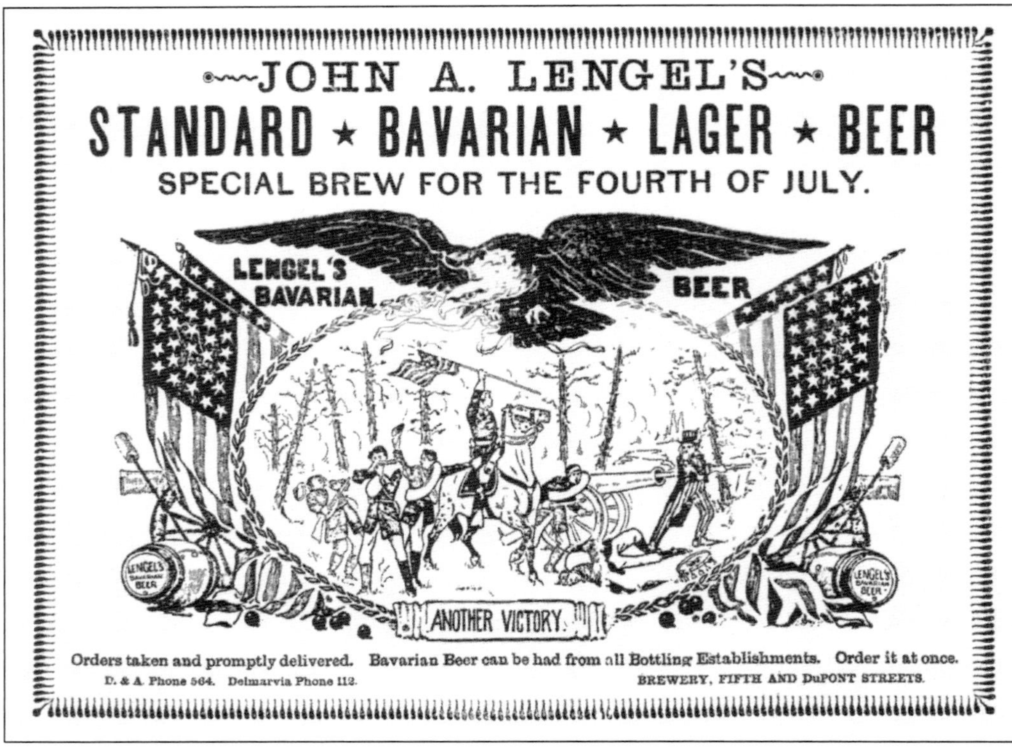

WILMINGTON *SUNDAY STAR* ADVERTISEMENT, JULY 3, 1898. A native of Baden-Württemberg, Lengel operated a weiss and lager beer brewery in the Germantown section of Philadelphia before coming to Wilmington. He made large capital investments in the Wilmington brewery to improve quality and increase the facility's production. In 1894, the business was incorporated as the Bavarian Brewery Company, Inc., with Lengel serving as president. (WPL.)

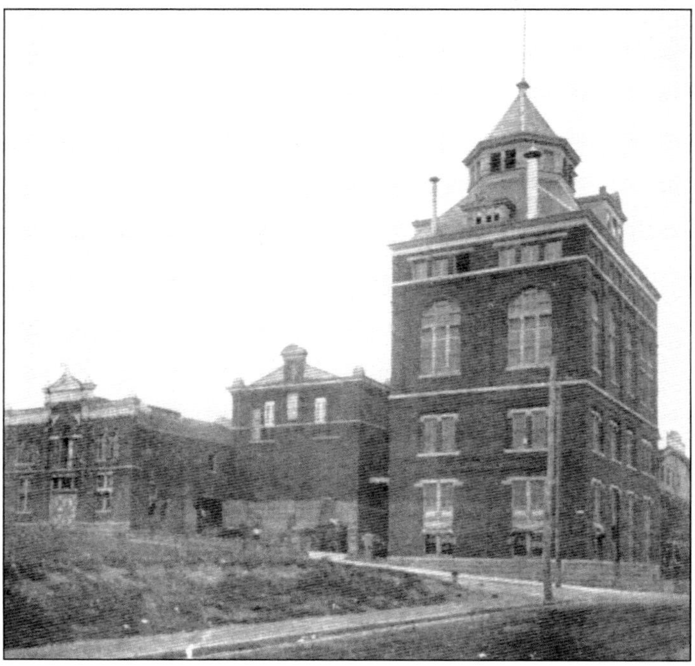

BAVARIAN BREWERY, WILMINGTON, C. 1899. The Bavarian Brewery added a large five-story brew and stock house (pictured at far right) in 1897, increasing its annual production capacity to 20,000 barrels. The brewery delivered its flagship lager beer, porter, and seasonal beers to saloons and hotels in Wilmington and the surrounding area. Bavarian's bottled products were available for purchase from bottling companies and liquor retailers throughout the city. (WPL.)

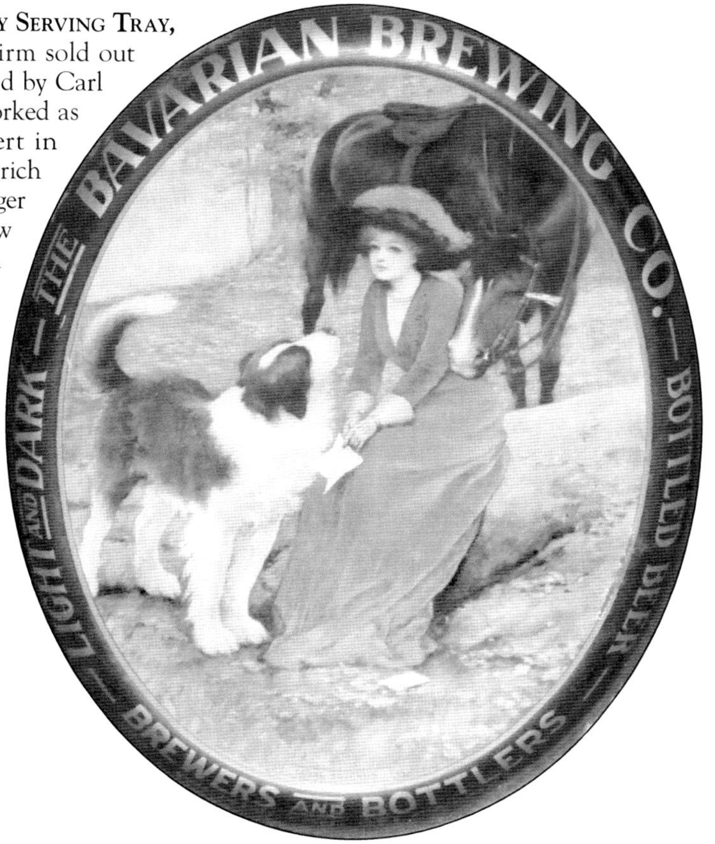

Bavarian Brewing Company Serving Tray, c. 1915. In 1898, Lengel's firm sold out to a group of investors headed by Carl H. Eisenmenger, who had worked as brewmaster for Jacob Ruppert in Manhattan and Christian Heurich in Washington, DC. Eisenmenger served as president of the new firm, called the Bavarian Brewing Company, Inc., and Lengel stayed on as vice president until retiring in 1901. (Photograph by Larry Handy; HK.)

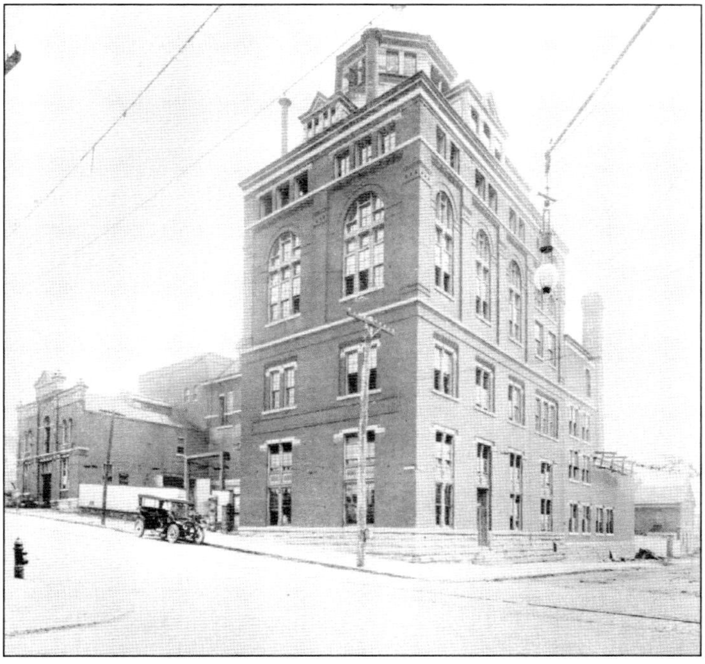

Bavarian Brewery, c. 1911. Under Eisenmenger's experienced guidance, the Bavarian Brewing Company increased its share of the local market with its lager beer, porter, and seasonal beers. Two of Bavarian's specialties were its Bavarian (light) and Maerzen (dark) lagers, which were available throughout Delaware and in Chester County, Pennsylvania. The brewery's annual output totaled 60,000 barrels. (HML.)

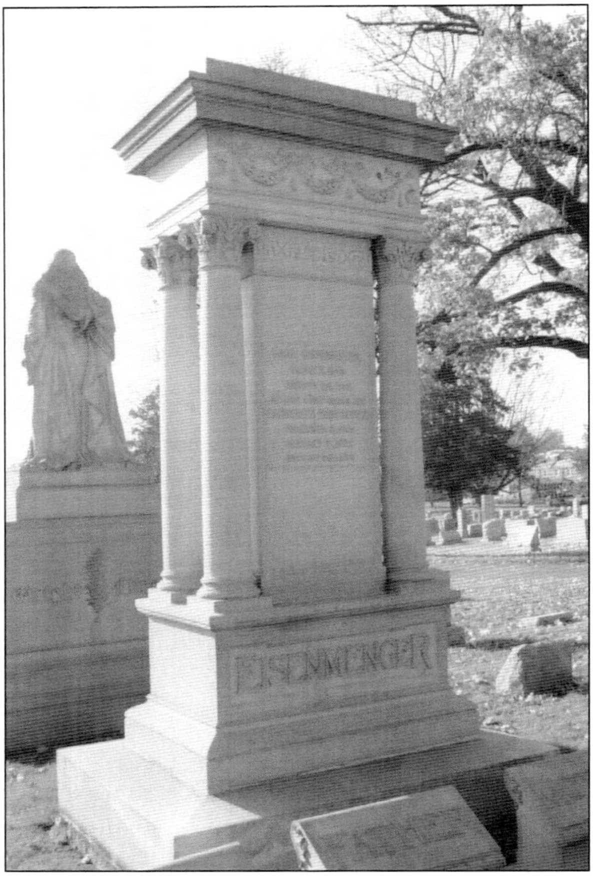

EISENMENGER MONUMENT, RIVERVIEW CEMETERY, 1997. Poor health forced Eisenmenger's retirement in 1908, and he died one year later. The brewing company reorganized with Eisenmenger's wife, Magdalene, taking over as president, their son Carl Herman Eisenmenger as general manager, and nephew John Hehl as vice president. Longtime Bavarian employee Jacob Steiger assumed the role of brewmaster. In 1911, Magdalene Eisenmenger stepped aside, and her son became president. (Author's collection.)

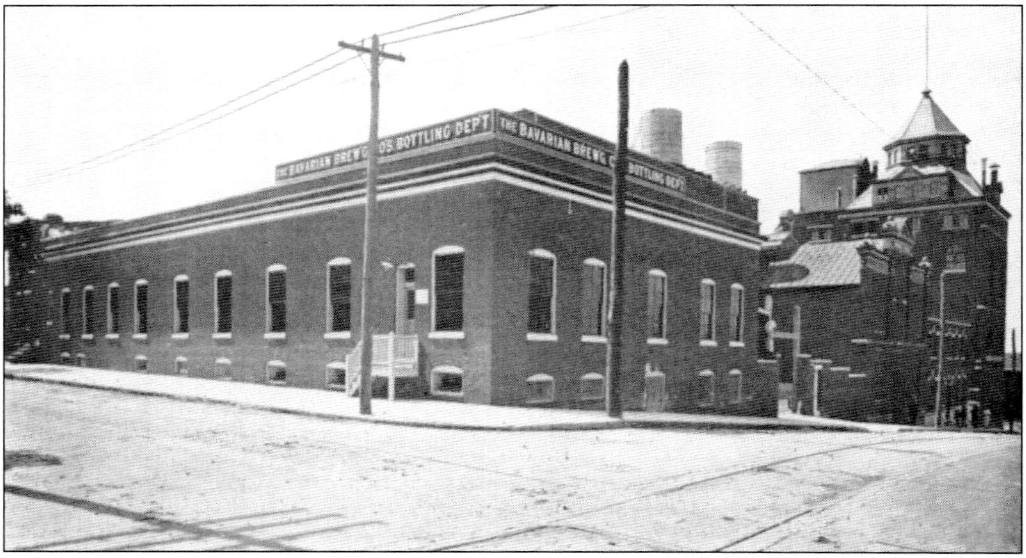

BAVARIAN BREWERY, 1914. Over the next several years, Bavarian became a worthy competitor to the Stoeckle and Hartmann & Fehrenbach brewing empires. The company greatly expanded its physical plant in 1913, adding a new four-story annex containing a cooper shop, stock room, and boiler house along Fifth Street, between DuPont and Clayton Streets. (Beer Institute.)

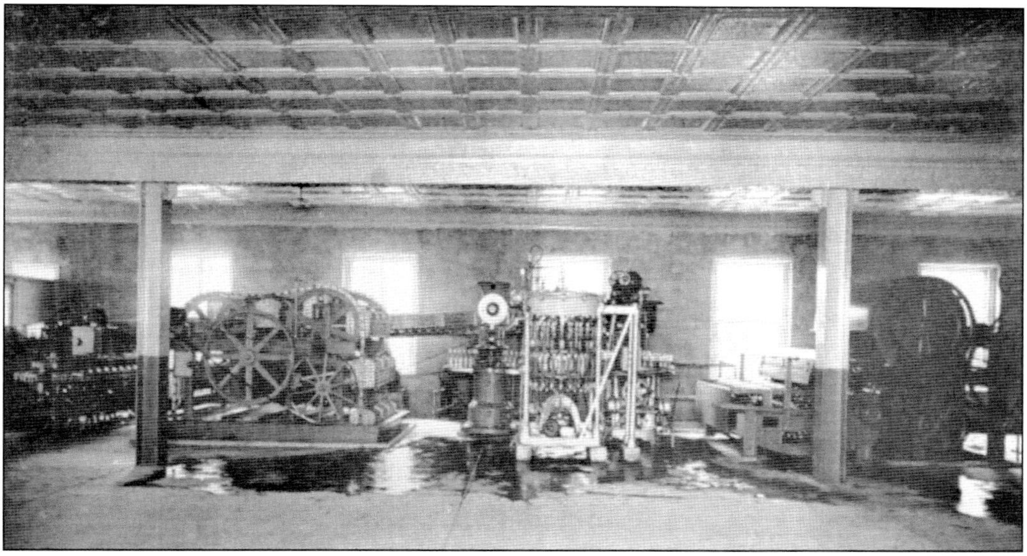

Bavarian Brewery Bottling House, 1914. The brewery constructed a two-story office building and bottling and stock house at the southeast corner of Sixth and DuPont Streets in 1914. This allowed the brewery to double capacity and distribute its bottle product directly to customers' homes. (Beer Institute.)

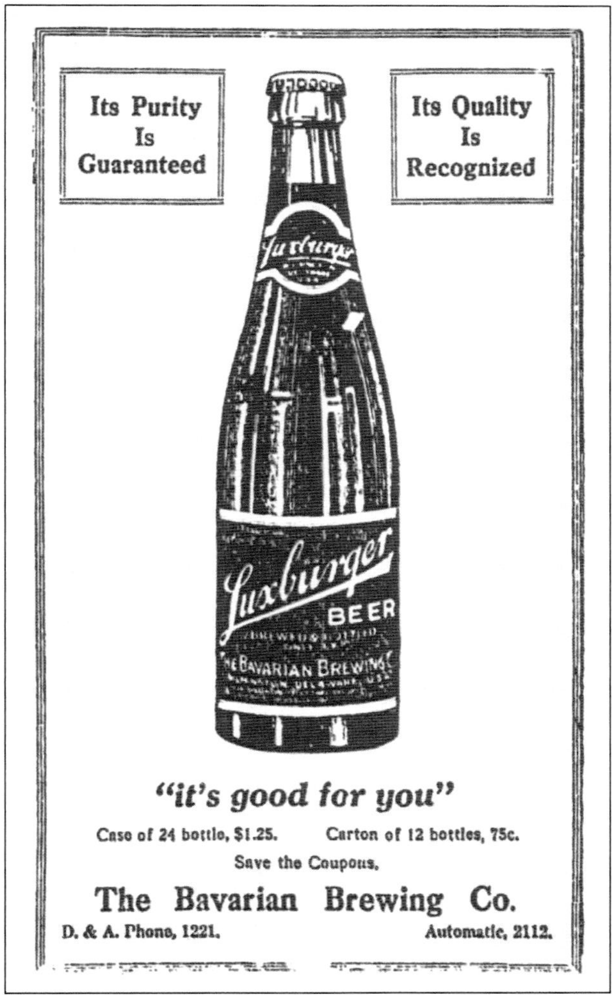

***Wilmington Sunday Star* Advertisement, August 15, 1915.** The brewery produced its Green Label, Bavarian, and Luxburger beers until the introduction of Prohibition. In the run up to Prohibition in 1919, Eisenmenger changed the name of the company to Peninsula Products Company and began producing soft drinks. (Author's collection.)

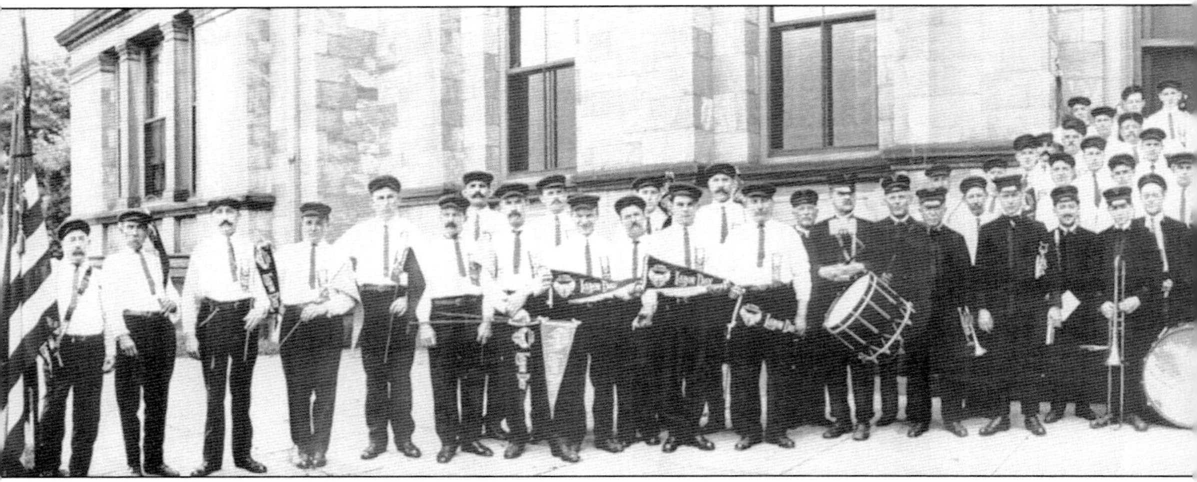

INTERNATIONAL UNION OF UNITED BREWERY WORKMEN, LOCAL UNION 267, WILMINGTON, C. 1910. This photograph was taken to commemorate the gathering of Local Union 267 at the annual Labor Day parade in Wilmington. The predecessor of the IUUBW, the National Union

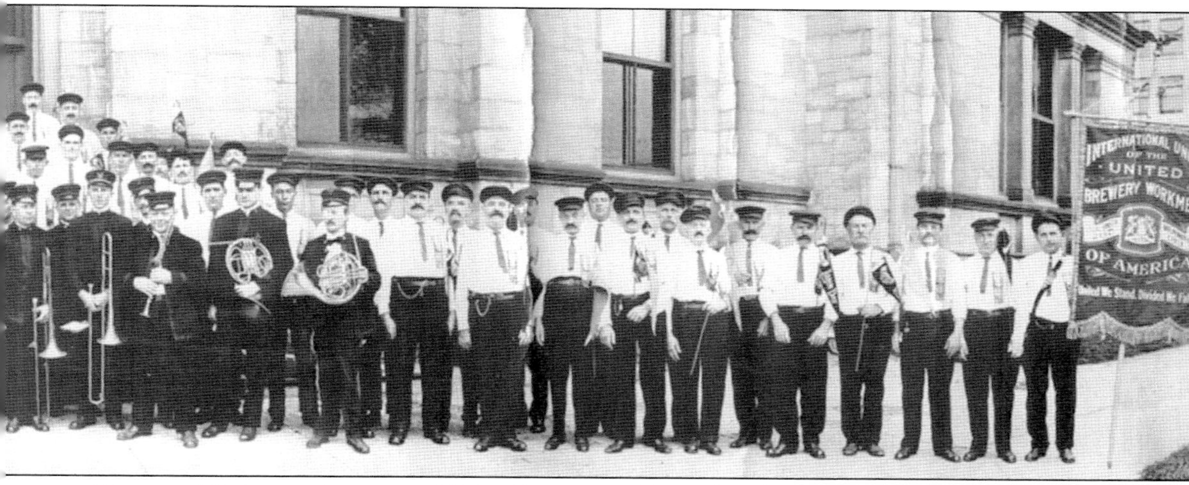

of Brewery Workmen, formed in 1886. The union affiliated with the American Federation of Labor the following year, making it one of the first industrial unions in the country. In 1910, the Wilmington L.U. 267 numbered approximately 70 men. (Author's collection.)

CHRISTOPHER BAUER,

PROPRIETOR OF THE

Bavaria Park Hotel,

ALSO DEALER IN FINE

Wines, Liquors, Beer, Cigars, Etc.

Park and Dancing Hall For Rent for Parties and Picnics.

THE BEST BOWLING ALLEYS IN THE CITY.

S. W. Cor. Fifth and DuPont Sts., WILMINGTON, DEL.

WILMINGTON CITY DIRECTORY, 1892. Situated across the street from the brewery, Excelsior Park opened in 1888. The park, which maintained a close affiliation with the brewery, changed its name to reflect changes in the brewery's name, becoming Bavaria Park and, finally, Bavarian Park. The site was a popular entertainment area, particularly for Wilmington's German community, and included a park, pavilion, hotel, saloon, and bowling alleys. Bavarian Park closed for good around 1910. (WPL.)

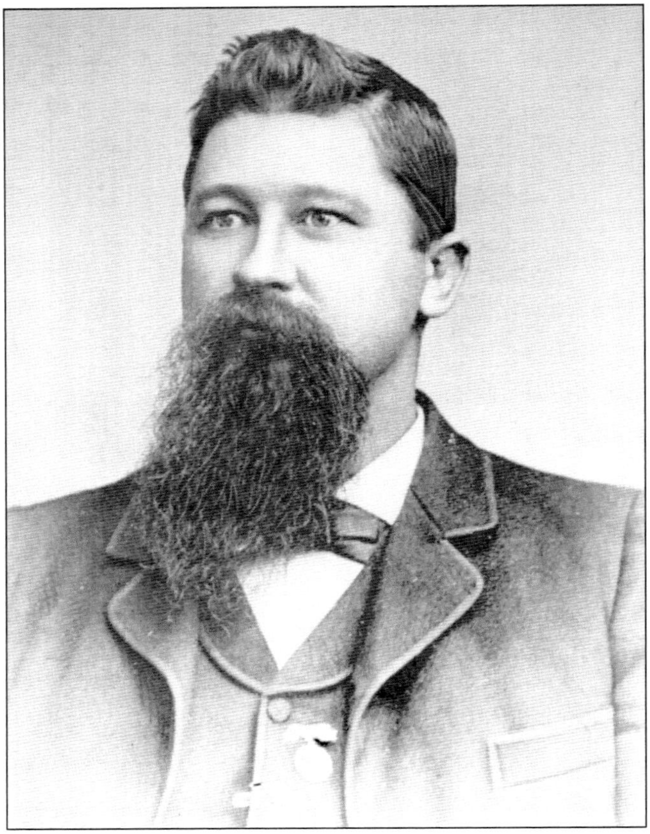

Peter Ebner. A native of Memel, Prussia, Peter Ebner arrived in Wilmington in 1877. He worked in the restaurant business for 10 years before opening a bottling plant on the southeast corner of Fourth and Union Streets. Ebner bottled and distributed beer for Stoeckle, Bavarian, Hartmann & Fehrenbach, and others. A pillar of Wilmington's German community, Ebner suffered a stroke in 1900 and was succeeded in business by his sons. (WPL.)

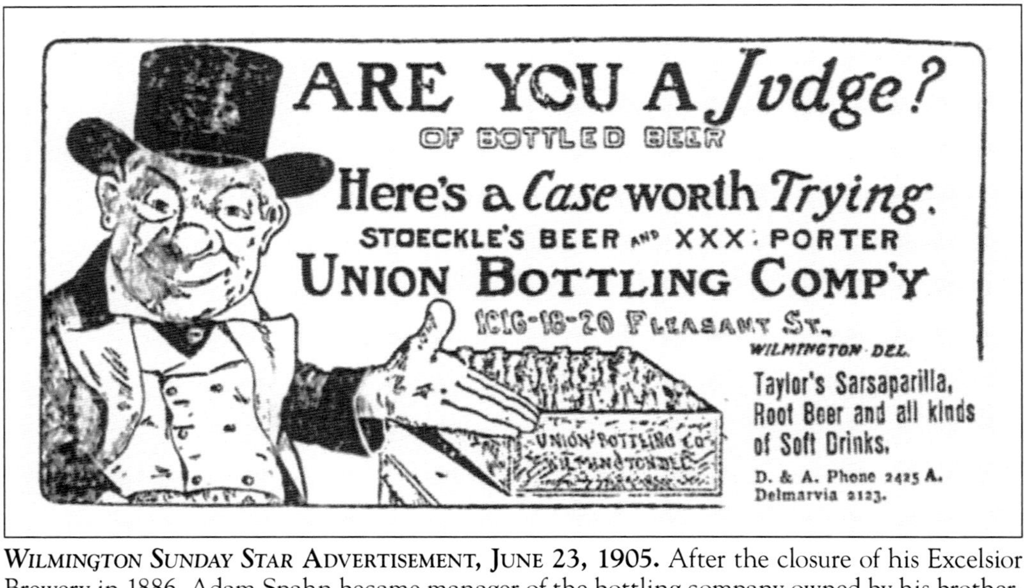

***Wilmington Sunday Star* Advertisement, June 23, 1905.** After the closure of his Excelsior Brewery in 1886, Adam Spahn became manager of the bottling company owned by his brother-in-law Peter Ebner. He entered a bottling partnership with Joseph Merkel in 1898 at 1016–1020 Pleasant Street, which dissolved in 1902. Spahn then formed the Union Bottling Company and served as its president until his retirement in 1908. Union bottled and sold only Stoeckle's beer. (WPL.)

JOHN P. DONAHOE. Born in County Tyrone, Ireland, Donahoe came to Wilmington as a child in 1842. He worked as a cooper before enlisting with the 1st Regiment of the Delaware Volunteers during the Civil War. Donahoe's heroic military career ended with his capture by Confederate troops. Upon his release, he returned to Wilmington and eventually entered a bottling partnership with William H. Robinson in 1872 at 521 Orange Street. (DHS.)

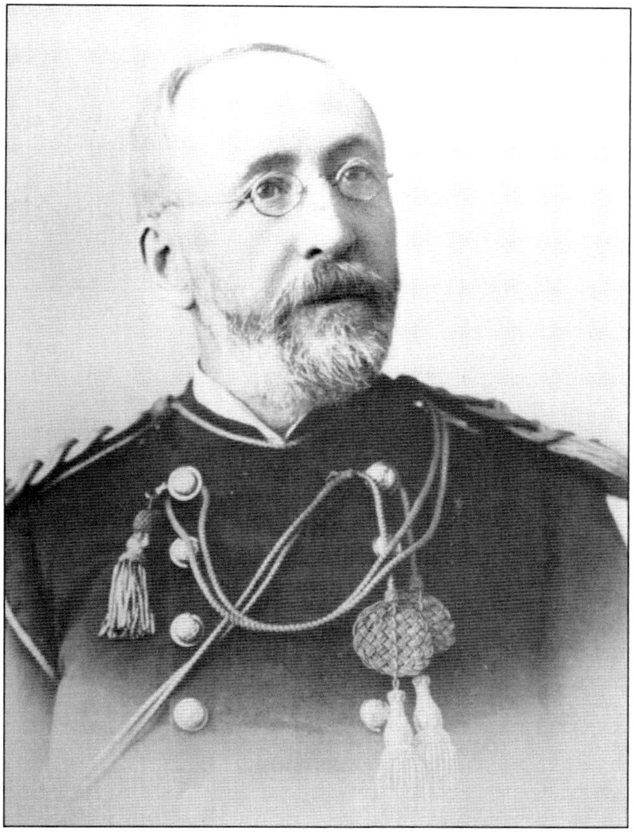

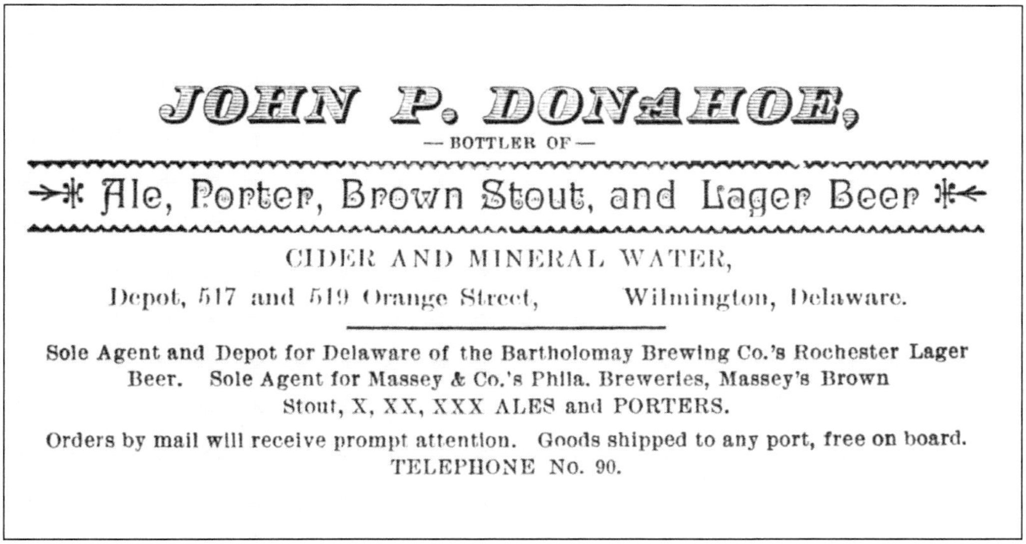

WILMINGTON CITY DIRECTORY ADVERTISEMENT, 1884. Donahoe purchased Robinson's interests in 1880 and constructed a sizable three-story bottling plant at 517–519 Orange Street, which he operated until his retirement 21 years later. Donahoe maintained exclusive bottling agreements with out-of-state breweries, including Massey of Philadelphia and Bartholomay of Rochester, New York. He also served several terms in the 1890s as a state senator and representative, including a stint as Speaker of the House. (WPL.)

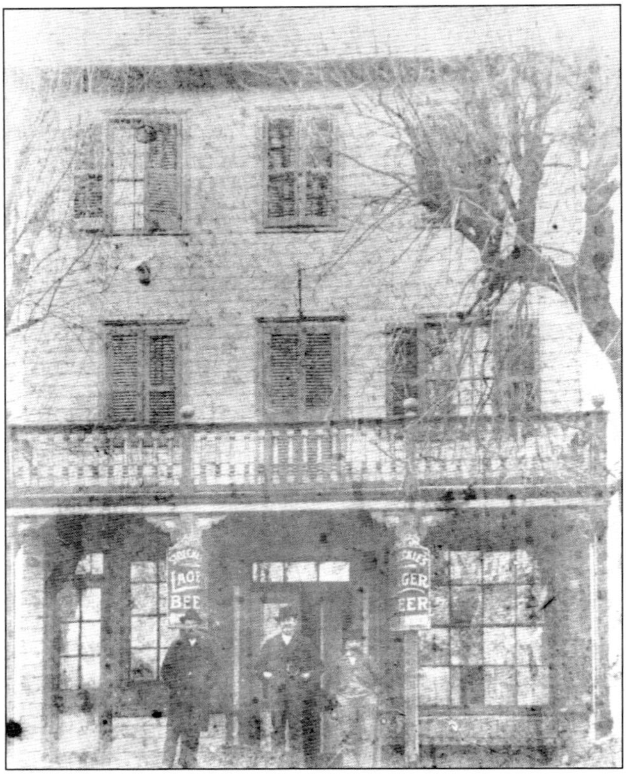

Tom Toy's Tavern (William Penn Hotel), c. 1885. Also known as the William Penn Hotel, John Thomas Toy operated his hotel, saloon, and grocery in Henry Clay Village, near Wilmington, from 1868 until his retirement around 1906. The first-floor saloon was a popular meeting place for men to discuss politics over a Stoeckle lager beer. Patrick Dougherty ran the tavern until 1917, when rural New Castle County went dry. (HML.)

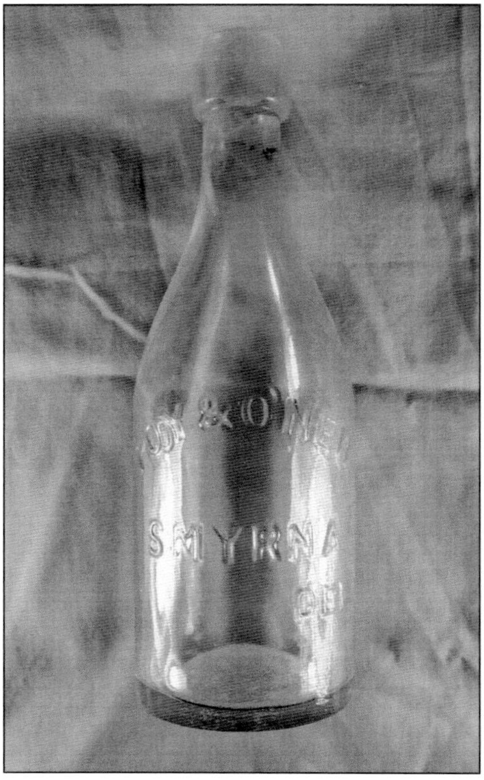

Toy and O'Neil Bottle, c. 1870. As early as 1869, Thomas Toy's brother Daniel and John O'Neil operated a bottling plant and brewery on the southeast corner of Upham and West Commerce Streets in Smyrna. The firm bottled mineral water as well as its own brands of ale and porter. O'Neil left the business after 1872, and Toy ran it alone until 1875, when he returned to his native Wilmington. (JK.)

GRAND UNION HOTEL, WILMINGTON, C. 1895. Henry Blouth came to New York from Bavaria in 1869, eventually settling in Troy. While on a trip to Wilmington in 1878, he met and fell in love with Caroline Stoeckle, daughter of brewer Joseph Stoeckle. They married and moved to Wilmington in 1883. Blouth purchased a lot on the northeast corner of Front and French Streets and built the lavish Grand Union Hotel. (DHS.)

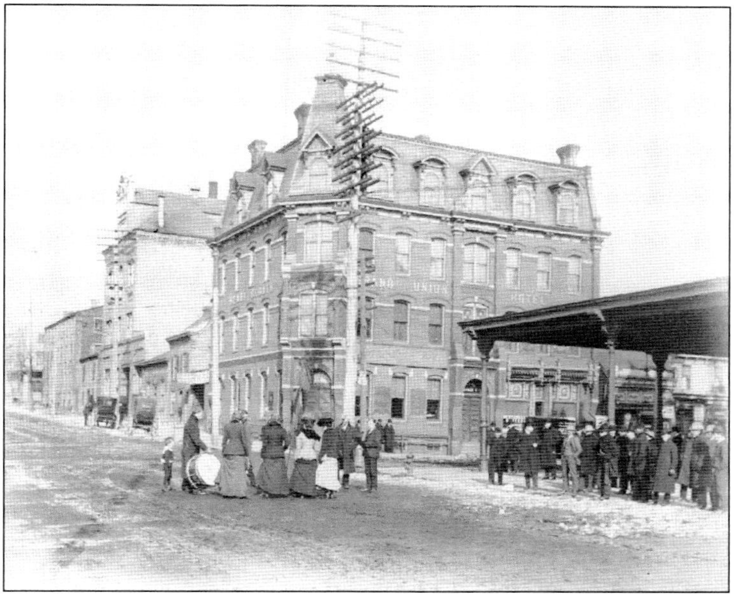

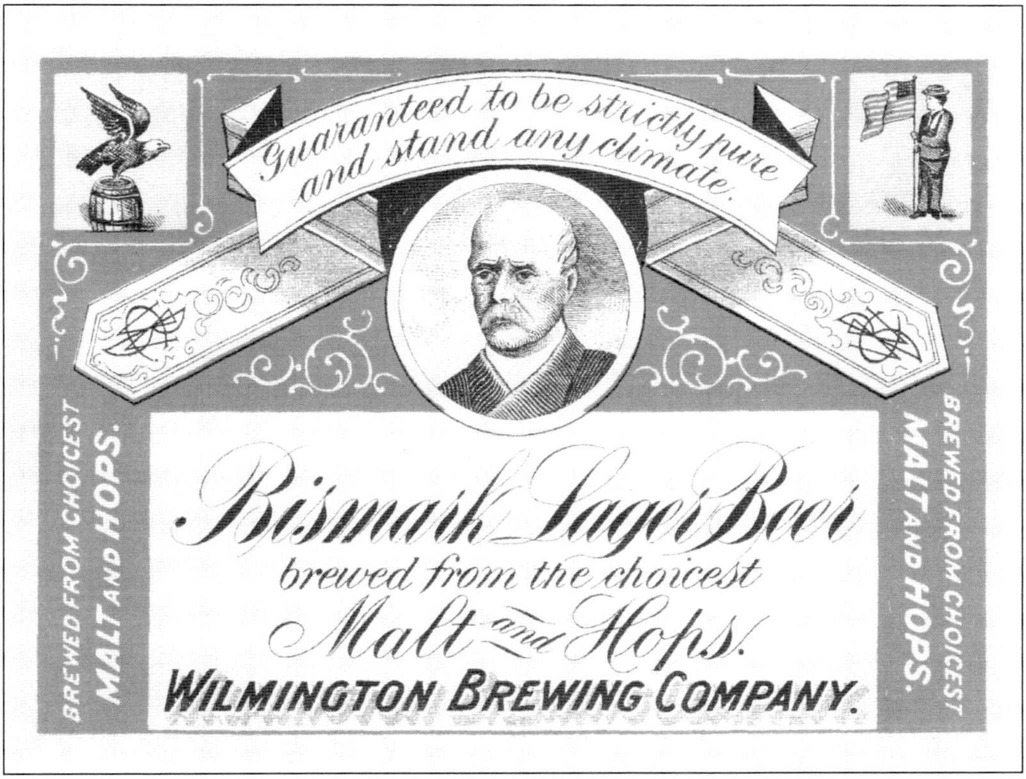

WILMINGTON BREWING COMPANY BEER LABEL, C. 1910. Blouth purchased several buildings just north of the Grand Union Hotel on French Street and in 1902 opened his own brewery. The Wilmington Brewing Company, which had a capacity of about 20,000 barrels, experienced steady growth until Blouth's unexpected death in 1913. His wife promptly closed the brewery and sold the machinery to her family's brewing company. (BKBL.)

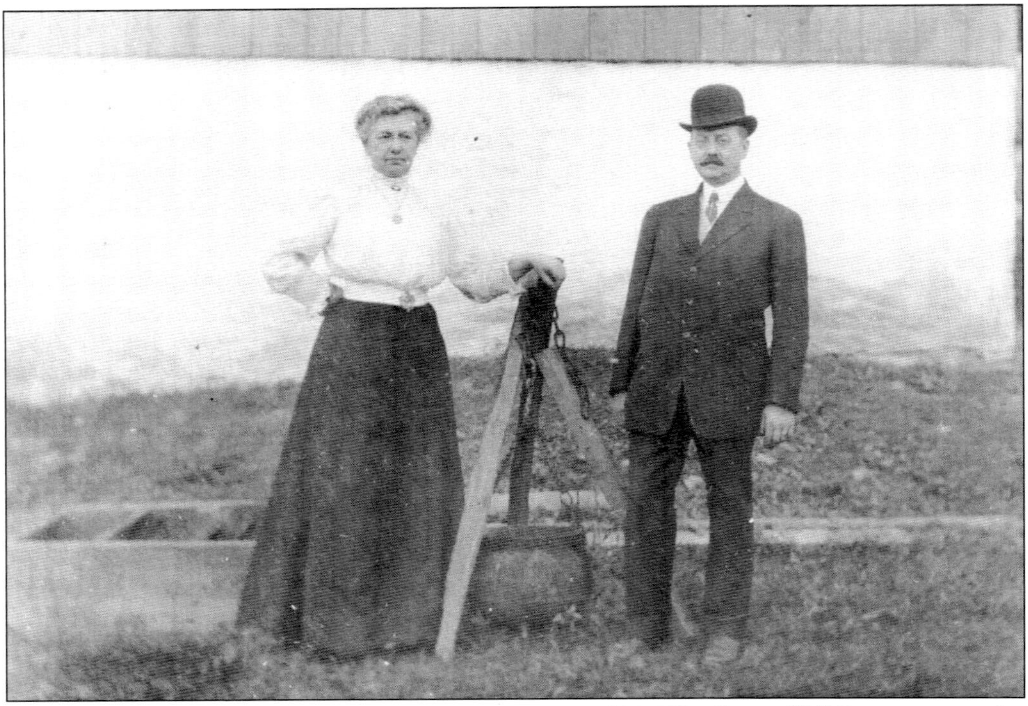

F. Hermann and Mary Biedermann, Wooddale, c. 1900. The Spring Hill Brewery, near the village of Wooddale, was a rare example of a 19th-century commercial brewery operating outside of Wilmington. In 1881, F. Hermann Biedermann purchased brewing equipment from his son-in-law Frederick Wurster, who had very briefly run a small lager brewery in the back of his saloon at 14 East Second Street in Wilmington. (LRW.)

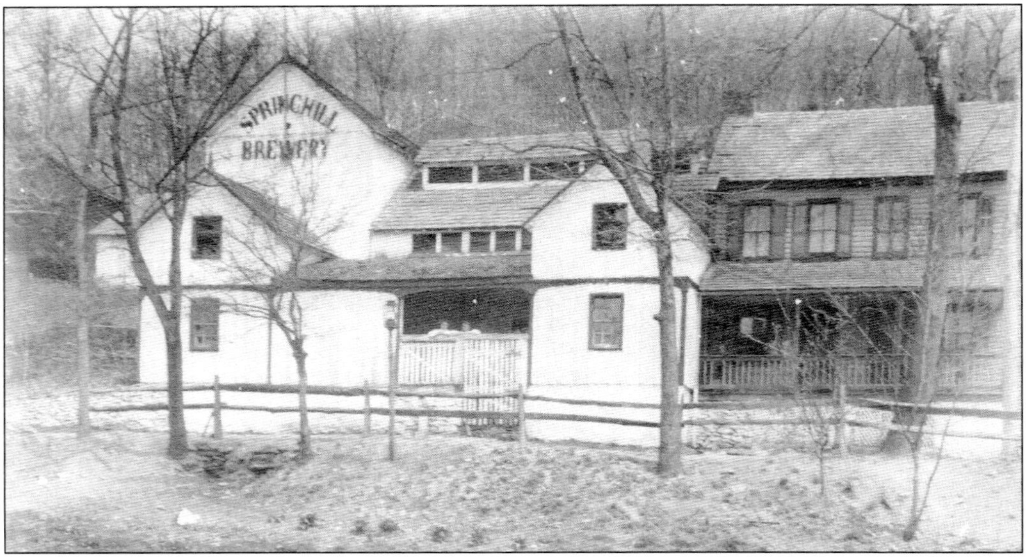

Spring Hill Brewery, Wooddale, c. 1890. Biedermann constructed a brewery on his property along Red Clay Creek and began supplying his draft beer to saloons in and around Wooddale. Biedermann's brewery was a successful small operation, with an annual capacity of less than 500 barrels. Hermann never intended to expand his business and was quite proud of not shipping his beer into Wilmington. (LRW.)

GEORGE J. BIEDERMANN. F. Hermann Biedermann retired in 1888 and his son George J. took over the brewery. George had both formal and practical training in the art of brewing and possessed a keen business mind. He gave the brewery its Spring Hill name and installed a bottling plant to allow the business to expand its reach. Unfortunately, George died unexpectedly in 1905. (LRW.)

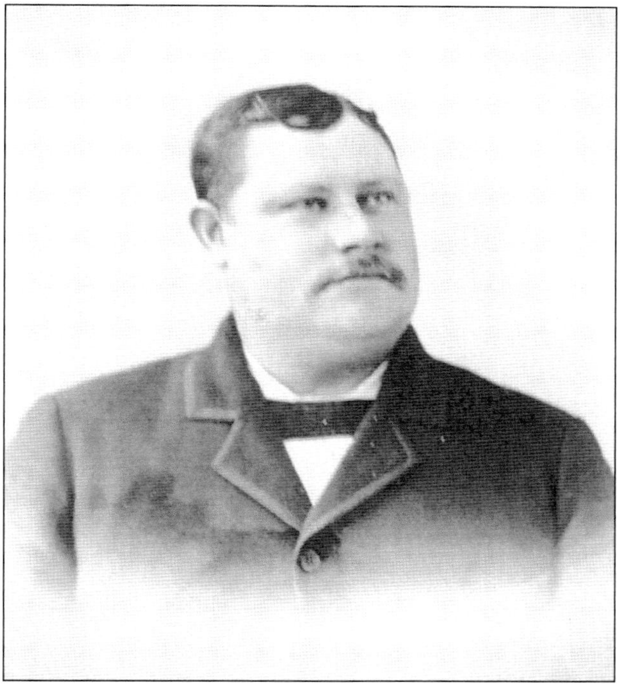

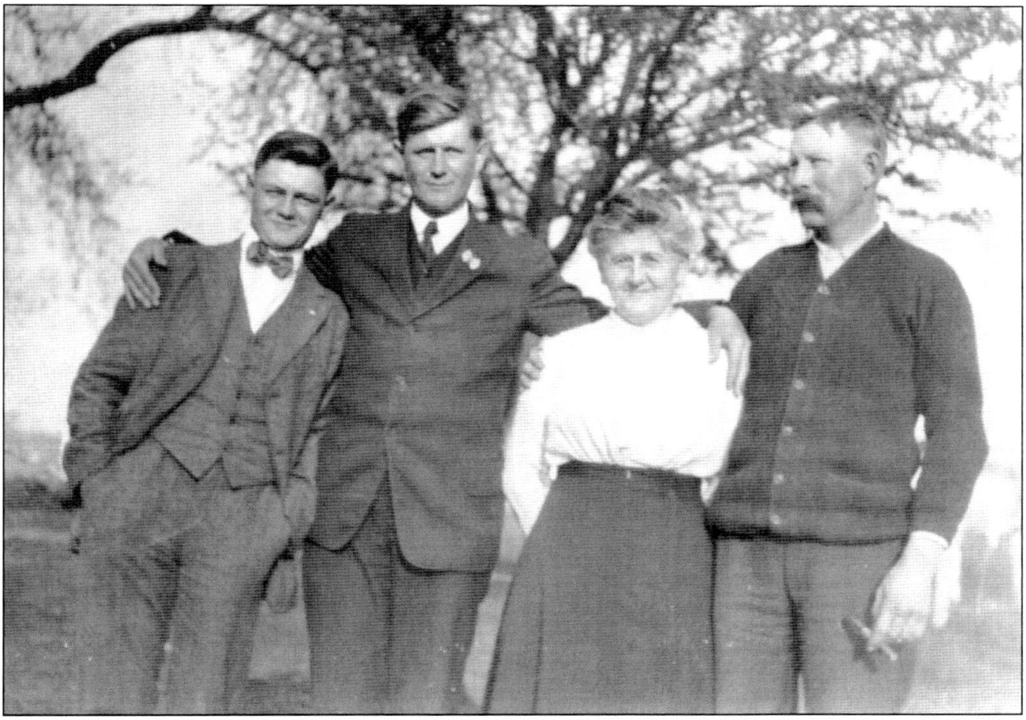

BIEDERMANN FAMILY, C. 1920. Pictured here are, from left to right, George Biedermann's sons, Harvey F. and George H., wife Bertha (Bauer), and brother Herman F. Biedermann. George's brother, Herman F., assumed control of the Spring Hill Brewery and ran it until it was destroyed by fire in 1911. He then got out of the brewing business and operated a farm near Hockessin, called Wyndmore. (LRW.)

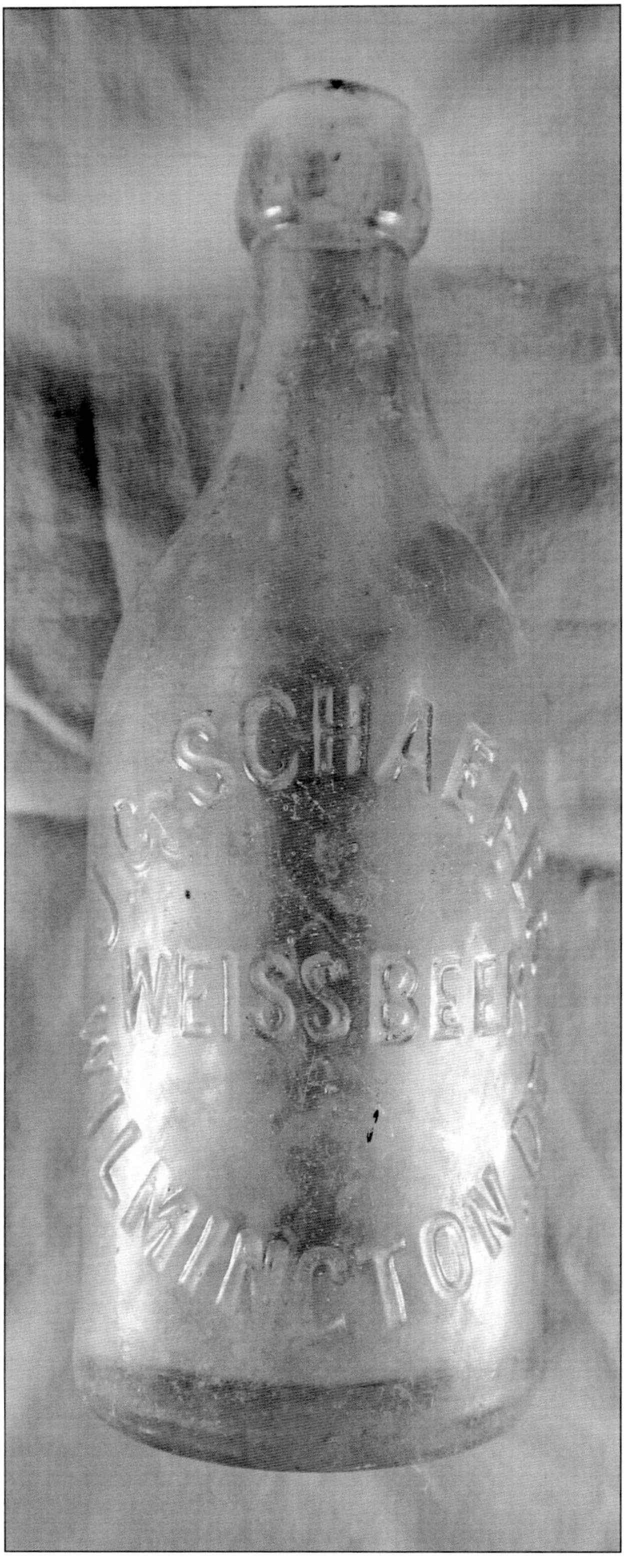

John G. Schaefer Bottle, c. 1890. A native of Bavaria, John Gustav Schaefer operated saloons in Wilmington in the 1860s and 1870s. He began brewing weiss beer in the back of his Weeping Willow tavern at Eleventh and Adams Streets in 1880. Demand for his weiss was sufficient enough to inspire Schaefer to open a small 500-barrel brewery on the northwest corner of Seventeenth and Union Streets in 1885. John died in 1891, and his wife, Mary, took control of the brewery and bottling house. She and brewer Robert McCune very capably ran the Diamond State Weiss Beer Brewery until her retirement in 1908. Mary Schaeffer sold the plant to saloon owner Edward Krause, who continued brewing weiss beer and bottling soft drinks under the Delaware Bottling Company moniker. (JK.)

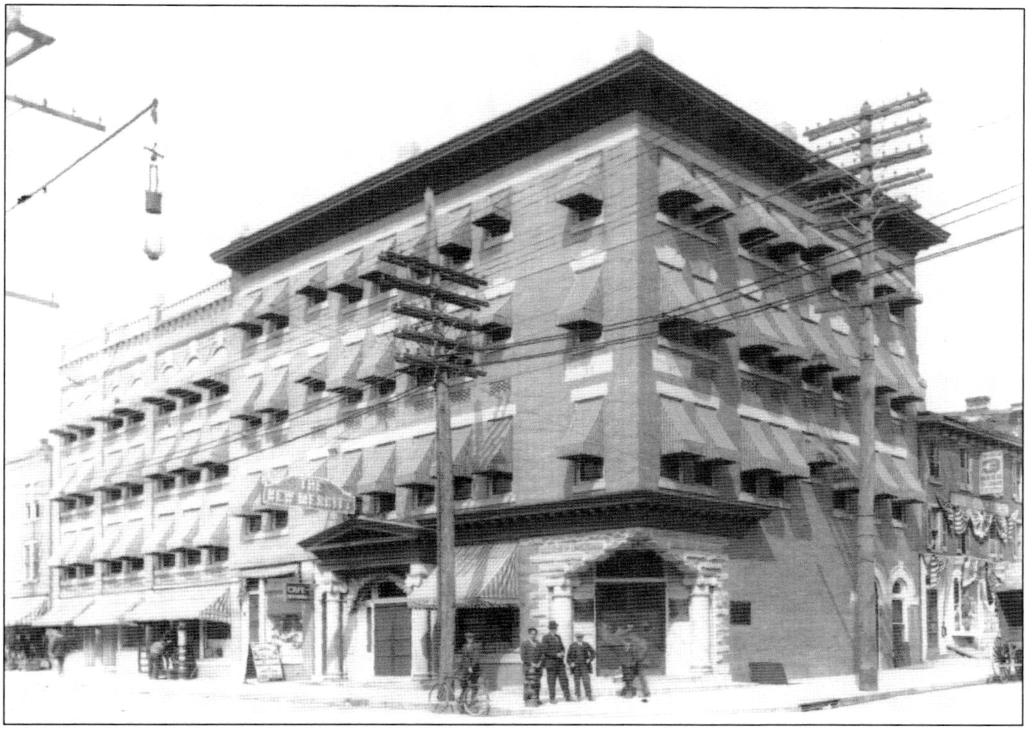

Hotel Merritt, Wilmington, c. 1911. In 1910, Krause purchased the old Merritt House Hotel on the northwest corner of Front and French Streets from John Fielding. In 1911, he decided to devote his time exclusively to the hotel and saloon business and close the bottling plant and brewery at Seventeenth and Union Streets. Krause operated the Hotel Merritt until about 1924. (DHS.)

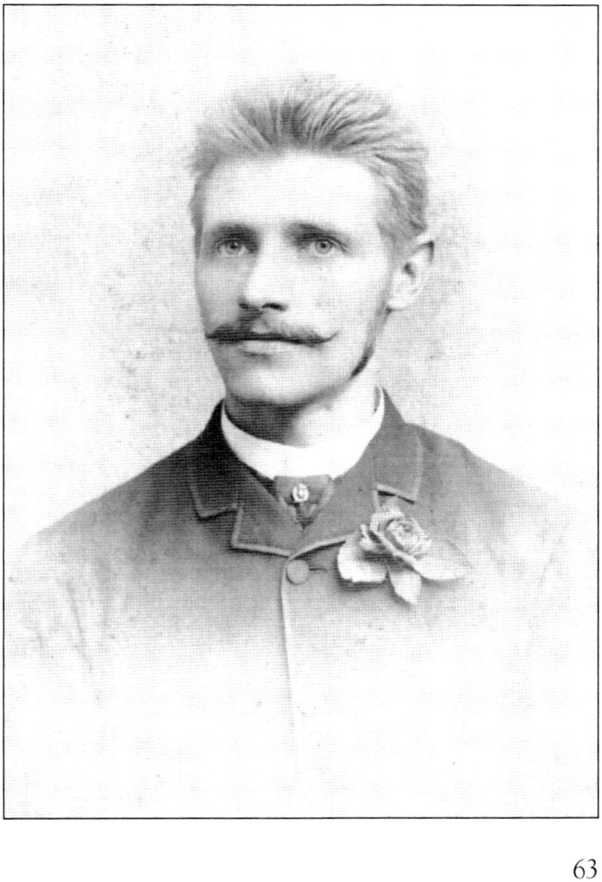

Maryan F. Poniecki. After having worked at several trades upon arriving in Wilmington from Poland, Poniecki started a beer- and soda-bottling house at 1800 West Fourth Street in 1903. The next year, he moved bottling operations to the southwest corner of Maryland Avenue and Chestnut Street, where he also opened the White Eagle Hotel and saloon. He got out of bottling in 1905 and focused on his saloon business. (ES.)

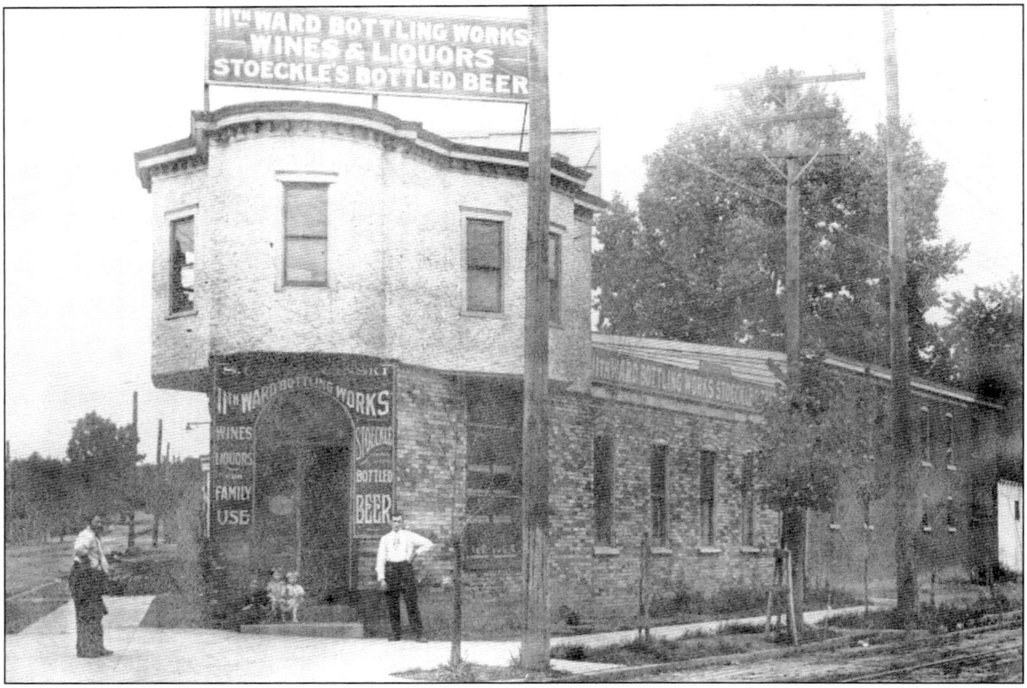

ELEVENTH WARD BOTTLING WORKS, BEECH STREET, c. 1911. Stanley L. Sobocinski, at far right in this photograph, immigrated from Lomza, Poland, and settled in Wilmington. He took over the bottling house at 1800 West Fourth Street from his father-in-law, Maryan Poniecki, in 1904. In 1910, he opened Eleventh Ward Bottling Works at Maryland Avenue and Van Buren Street. (ES.)

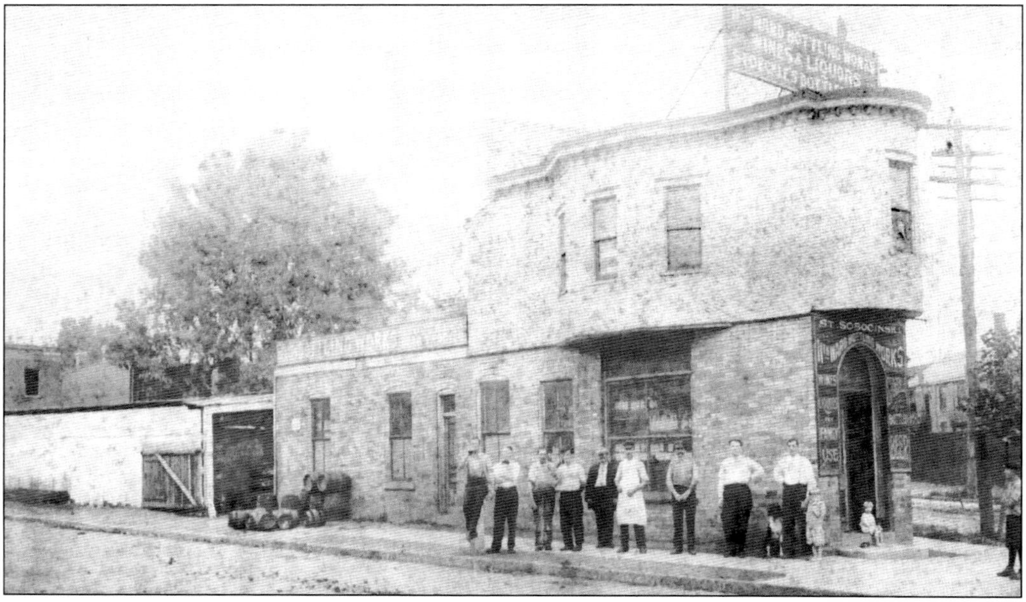

ELEVENTH WARD BOTTLING WORKS, MARYLAND AVENUE, c. 1911. Sobocinski operated a retail liquor store and bottled soft drinks and Stoeckle's beer in the back. In 1911, he purchased Edward Krause's brewing equipment and began brewing weiss beer on site. Brewing at this location ceased once Sobocinski sold the business to Bronislaw Lewandowski in 1915. Lewandowski would operate the bottling plant for nearly 40 years. (ES.)

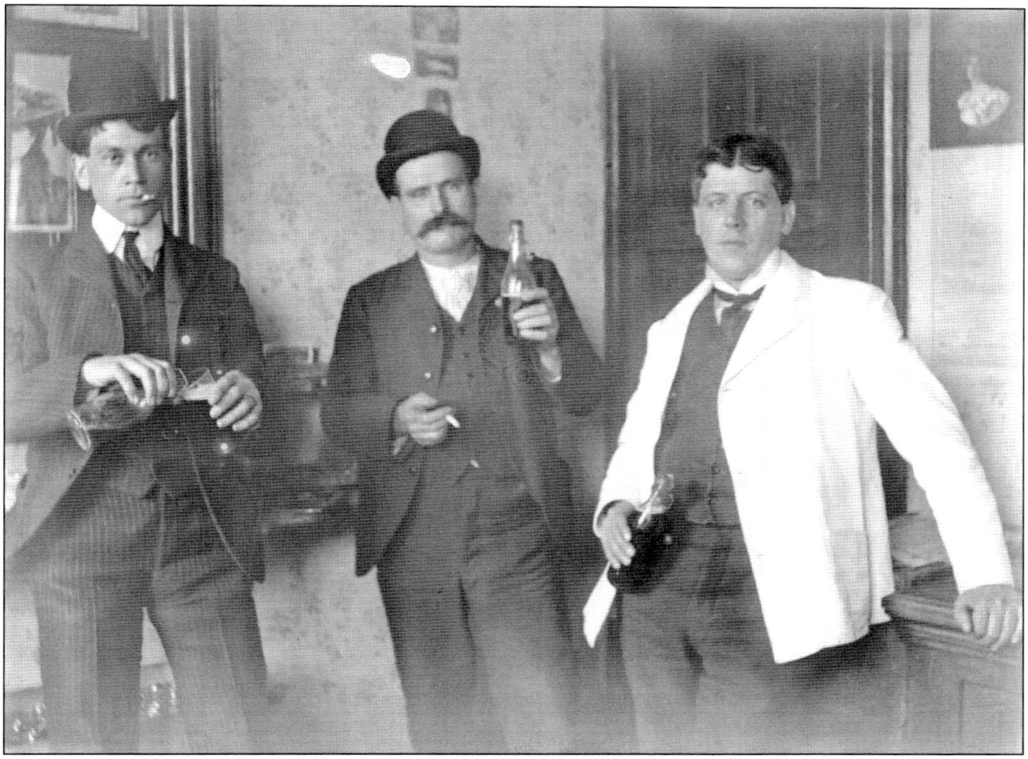

Unidentified Saloon, Wilmington, c. 1905. Taverns and saloons have played key roles in the cultural, political, and social lives of Americans since the 17th century. As the population in Delaware's towns and cities escalated in the mid- to late 1800s, so did the number of watering holes where men could seek temporary relief from the day's hard labor. By 1890, there were more than 180 drinking establishments and liquor dealers in Wilmington alone. (DHS.)

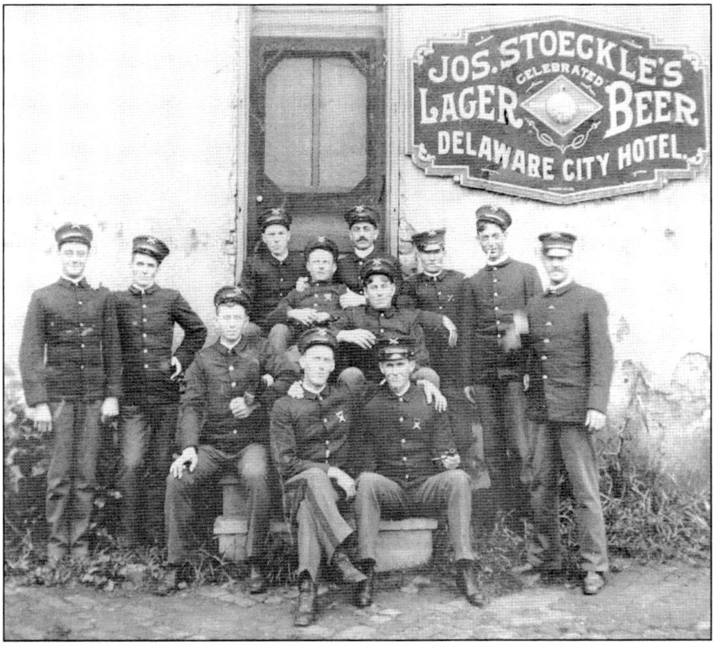

Delaware City Hotel, c. 1907. Established in 1828, the Delaware City Hotel is only two years younger than the town itself. Situated at the foot of Clinton Street near the Delaware River, the hotel's tavern was said to have been one of the best stocked in rural New Castle County. Here, a group of Fort DuPont soldiers from the 112th Company, Coast Artillery Corps, unwinds beneath a Stoeckle beer sign. (JK.)

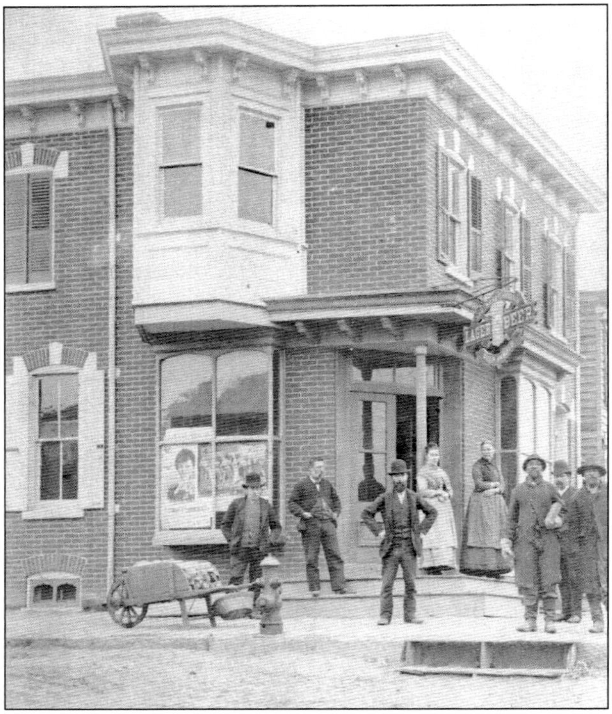

PHILLIP AMBOLD'S SALOON, WILMINGTON, C. 1890. Ambold, who was born in Baden, made his way to Wilmington by the 1870s. He served as proprietor of several saloons in the city from the mid-1880s until the early 1890s. At this unidentified location, Ambold was advertising Hartmann & Fehrenbach's lager beer. (Author's collection.)

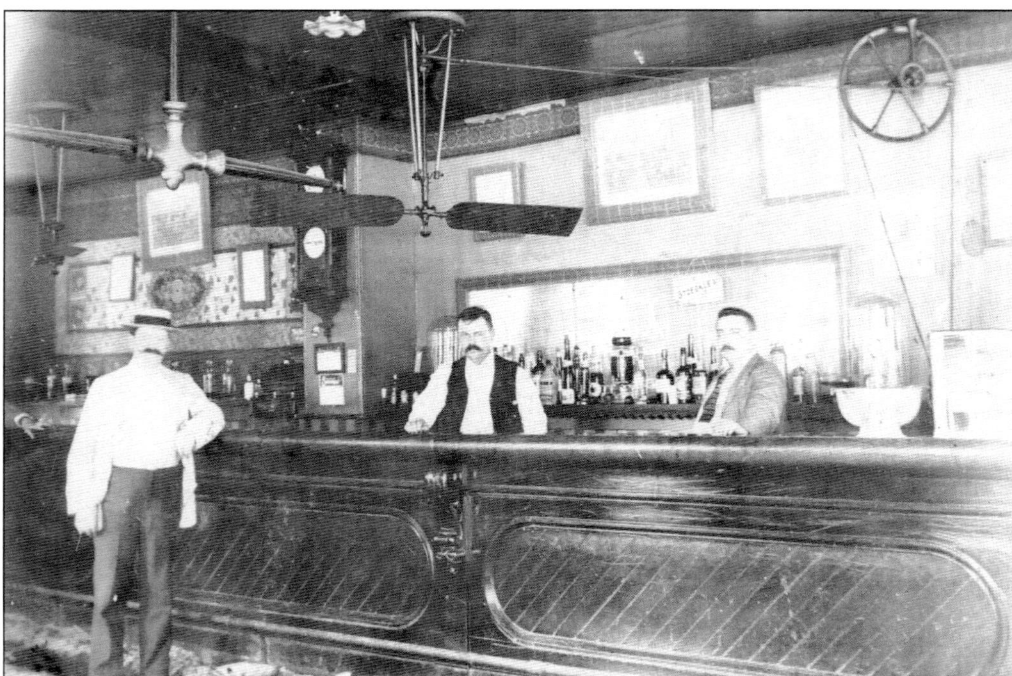

BAYARD HOTEL, DOVER, C. 1905. Bartender Frank Van Sant, in the center of the photograph, poses with a Stoeckle beer sign on the mirror behind him. Situated on the southwest corner of Loockerman Street and Governors Avenue, this hotel was within a short stroll of Dover's train station and became a popular destination for weary travelers. The building was demolished in 2011. (DPA.)

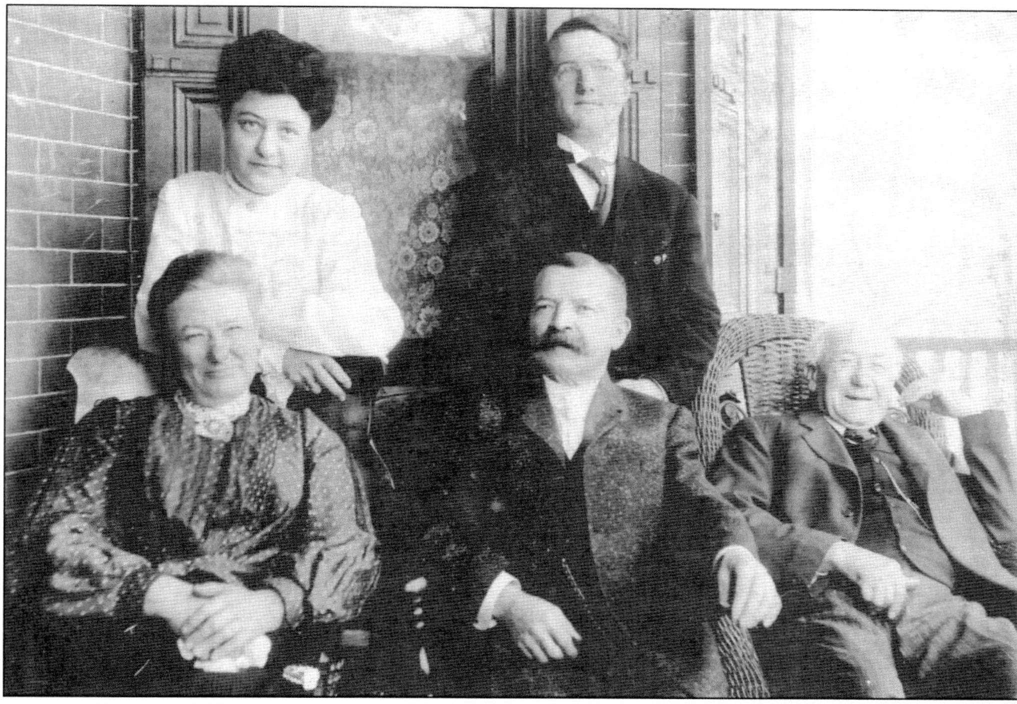

Anton Hauber, Wilmington, c. 1904. Württemberg native Anton Hauber (seated at center) opened his first saloon in Wilmington in 1879 before relocating the business two times. Wartime Prohibition in 1917 ended Hauber's nearly four-decade-long career in the saloon trade, but by then he was ready for retirement. Also pictured are Hauber's wife, Amelia; his children, Flora and Arthur; and his father-in-law, Henry Grebe. (Delaware Saengerbund and Library.)

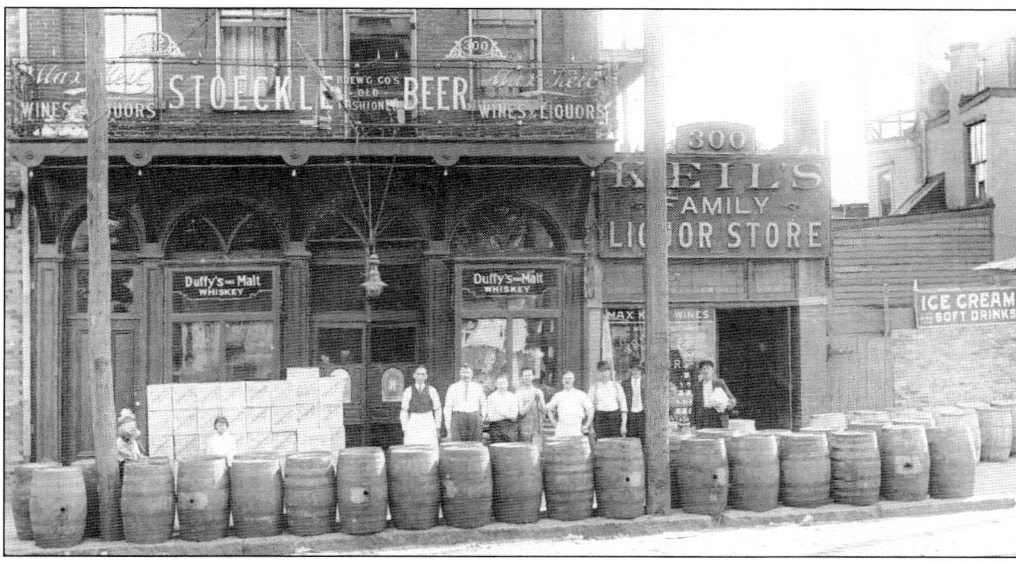

Max Keil's Wine and Liquor House, Wilmington, 1906. Born Mendel Kuchen in Beicz, Austria, Max Keil opened a saloon and liquor store at 300–302 East Fourth Street in 1906. As indicated by the saloon's marquee, Keil sold Stoeckle beer. At the onset of Prohibition, Keil headed the Keil Motor Company automobile dealership, and after repeal, he started a chain of retail liquor stores. (DHS.)

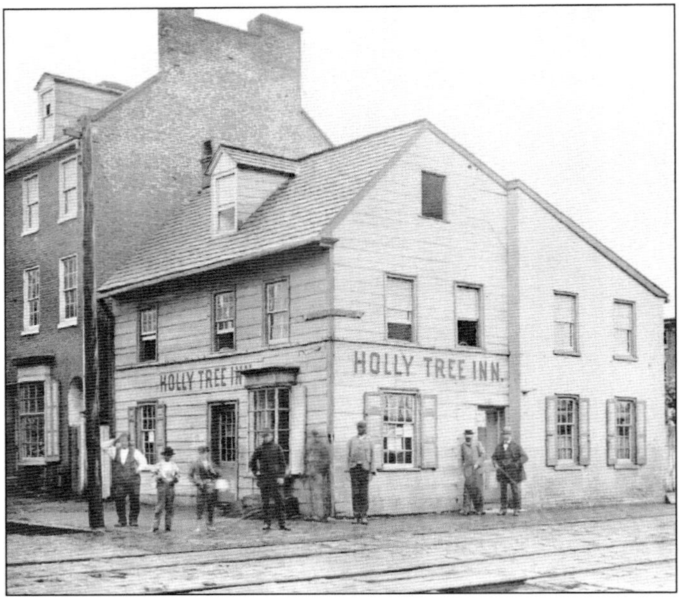

Holly Tree Inn, Wilmington, c. 1875. Beginning in the mid-1870s, Women's Christian Temperance Union (WCTU) groups opened Holly Tree Inns like the one pictured here on the northeast corner of Water and Market Streets. Coffee houses such as these offered male patrons harmless refreshments and lunches, while serving as outlets for temperance propaganda and meetings. Organized by the Holly Tree Inn Association, the inn had a short run from 1875 until 1877 and later served as a saloon. (DHS.)

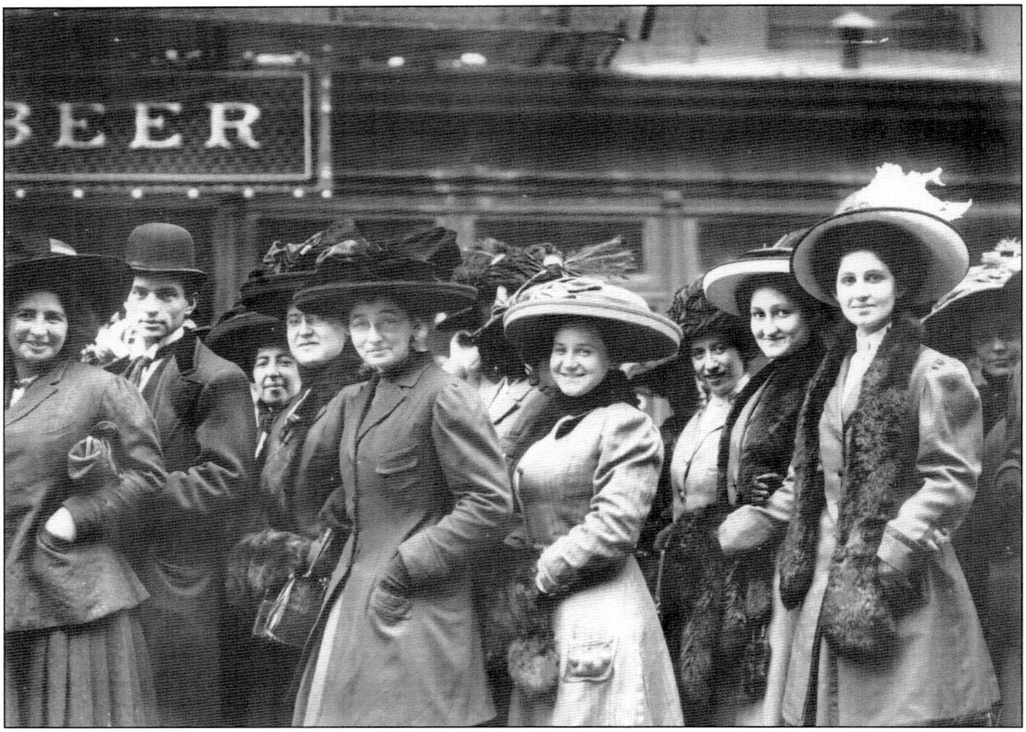

Picket of Volunteers. From the mid-1870s until the early 1890s, the WCTU was the torchbearer of the temperance movement in the United States. Along with public education campaigns, WCTU members also resorted to more extreme tactics such as organized picketing and blocking the entrances of saloons and retail liquor establishments. The WCTU of Delaware organized in 1880 and had branches in nearly every town from Delmar to Wilmington by 1885. (HML.)

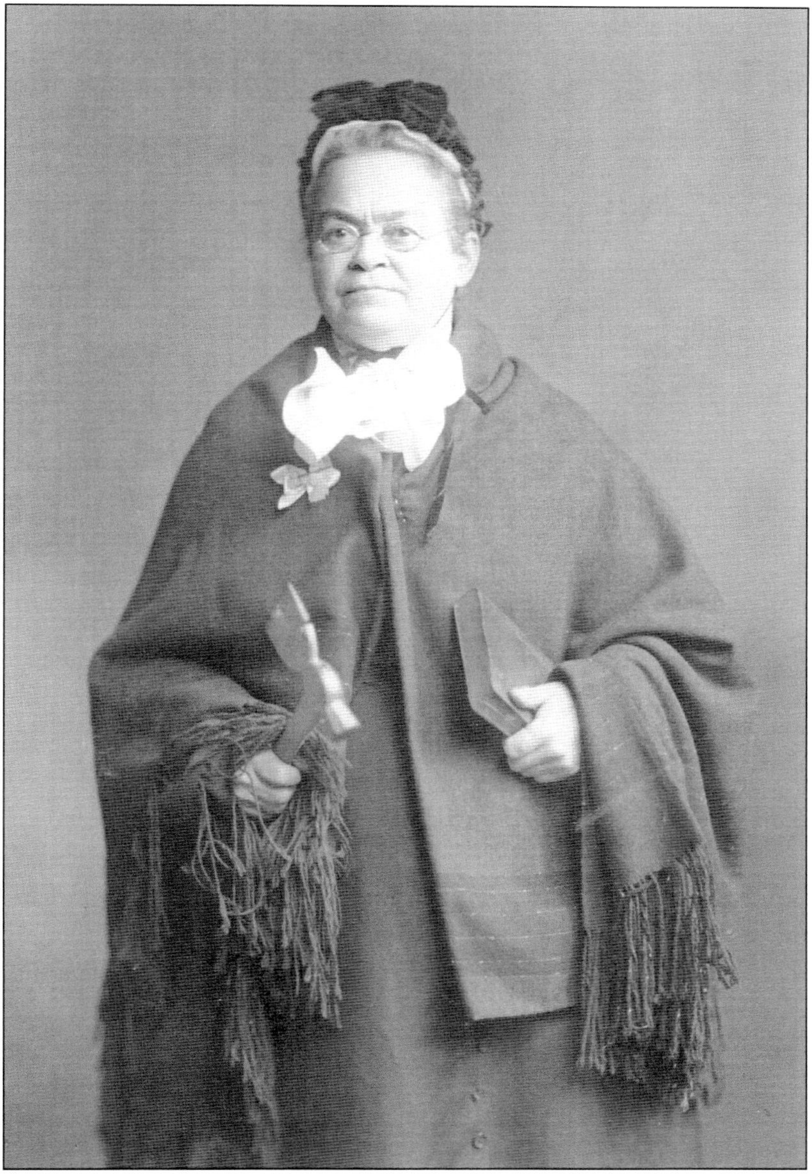

CARRIE AMELIA NATION, C. 1910. The WTCU's most radical member was Carrie Nation, who first gained attention in Kansas in 1900 with her campaign of "hatchetations." Sometimes accompanied by a band of righteous cohorts known as the Home Defenders, Nation would enter a saloon praying or singing hymns and begin smashing the bottles and bar fixtures with a hatchet and bricks. She was arrested more than 30 times between 1900 and 1910. Nation developed an international reputation and found success on the lecture circuit, where she sold her books, photographs, and hatchet pins to pay her fines. She drew large crowds to the two rallies she held in Millcreek Hundred in August 1904. An estimated crowd of 10,000 witnessed Nation speak on August 4 at Whiteman's Grove near Newark, and another 15,000 attended two lectures at Brandywine Springs Park two days later. The throngs heard Nation rail against brewers, saloon owners, tobacco makers, and "the rotten, riotous, rum-soaked Republicans with Roosevelt, the beer-guggling Dutchman, at their head." Nation sold out her entire supply of books and pins while in Delaware. (Kansas Historical Society.)

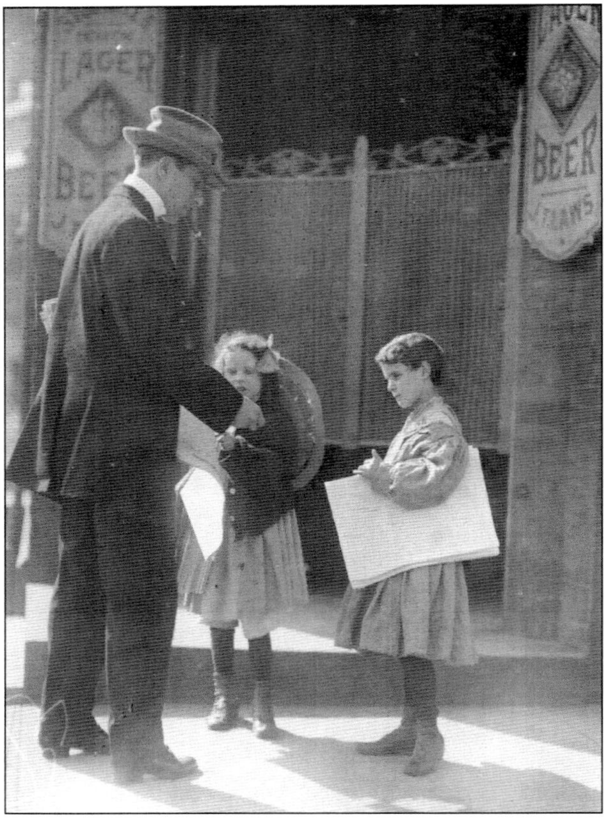

James T. Laws's Saloon, Wilmington, 1910. Two girls are pictured here selling newspapers outside of Laws's establishment at 401 Shipley Street, which, as the sign indicates, sold Stoeckle's lager. Temperance advocates long held that saloons were having a pernicious effect on the American family, with women and children being the chief victims of the products they peddled. They were vilified as dens of iniquity and hovels from which children should be protected. (LOC.)

The Gilpin House, New Castle, 1914. Stoeckle beer signs hang outside of the Gilpin House, which was run by John B. Truitt. Located at 210 Delaware Street opposite the Old Court House, a tavern operated at this site as early as 1741. The Gilpin House remains one of the oldest buildings in New Castle but has been altered several times. (New Castle Historical Society.)

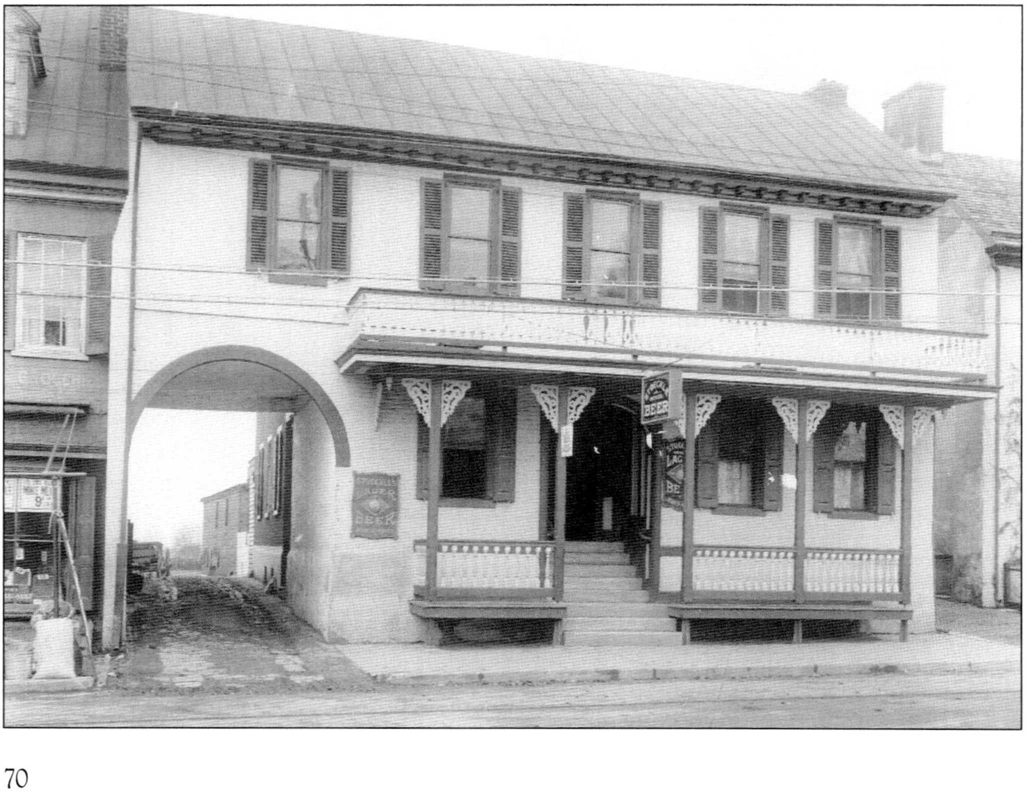

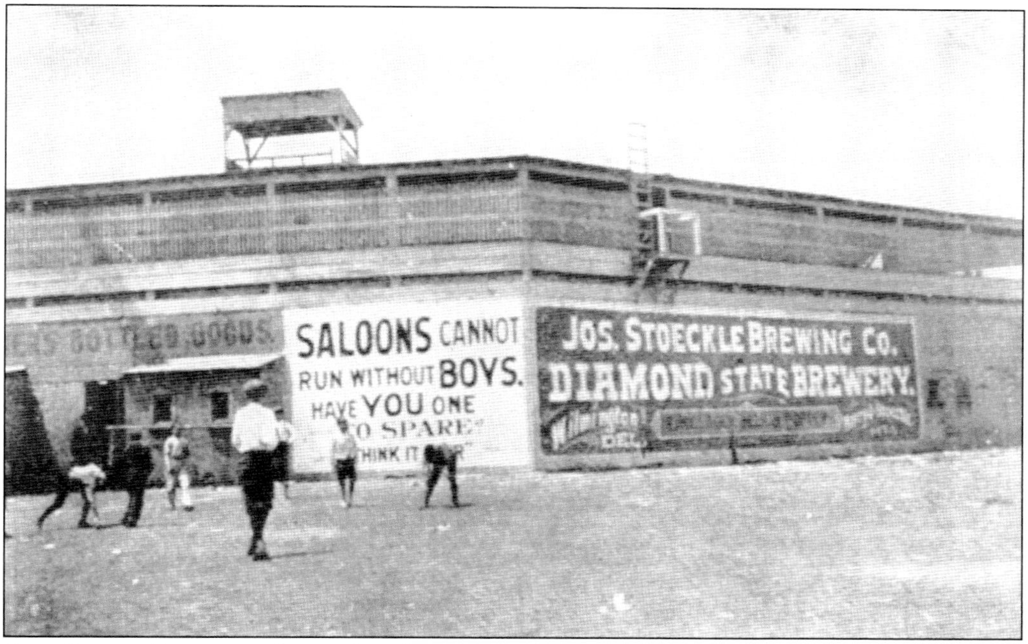

ANTI-LIQUOR POSTCARD, SOUTH SIDE BALLPARK, WILMINGTON, 1907. In February 1907, Delaware prohibitionists began lobbying the state legislature for local option measures. Each county and the City of Wilmington would have the ability by way of referendum to establish its own liquor regulations. In July, the Anti-Saloon League cannily placed its own advertisement between the Stoeckle Brewing Company and Ebner Bottling Company signs on the baseball grounds, which stirred controversy among the city's wet and dry advocates. (DPA.)

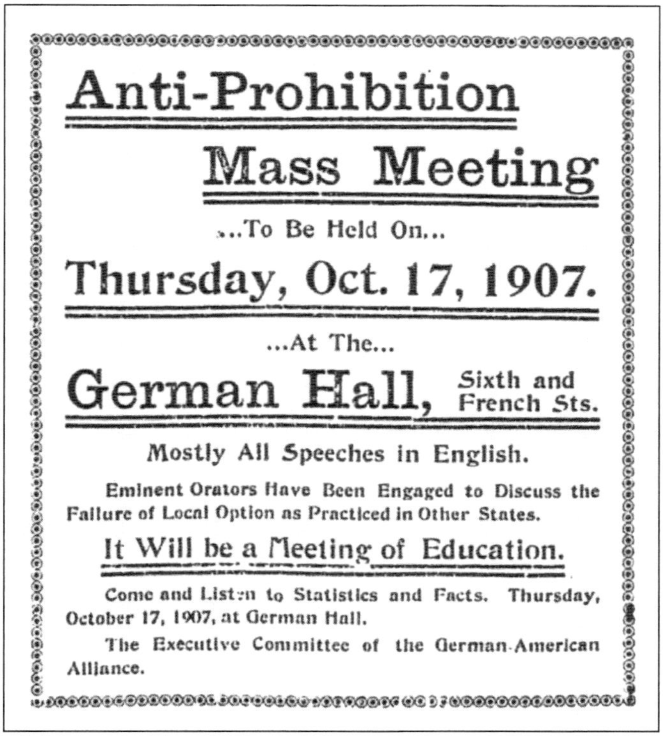

***WILMINGTON SUNDAY STAR* ADVERTISEMENT, OCTOBER 13, 1907.** A war of words proceeded throughout 1907, as Delaware prepared for a November 5 local option vote. In the end, both Sussex and Kent Counties voted overwhelmingly to go dry immediately, while rural New Castle County and Wilmington voted wet. Prohibition was under way in two lower counties, and Wilmington's brewers would be forced to adapt. (Author's collection.)

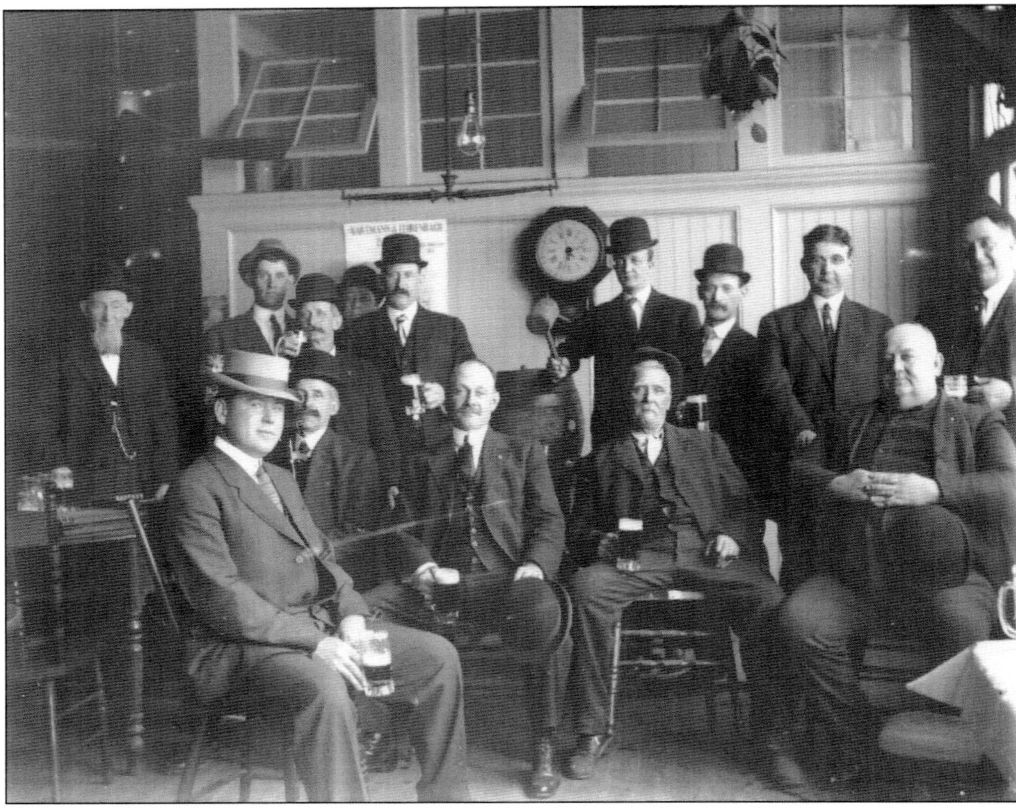

Atlantic Garden Saloon, Wilmington, c. 1910. In this photograph, a group of men pose in front of a Hartmann & Fehrenbach poster in Harry Schnepf's tavern at 224 King Street. As a result of successful efforts by anti-liquor groups, Schnepf and his counterparts in the saloon business were subjected to higher taxation, constant licensing challenges, and regulations prohibiting free lunches and takeaway growlers. (DHS.)

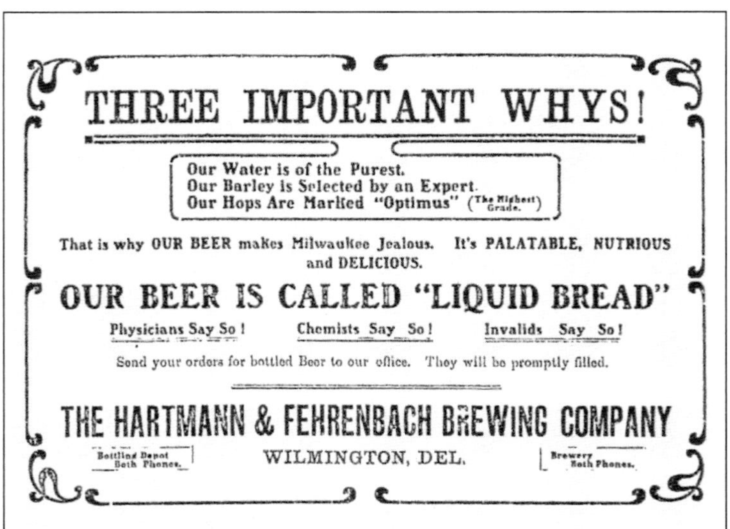

***Wilmington Sunday Star* Advertisement, June 6, 1907.** With their livelihood under direct attack, brewers attempted to sway public opinion by portraying their products as healthful alternatives to more spirituous drinks. Brewery advertisements, like the one pictured here from Hartmann & Fehrenbach, often touted beer's natural ingredients, nutritional value, and purity. (Author's collection.)

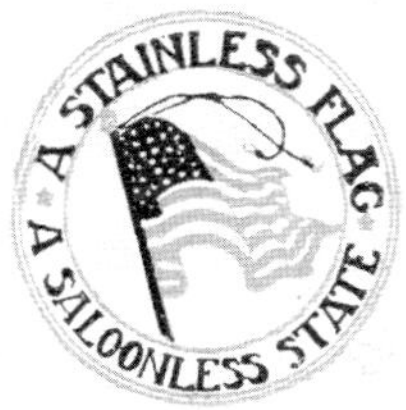

No Saloon In Delaware.

MISS MAGGIE S. WILSON.

(Tune—"Our Delaware")

On New Castle's granite hill-tops
And the smiling vales between,
On her sunlit plains and hillocks,
And the meadow lands so green,
Men are rising up in conflict
With a foe that's everywhere;
This their fearless, daring edict—
No saloon in Delaware.

CHORUS.

Oh, our Delaware! Our beloved Delaware!
For a stainless flag is waving
In beloved Delaware.
Oh, our Delaware! Our beloved Delaware!
Here's the loyal son that pledges—
No saloon in Delaware.

Where the wheatfields wave in beauty
In the peaceful land of Kent,
There true men will do their duty,
Doom the foe to banishment:
True-blue sons and fathers loyal,
Each the victory will share;
Each will give his mandate royal—
No saloon in Delaware.

Where old ocean's waves roll onward
On a silver-sanded beach,
And the orchard boughs lift sunward
Many a rosy-tinted peach,
Sussex manhood triumph's bringing,
Hear the shouts that fill the air;
They have set the chorus ringing—
No saloon in Delaware.

Anti-Saloon League Postcard, c. 1907. The Anti-Saloon League (ASL) organized nationally in 1893 with the express purpose of unifying and focusing anti-liquor factions and increasing sentiment against the liquor industry. The league used religious suasion and appeals to patriotism as part of an unrelenting public propaganda campaign. State by state, the ASL methodically and successfully worked with business leaders and politicians, eventually garnering support for legislative action. Since many of the breweries and saloons were owned and operated by those of German descent, the ASL found it useful to its cause to play upon anti-German sentiment in the lead-up to World War I. In 1913, with successful statewide campaigns behind them, including Delaware's 1907 local option vote, the ASL turned its focus toward national prohibition legislation. Another local option vote in 1917 rendered rural New Castle County dry. Wilmington, with more than half of the state's population and all three of its breweries, remained wet. (DPA.)

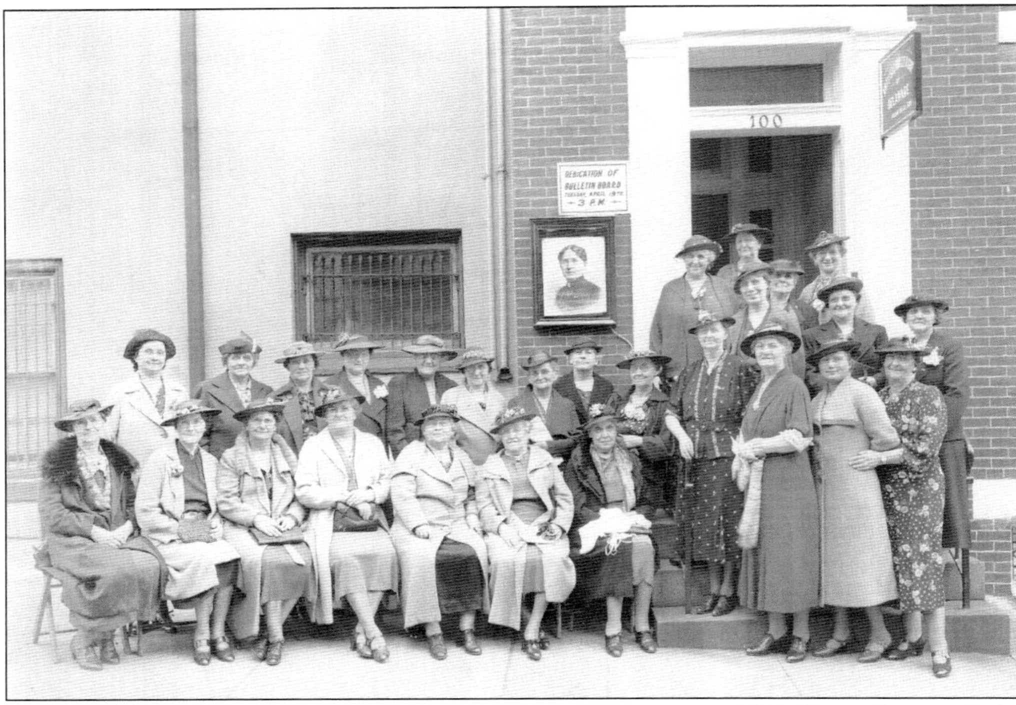

ANTI-SALOON LEAGUE OF DELAWARE HEADQUARTERS, WILMINGTON, 1938. Even after repeal, the Anti-Saloon League continued its dogged pursuit of anti-liquor regulations, though unsuccessfully. Here, members of the ASL are pictured in front of the state headquarters at 100 West Eight Street. Rev. Ivanhoe Willis served as the organization's superintendent. (Author's collection.)

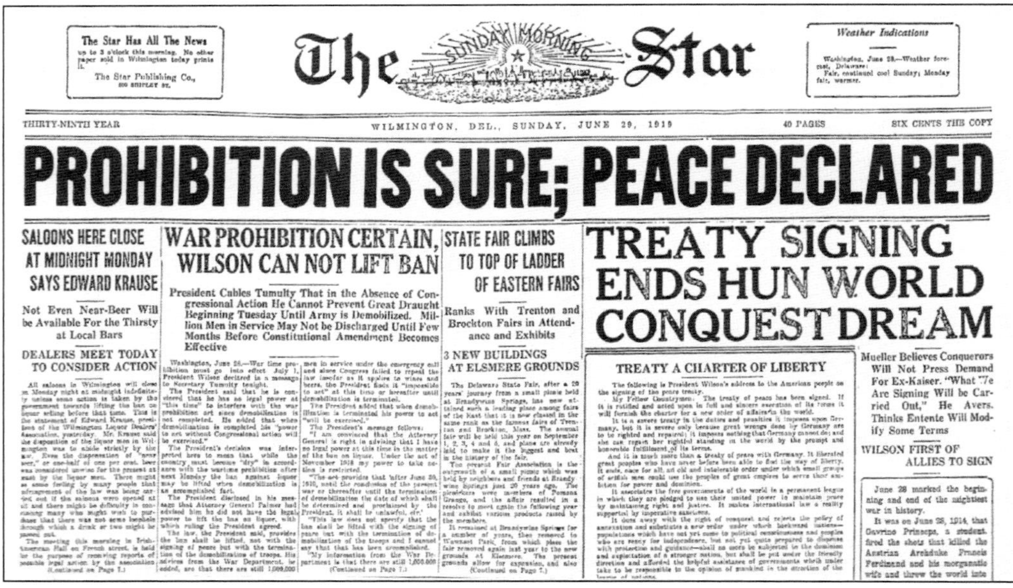

The Star Has All The News up to 3 o'clock this morning. No other paper sold in Wilmington today prints it. The Star Publishing Co., 800 Shipley St.

The Sunday Morning Star

Weather Indications — Washington, June 28.—Weather forecast, Delaware: Fair, continued cool Sunday; Monday fair, warmer.

THIRTY-NINTH YEAR — WILMINGTON, DEL., SUNDAY, JUNE 29, 1919 — 40 PAGES — SIX CENTS THE COPY

PROHIBITION IS SURE; PEACE DECLARED

SALOONS HERE CLOSE AT MIDNIGHT MONDAY SAYS EDWARD KRAUSE

Not Even Near-Beer Will be Available For the Thirsty at Local Bars

DEALERS MEET TODAY TO CONSIDER ACTION

WAR PROHIBITION CERTAIN, WILSON CAN NOT LIFT BAN

President Cables Tumulty That in the Absence of Congressional Action He Cannot Prevent Great Draught Beginning Tuesday Until Army is Demobilized. Million Men in Service May Not be Discharged Until Few Months Before Constitutional Amendment Becomes Effective

STATE FAIR CLIMBS TO TOP OF LADDER OF EASTERN FAIRS

Ranks With Trenton and Brockton Fairs in Attendance and Exhibits

3 NEW BUILDINGS AT ELSMERE GROUNDS

TREATY SIGNING ENDS HUN WORLD CONQUEST DREAM

TREATY A CHARTER OF LIBERTY

Mueller Believes Conquerors Will Not Press Demand For Ex-Kaiser. "What We Are Signing Will be Carried Out," He Avers. Thinks Entente Will Modify Some Terms

WILSON FIRST OF ALLIES TO SIGN

WILMINGTON SUNDAY STAR HEADLINE, JUNE 29, 1919. In December 1917, Congress passed the 18th Amendment, but ratification would not occur until January 1919. In the meantime, wartime Prohibition measures were enacted in an attempt to conserve grain, a full week after the armistice was signed. Since the troops had not yet been demobilized, Pres. Woodrow Wilson did not suspend the act. (Author's collection.)

Three

Brewing's Revival and Disappearance 1920–1955

While the implementation of Prohibition killed the legal brewing industry, it could not effectively prevent those who wanted a drink from purchasing it by illicit means or making it themselves. The demand for beer and other alcohol still existed. The Volstead Act simply drove its production underground and turned over a once-taxable industry to organized crime.

Delaware's Big Three breweries tried to convert production to soft drinks and near beer but were unable to sustain their operations for long. During the 13 long years of Prohibition, the owners and primary operators of the Diamond State and the Hartmann & Fehrenbach Breweries died, and their companies ceased operations; the Bavarian Brewery also closed. All three facilities fell into the hands of bootleggers, whose operations were invariably shut down by federal agents.

As the issues with Prohibition enforcement became increasingly more evident through the 1920s, the Association Against the Prohibition Amendment, led by Delawareans Pierre S. du Pont, Irenee du Pont, John J. Raskob, and others, mounted the successful national effort for repeal. When the 21st Amendment was finally implemented, Pierre du Pont served as the head of Delaware's new state liquor commission and helped shape the state's new alcohol policy.

Delaware adopted a new three-tiered distribution system, which segregated production from distribution in an effort to protect the public from the abuses of the past. Unfortunately for Delaware brewers, the new system allowed for wider distribution of other regional and national brands in the state for the first time. In the pre-Prohibition years, Delaware consumers had always demonstrated loyalty to the local breweries that served them, but that would no longer be the case, beginning in 1933.

In the early 1930s, the old Diamond State and Bavarian Breweries were renovated and reopened by new concerns. Ultimately though, Delaware's two lone breweries were put out of business by larger, better-funded, and more expertly marketed regional and national companies. The two facilities sat idle for much of the 1950s, fell into disrepair, and were eventually demolished. The 22-year spike in brewing activity in the First State after repeal would be followed by an interminably long 40-year drought.

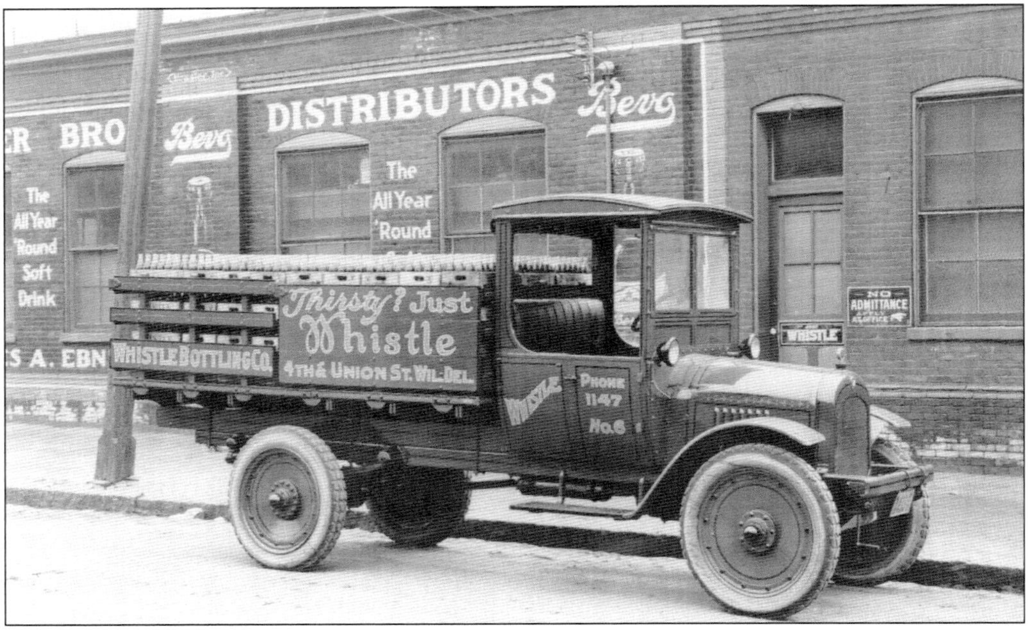

EBNER BROTHERS BOTTLING COMPANY, WILMINGTON, C. 1920. With the implementation of the Volstead Act in January 1920, the production, importation, and distribution of alcoholic beverages was outlawed. Wilmington's breweries and bottlers complied with the act and converted production to de-alcoholized near beer and soft drinks. In this photograph, an Ebner truck advertising Whistle soda is parked in front of its bottling house at Fourth and Union Streets. The Ebners also distributed Bevo, Anheuser-Busch's near beer. (DHS.)

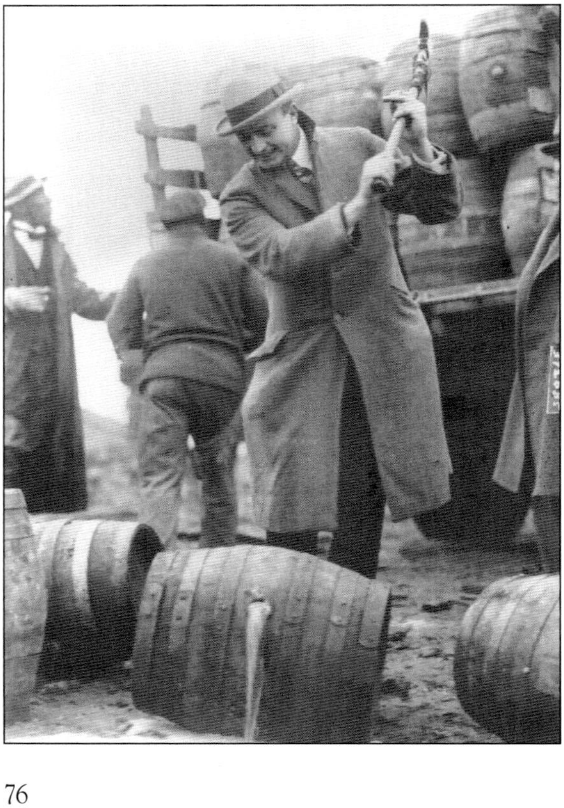

CITY PUBLIC SAFETY DIRECTOR SMEDLEY D. "DUCKBOARDS" BUTLER, PHILADELPHIA, 1924. Though they tried, Wilmington's three brewing companies could not sustain their large physical plants producing nonalcoholic beverages. The Hartmann & Fehrenbach and Bavarian Breweries eventually came under the control of illicit operators, and both were busted by federal agents for Prohibition violations. (LOC.)

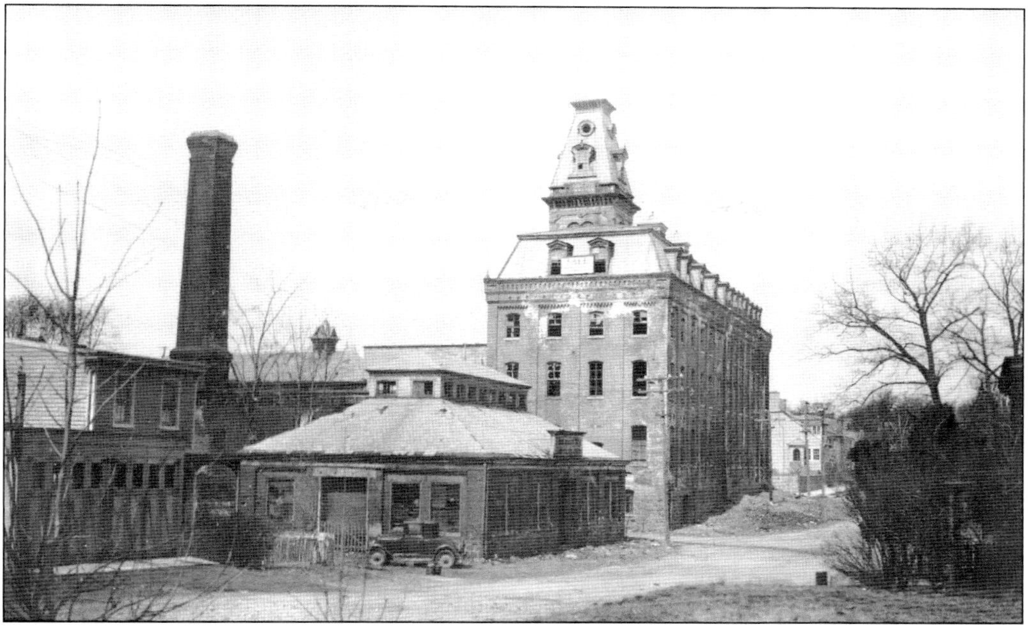

HARTMANN & FEHRENBACH BREWERY, 1932. This was the scene along Wawaset Street, as H&F's Brandywine Lager Brewery stood in total disrepair. The brewery had ceased legal operations in 1920, and the company's president, John G. Hartmann, died in 1927. The four-story brew and stock house was torn down in 1932 to make way for row houses. The bottling plant in the foreground is currently in use as a law office. (HML.)

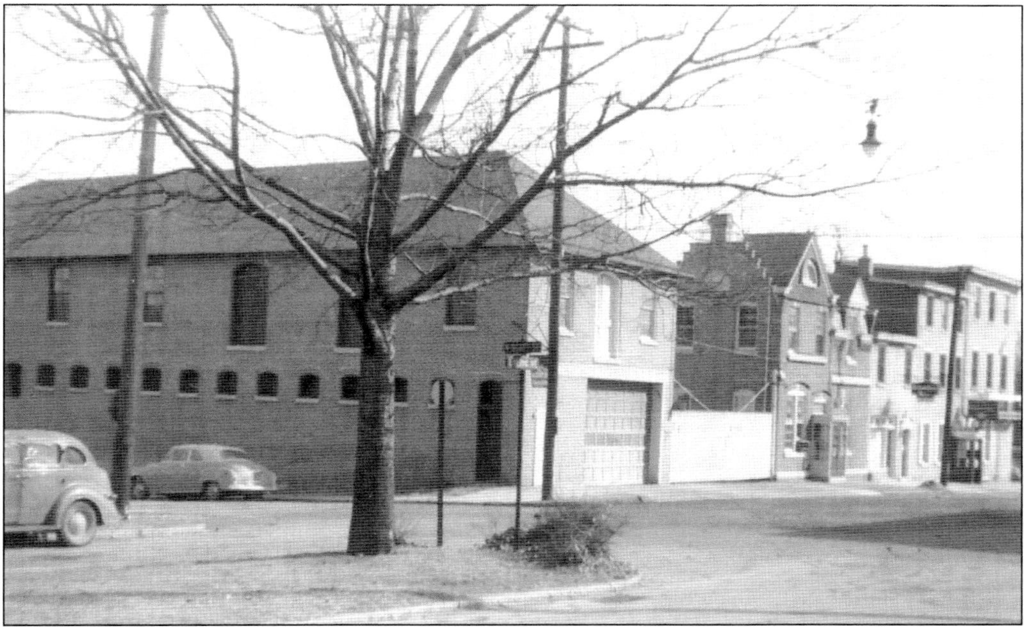

HARTMANN & FEHRENBACH BREWERY, 1955. The H&F livery stable appears here in the foreground on the northeast corner of Lovering Avenue and Scott Street. It survived Prohibition and housed a trucking company for many years. Next to it was the brewery office, which also survived until both buildings were taken down in 1968. The brewery hotel and saloon survive as Gallucio's Pub. (NBM.)

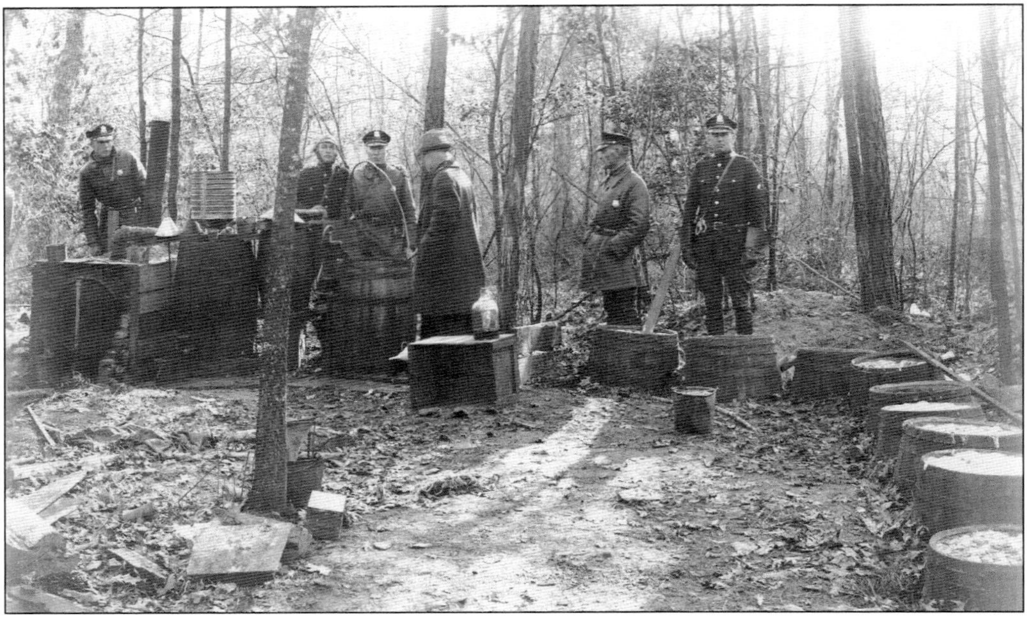

DELAWARE PROHIBITION AGENTS RAID ILLEGAL STILLS, 1920S. Scenes like the one pictured here were played out throughout Delaware during the 13 years of national Prohibition. The "noble experiment," which was undertaken to curb social ills, did not reduce Americans desire for alcohol; it simply drove its production and distribution underground and led to rampant crime and corruption. (DPA.)

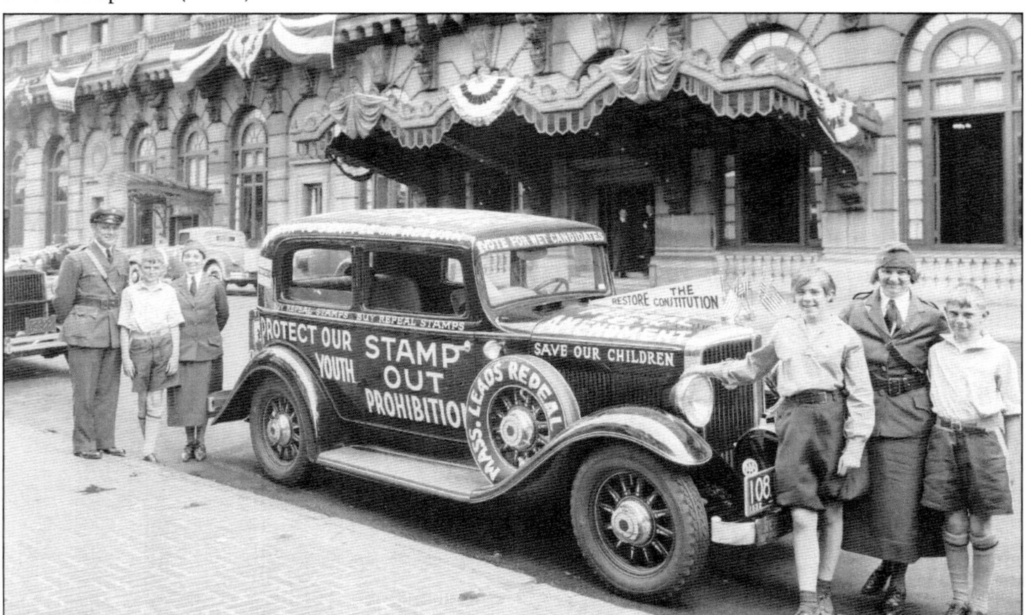

VEHICLE PROMOTING REPEAL OUTSIDE OF THE HOTEL DUPONT, WILMINGTON, C. 1930. Prohibition killed the brewing industry, which, in Delaware, had accounted for millions of dollars in revenue and hundreds of jobs. By the end of the 1920s, it had become clear that Prohibition was failing on all counts. As had been the case with the Prohibition movement, women and children became active participants in the effort for repeal. (HML.)

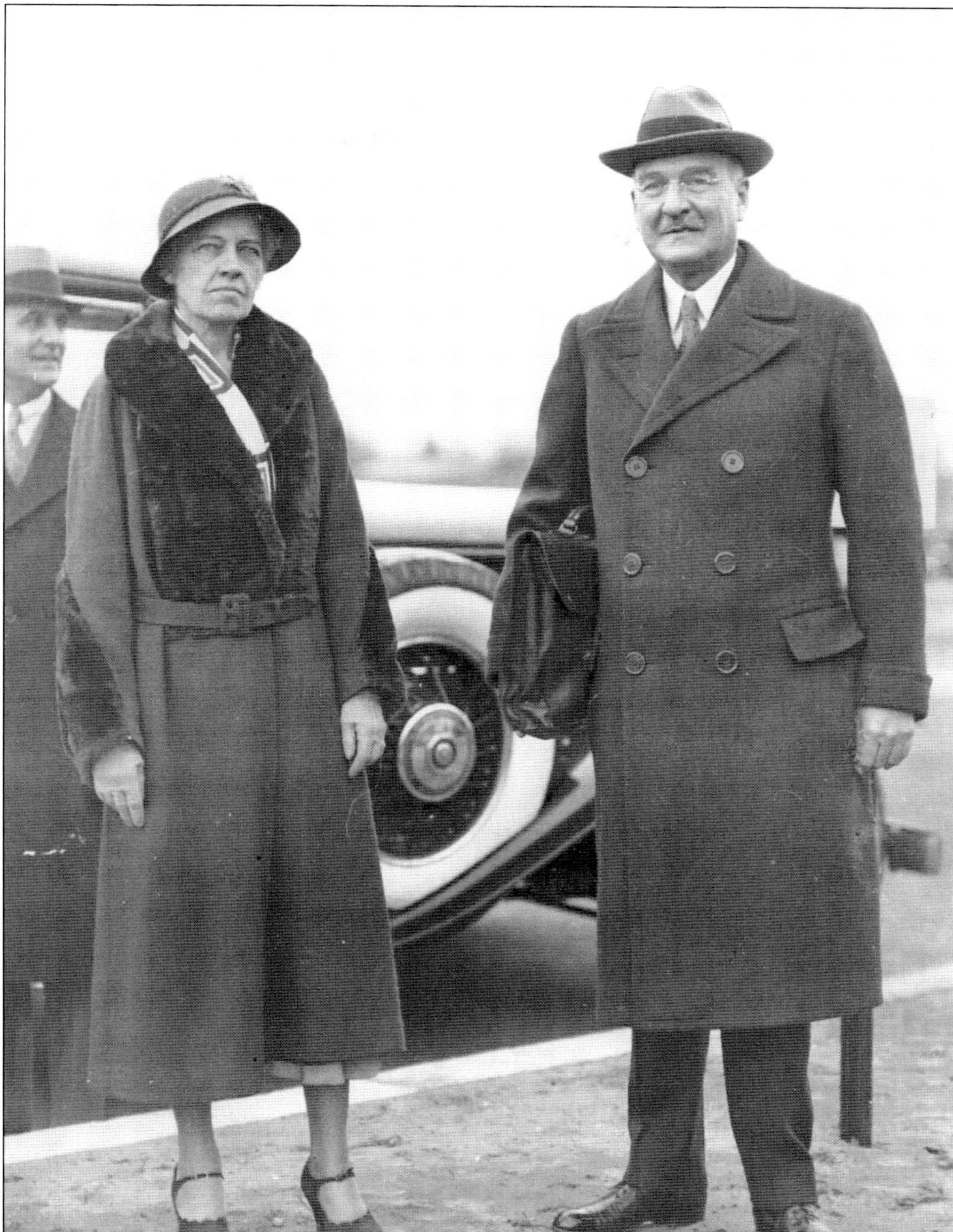

JEANETTE ECKMAN AND PIERRE S. DU PONT, DOVER, JANUARY 1933. Eckman, the executive secretary of the Women's National Organization of Prohibition Reform, and du Pont, leader of the National Association Against Prohibition, are seen here before the hearings that overturned Delaware's Klair Law. More restrictive than the Volstead Act, the Klair Law actually prohibited possession of alcohol in the First State. Delaware's du Pont, initially in favor of Prohibition, became one of the United States' most prominent and ardent proponents for repeal. (DHS.)

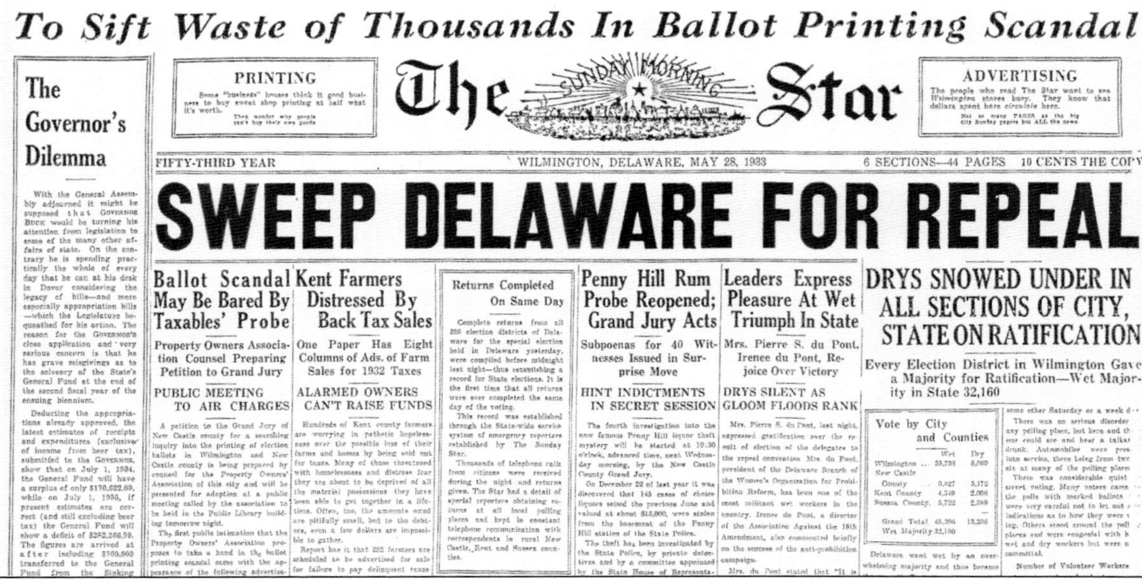

To Sift Waste of Thousands In Ballot Printing Scandal

PRINTING

Some "business" houses think it good business to buy sweat shop printing at half what it's worth.

Then wonder why people can't buy their own goods

The Sunday Morning Star

ADVERTISING

The people who read The Star want to see Wilmington stores busy. They know that dollars spent here *circulate* here.

Not so many PAGES as the big city Sunday papers but ALL the news.

FIFTY-THIRD YEAR | WILMINGTON, DELAWARE, MAY 28, 1933 | 6 SECTIONS—44 PAGES | 10 CENTS THE COPY

SWEEP DELAWARE FOR REPEAL

The Governor's Dilemma

With the General Assembly adjourned it might be supposed that GOVERNOR BUCK would be turning his attention from legislation to some of the many other affairs of state. On the contrary he is spending practically the whole of every day that he can at his desk in Dover considering the legacy of bills—and more especially appropriation bills—which the Legislature bequeathed for his action. The reason for the GOVERNOR'S close application and very serious concern is that he has grave misgivings as to the solvency of the State's General Fund at the end of the second fiscal year of the ensuing biennium.

Deducting the appropriations already approved, the latest estimates of receipts and expenditures (exclusive of income from beer tax), submitted to the GOVERNOR, show that on July 1, 1934, the General Fund will have a surplus of only $170,622.09, while on July 1, 1935, if present estimates are correct (and still excluding beer tax) the General Fund will show a deficit of $282,266.99. The figures are arrived at after including $700,000 transferred to the General Fund from the Sinking

Ballot Scandal May Be Bared By Taxables' Probe

Property Owners Association Counsel Preparing Petition to Grand Jury

PUBLIC MEETING TO AIR CHARGES

A petition to the Grand Jury of New Castle county for a searching inquiry into the printing of election ballots in Wilmington and New Castle county is being prepared by counsel for the Property Owners' Association of this city and will be presented for adoption at a public meeting called by the association to be held in the Public Library building tomorrow night.

The first public intimation that the Property Owners' Association proposes to take a hand in the ballot printing scandal came with the appearance of the following advertise-

Kent Farmers Distressed By Back Tax Sales

One Paper Has Eight Columns of Ads. of Farm Sales for 1932 Taxes

ALARMED OWNERS CAN'T RAISE FUNDS

Hundreds of Kent county farmers are worrying in pathetic hopelessness over the possible loss of their farms and homes by being sold out for taxes. Many of those threatened with homelessness and distress fear they are about to be deprived of all the material possessions they have been able to get together in a lifetime. Often, too, the amounts owed are pitifully small, but to the debtors, even a few dollars are impossible to gather.

Report has it that 252 farmers are scheduled to be advertised for sale for failure to pay delinquent taxes

Returns Completed On Same Day

Complete returns from all 226 election districts of Delaware for the special election held in Delaware yesterday, were compiled before midnight last night—thus establishing a record for State elections. It is the first time that all returns were ever completed the same day of the voting.

This record was established through the State-wide service system of emergency reporters established by The Sunday Star.

Thousands of telephone calls from citizens were received during the night and returns given. The Star had a detail of special reporters obtaining returns at all local polling places and kept in constant telephone communication with correspondents in rural New Castle, Kent and Sussex counties.

Penny Hill Rum Probe Reopened; Grand Jury Acts

Subpoenas for 40 Witnesses Issued in Surprise Move

HINT INDICTMENTS IN SECRET SESSION

The fourth investigation into the now famous Penny Hill liquor theft mystery will be started at 10:30 o'clock, advanced time, next Wednesday morning, by the New Castle County Grand Jury.

On December 22 of last year it was discovered that 145 cases of choice liquors seized the previous June and valued at about $15,000, were stolen from the basement of the Penny Hill station of the State Police.

The theft has been investigated by the State Police, by private detectives and by a committee appointed by the State House of Representa-

Leaders Express Pleasure At Wet Triumph In State

Mrs. Pierre S. du Pont, Irenee du Pont, Rejoice Over Victory

DRYS SILENT AS GLOOM FLOODS RANK

Mrs. Pierre S. du Pont, last night, expressed gratification over the result of election of the delegates to the repeal convention. Mrs. du Pont, president of the Delaware Branch of the Women's Organization for Prohibition Reform, has been one of the most militant wet workers in the country. Irenee du Pont, a director of the Association Against the 18th Amendment, also commented briefly on the success of the anti-prohibition campaign.

Mrs. du Pont stated that "It is

DRYS SNOWED UNDER IN ALL SECTIONS OF CITY, STATE ON RATIFICATION

Every Election District in Wilmington Gave a Majority for Ratification—Wet Majority in State 32,160

Vote by City and Counties

	Wet	Dry
Wilmington ...	25,738	5,060
New Castle County ...	9,827	3,172
Kent County	4,349	2,006
Sussex County.	5,722	2,589
Grand Total	45,396	13,236
Wet Majority	32,160	

Delaware went wet by an overwhelming majority and thus became

some other Saturday or a week d...

There was no serious disorder any polling place, but here and th... one could see and hear a talkat... drunk. Automobiles were pres... into service, there being from tw... six at many of the polling places.

There was considerable quiet secret voting. Many voters came ... the polls with marked ballots ... were very careful not to let out ... indications as to how they were v... ing. Others stood around the poll... places and were congenial with b... wet and dry workers but were n... committal.

Number of Volunteer Workers

WILMINGTON SUNDAY STAR HEADLINE, MAY 28, 1933. In March 1933, Pres. Franklin Roosevelt signed the Cullen-Harrison Act, authorizing sales of 3.2-percent beer and wine. A Delaware statewide referendum in May 1933 resulted in a 70-percent-majority vote in favor of repeal. The state legislature formally ratified the 21st Amendment the following month. It would take additional state regulation and another six months before a brewery in Delaware would organize and begin selling beer. In the meantime, brewing companies from Philadelphia; New York; St. Louis, Missouri; and Milwaukee, Wisconsin, were quick to supply their products to thirsty Delawareans. (Author's collection.)

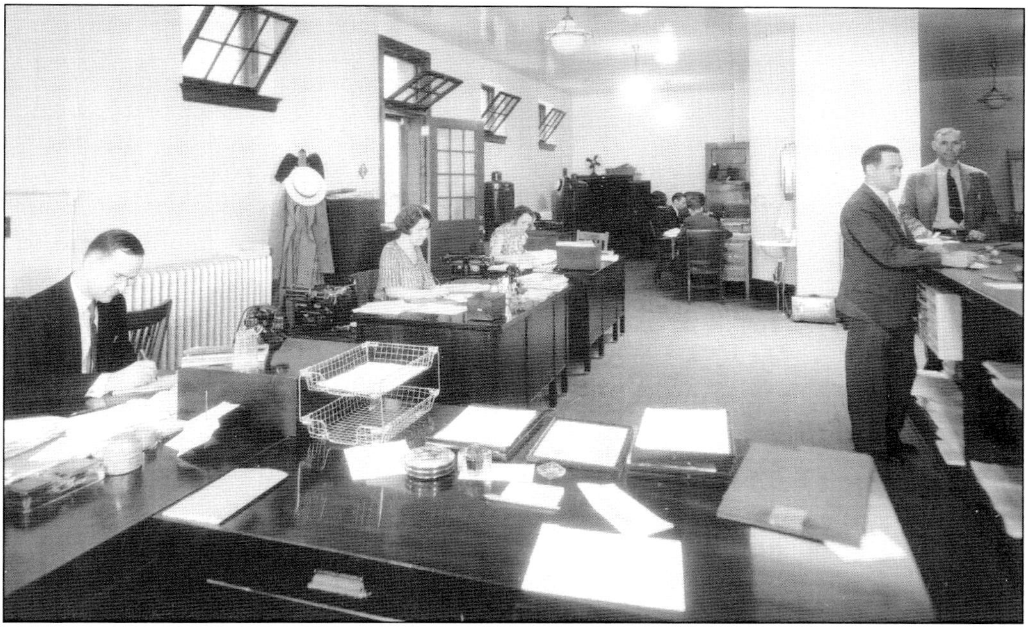

Delaware Liquor Commission Office, Wilmington, August 1933. Delaware's Liquor Control Act of 1933 created a commission to regulate the manufacture and sale of intoxicating beverages. Pierre du Pont was appointed the first liquor commissioner and helped to establish a new distribution system designed to curb the abuses of the pre-Prohibition era. The new three-tier system established a distribution chain from producers to distributors to retailers. (HML.)

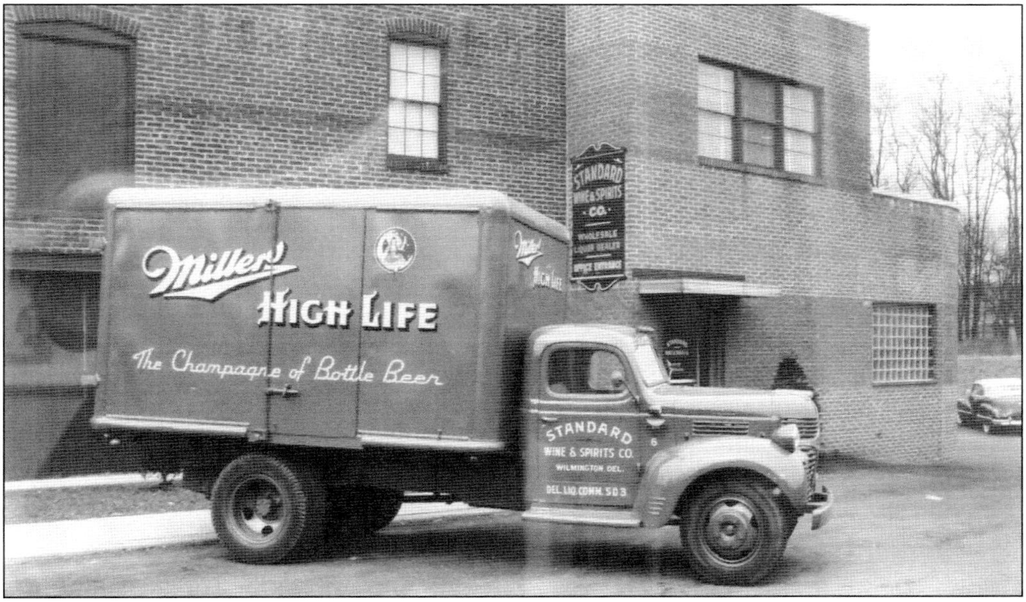

Standard Wine & Spirts Company Truck, Wilmington, c. 1953. The Delaware Liquor Commission issued the first liquor license to distributor James V. Tigani in 1933. After four years of successful operation, Tigani and Son changed the company name to Standard Wine & Spirits Company. A beer-delivery truck is pictured here in front of Standard's former warehouse at Twenty-seventh and Broom Streets. Still in operation, the company remains the largest distributor in Delaware. (Standard Distributing Company.)

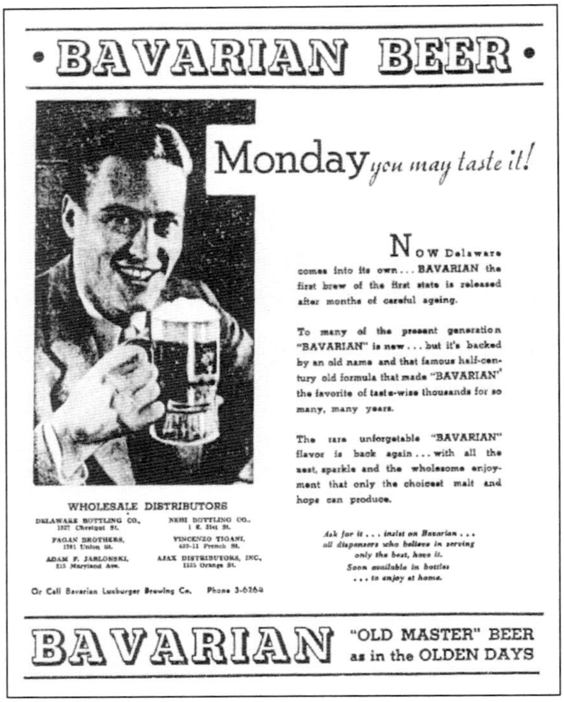

WILMINGTON SUNDAY STAR ADVERTISEMENT, NOVEMBER 26, 1933. Following the 1925 dissolution of the Peninsula Products bottling company, Carl H. Eisenmenger leased the old Bavarian Brewery. Wilmington Coca-Cola Bottling ran the plant from 1925 until 1930, when Brown Beverages Corporation took over for two years. After repeal, Eisenmenger hastily formed the Bavarian-Luxburger Brewing Company, was granted state and federal brewing licenses, and began re-tooling his brewery for production. By late November, Bavarian-Luxburger had its beer to market. (Author's collection.)

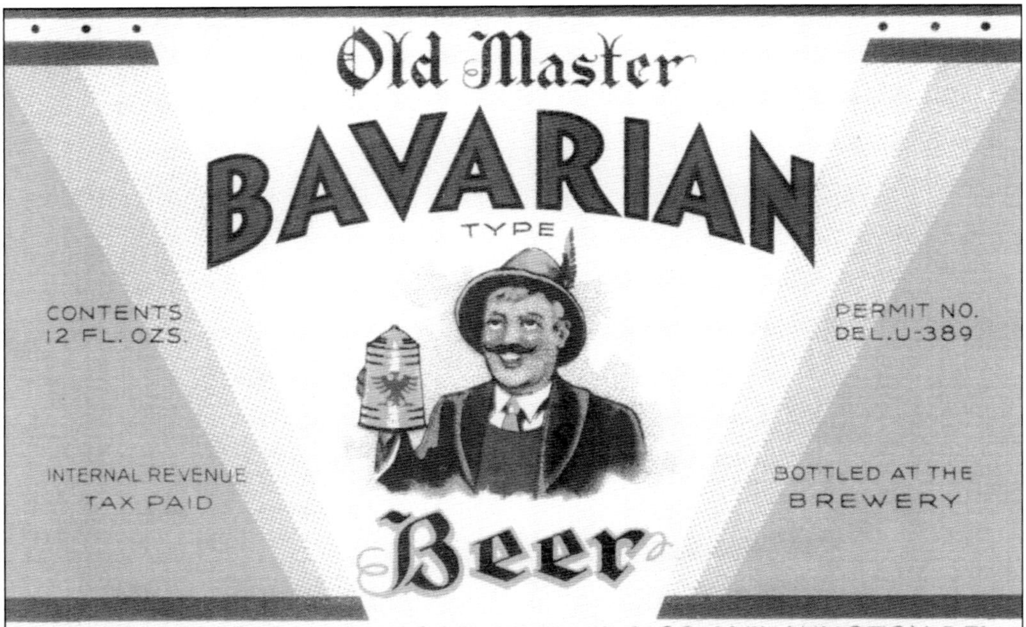

BAVARIAN-LUXBURGER LABEL, C. 1934. In its 18 short months of operation, the brewery turned out two flagship beers, Luxburger and Old Master Bavarian, in addition to a bock in the spring of 1934. Underfunded and unable to compete with other regional and national brands that had quickly established themselves throughout Delaware, the Bavarian-Luxburger Brewing Company went out of business in June 1935. Eisenmenger retired from brewing and began tending a farm in Arden. (Author's collection.)

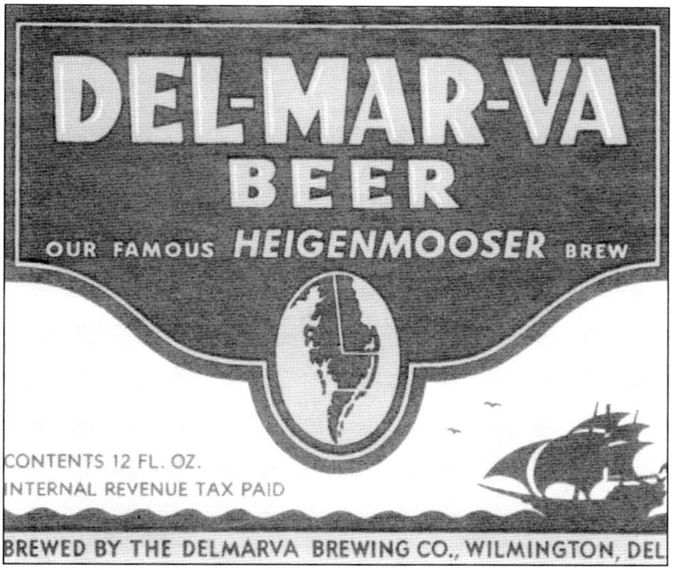

Delmarva Beer Label, c. 1937. The Bavarian Brewery sat idle for 29 months until Eisenmenger sold the plant to a new venture called the Delmarva Brewing Company, Inc. Substantial updates to the brewery at Fifth and DuPont Streets were made through the winter of 1937, increasing brewing capacity to 153,000 barrels per year. The firm hired Karl Heigenmooser as brewmaster and by June began distributing Delmarva Famous Pilsner and Heigenmooser beer in Delaware. (Author's collection.)

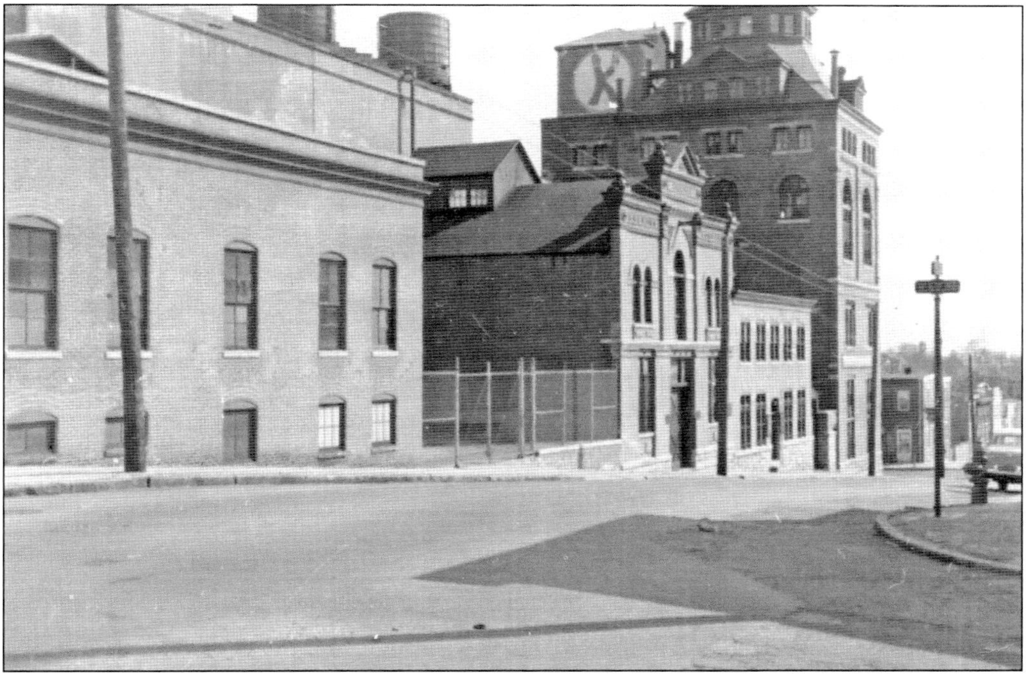

Bavarian Brewery, Wilmington, c. 1951. In addition to its flagship beers, Delmarva produced its export Wurzburger, bock, and Delaware Reserve beers. Unfortunately, the company was beset with financial difficulties from the outset. Only 10 percent of its sales came from outside of Delaware. Wartime restrictions on grain and supplies imposed further strains on sales, and Delmarva went out of business in June 1944. (NBM.)

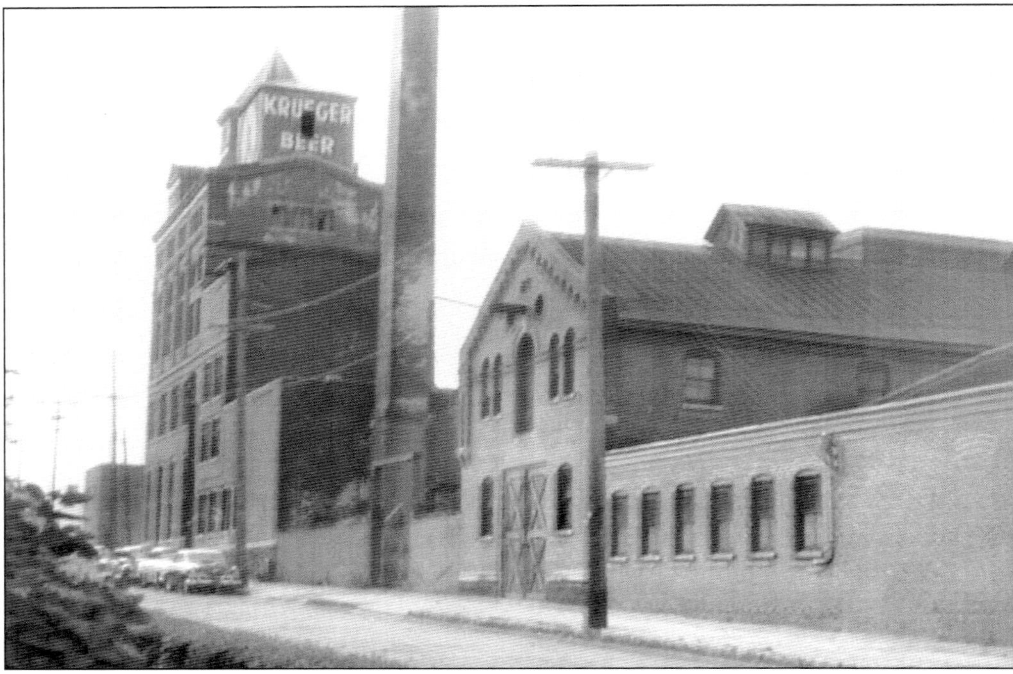

View of the Krueger Brewery, Wilmington, c. 1951. In July 1944, the G. Krueger Brewing Company of Newark, New Jersey, purchased the brewery from Delmarva and formed a wholly owned subsidiary, the Krueger Brewery Company, Delaware. Krueger was best known for having been the first brewery in the world to can beer, which it began doing in 1935. (NBM.)

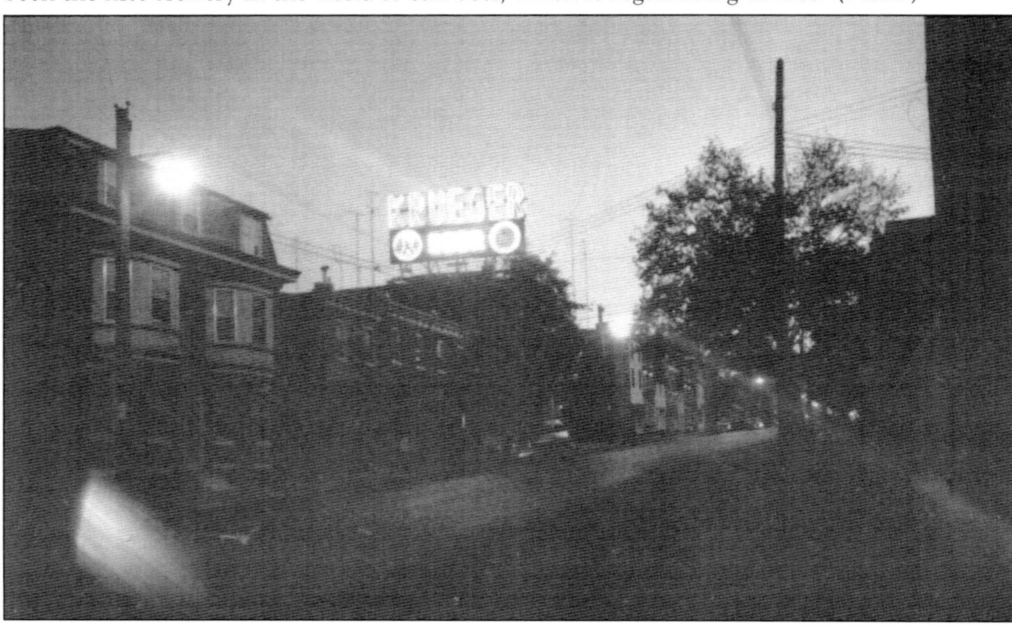

Krueger Sign Shines over Wilmington, c. 1950. Krueger utilized the Wilmington branch to serve its southernmost markets in the post–World War II era, which included Delaware, Maryland, Virginia, and West Virginia. They re-tooled the brewery for canning but also continued to utilize the existing bottling operations. The Wilmington brewery produced the flagship Krueger Beer, as well as Extra Light Lager and Extra Light Dry. (DHS.)

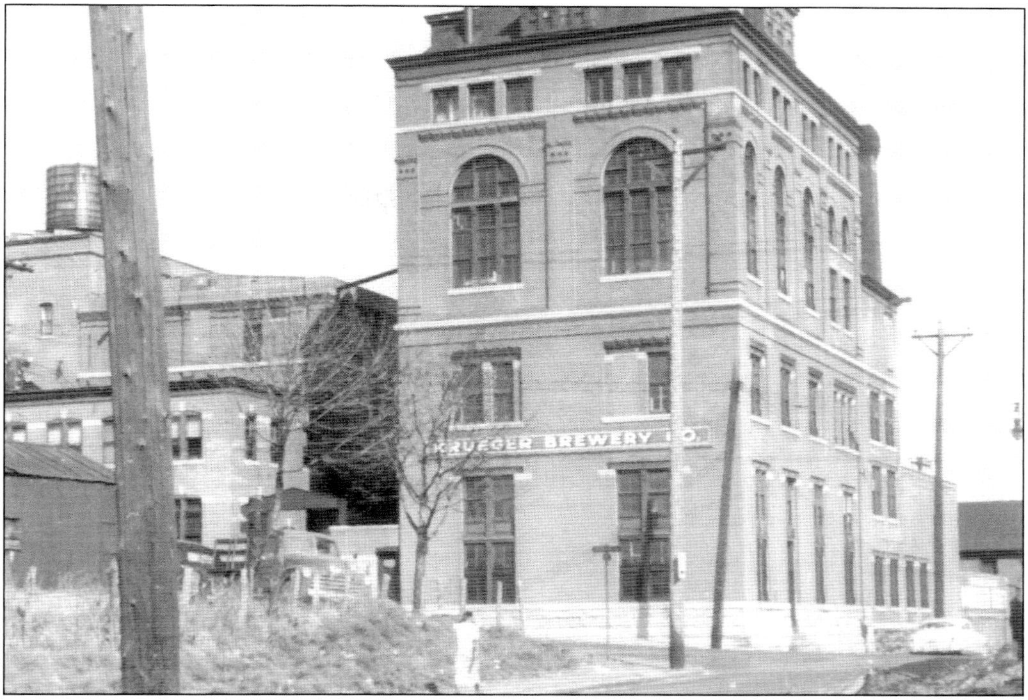

KRUEGER BREWERY, C. 1955. Just after World War II, Krueger made substantial capital investments in its Newark, New Jersey, brewery to increase its annual capacity to 750,000 barrels a year. By the end of 1950, Krueger concluded that its Wilmington brewery had become too outdated and obsolete to operate at a profit. In 1951, the parent company transferred all production to its New Jersey headquarters and shuttered the Wilmington branch. (NBM.)

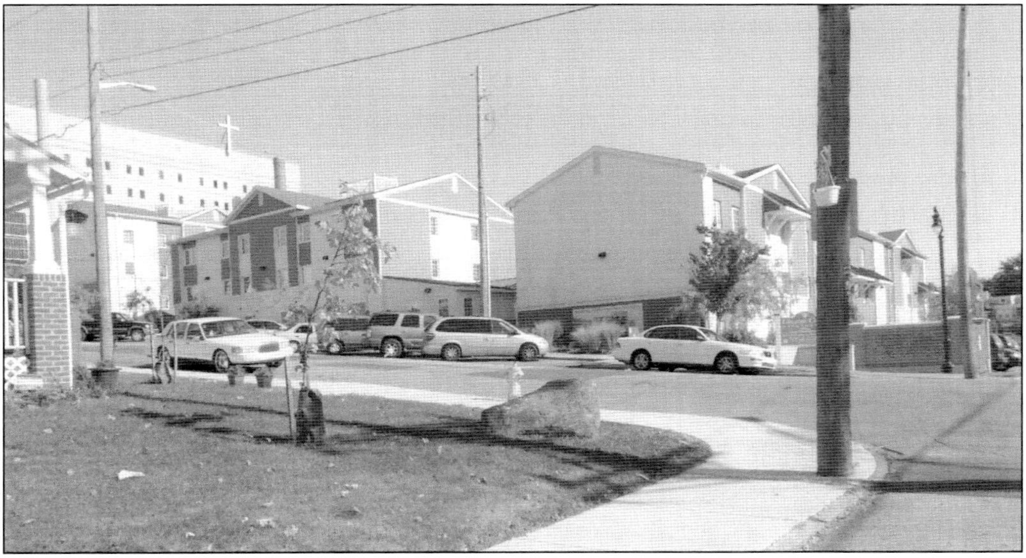

SITE OF THE FORMER KRUEGER BREWERY, 2012. Portions of the old brewery at Fifth and DuPont Streets were used by other businesses for non-brewing purposes through the 1950s. By the end of the decade, the complex fell into disrepair, was condemned, and became an abandoned eyesore. It was torn down in November 1964 to make way for public housing, which has recently been replaced by an apartment complex. (Author's collection.)

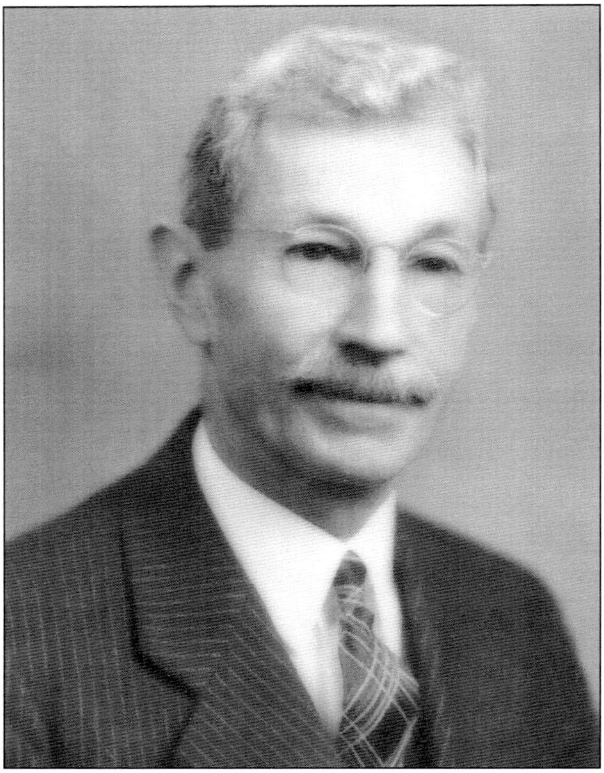

VICTOR E. ULLMANN, C. 1930. For many years, Ullmann worked as a cooper for the Joseph Stoeckle Brewing Company, and he had the good fortune of marrying Joseph Stoeckle's daughter Louisa. After leaving the brewery in 1905, Ullmann started a clay products manufacturing company near Newark. He assisted the Stoeckle heirs with management of the Wilmington brewery property at Fifth and DuPont Streets after it shut down in the 1920s. (James Prettyman.)

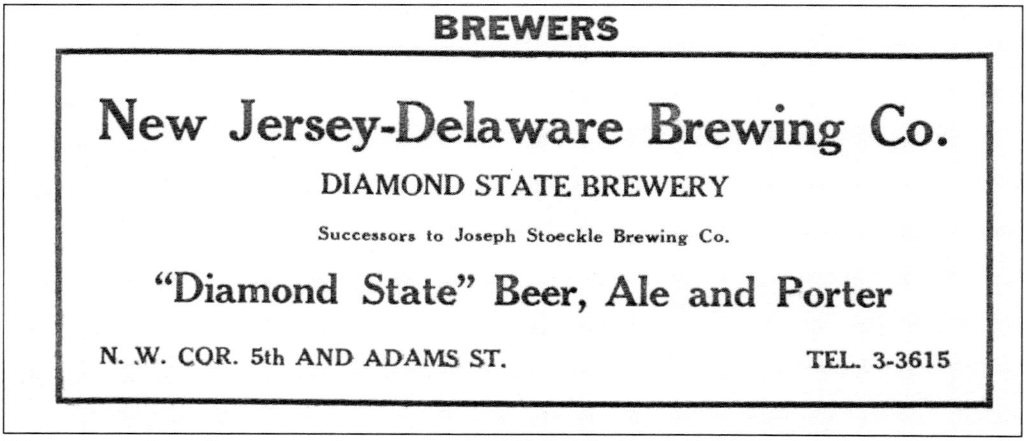

WILMINGTON CITY DIRECTORY ADVERTISEMENT, 1934. The Stoeckle family maintained ownership of the brewery through the Prohibition era. With repeal imminent, Ullmann and a group of investors organized a stock company, the New Jersey-Delaware Brewing Company, in early 1933 and purchased the idle Stoeckle brewery from the founder's heirs. Before the company could raise the required capital to begin operating, chief organizer and vice president Guy de la Rigaudiere died. (WPL.)

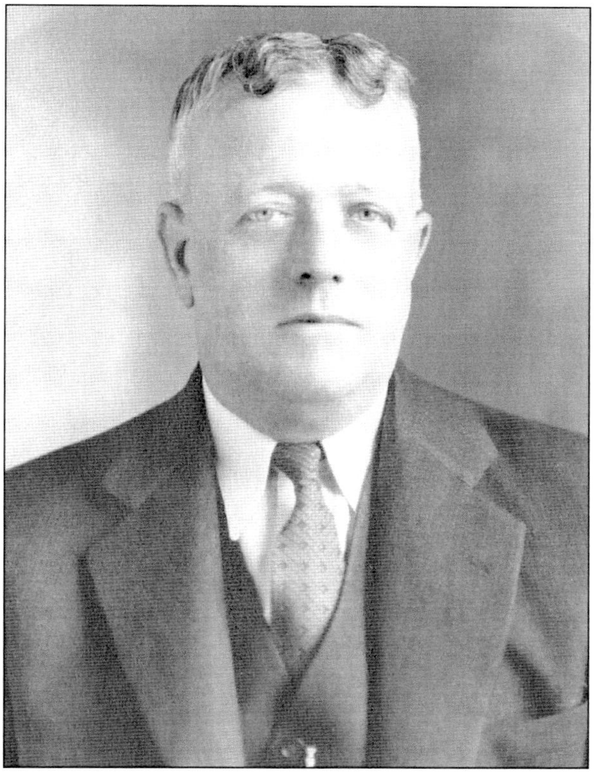

ADOLPH G. DANGEL, C. 1925. The New Jersey-Delaware Brewing Company floundered through 1934, unable to raise the needed capital. The firm reorganized and brought in Harry Wachtel from Philadelphia as chief organizer and vice president. Adolph Dangel, one of the company's chief investors and a longtime friend of the Stoeckle family, was elected president, and Wilmington attorney Joseph Errigo was elected secretary-treasurer. (WHD.)

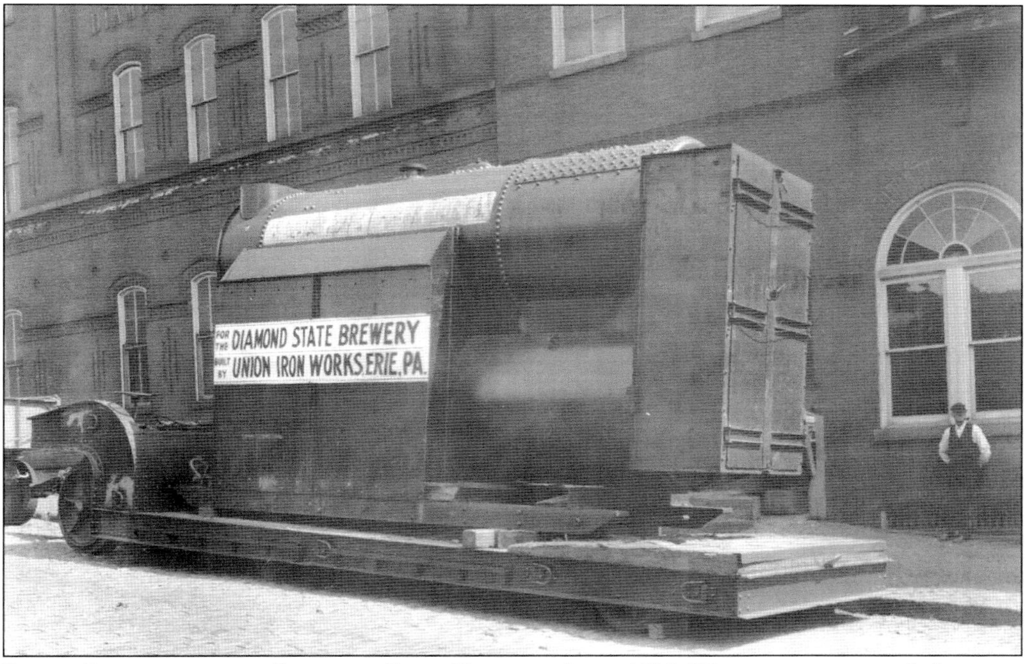

BOILER DELIVERY AT THE DIAMOND STATE BREWERY, JUNE 1935. The company struggled to raise capital and by early 1935 had purchased less than a third of the equipment necessary to retool the old brewery. In the spring of 1935, the company restructured its debt and obtained credit and loans to purchase the remainder of the equipment needed to get the brewery running. (DHS.)

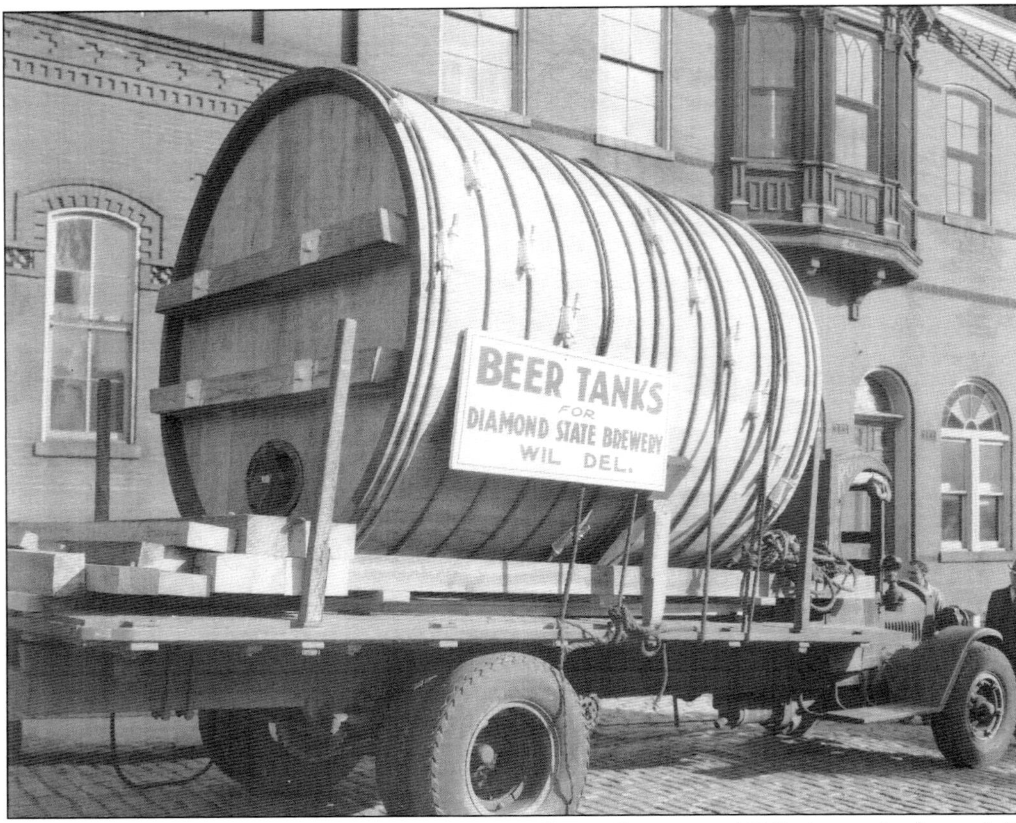

Fermenting Tank Delivery at the Diamond State Brewery, 1935. A new boiler and 30 fermenting tanks were added to the brewery, and a new refrigerating plant was constructed. Once operating, the Diamond State Brewery's annual capacity would be 200,000 barrels, with total anticipated annual production set at 50,000 barrels. In the spring of 1936, the company changed its name to the Diamond State Brewery, Inc., and secured the licenses needed to begin operating. (DHS.)

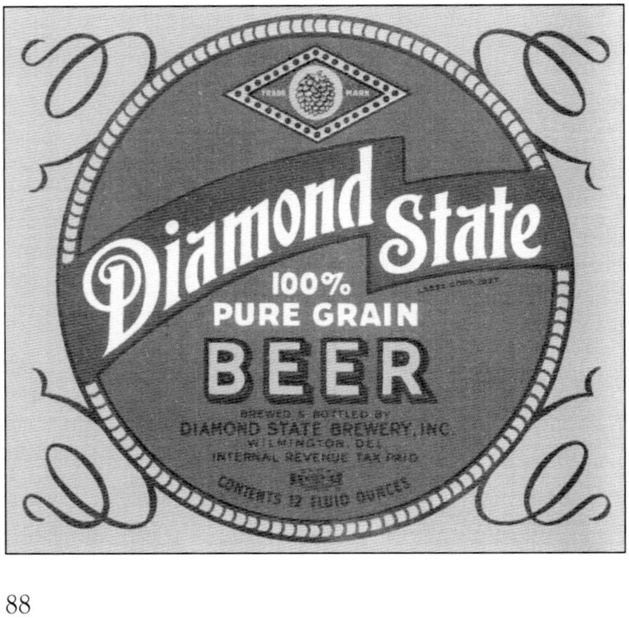

Diamond State Beer Label, 1941. The Diamond State Brewery finally opened for production in November 1936 and began shipping its Diamond State pure grain beer in kegs to Delaware distributors the next month. Later, it began selling bottled and canned beer. The Pure Grain Beer was advertised to have been an old-fashioned lager beer brewed using the old Stoeckle method of brewing. (Author's collection.)

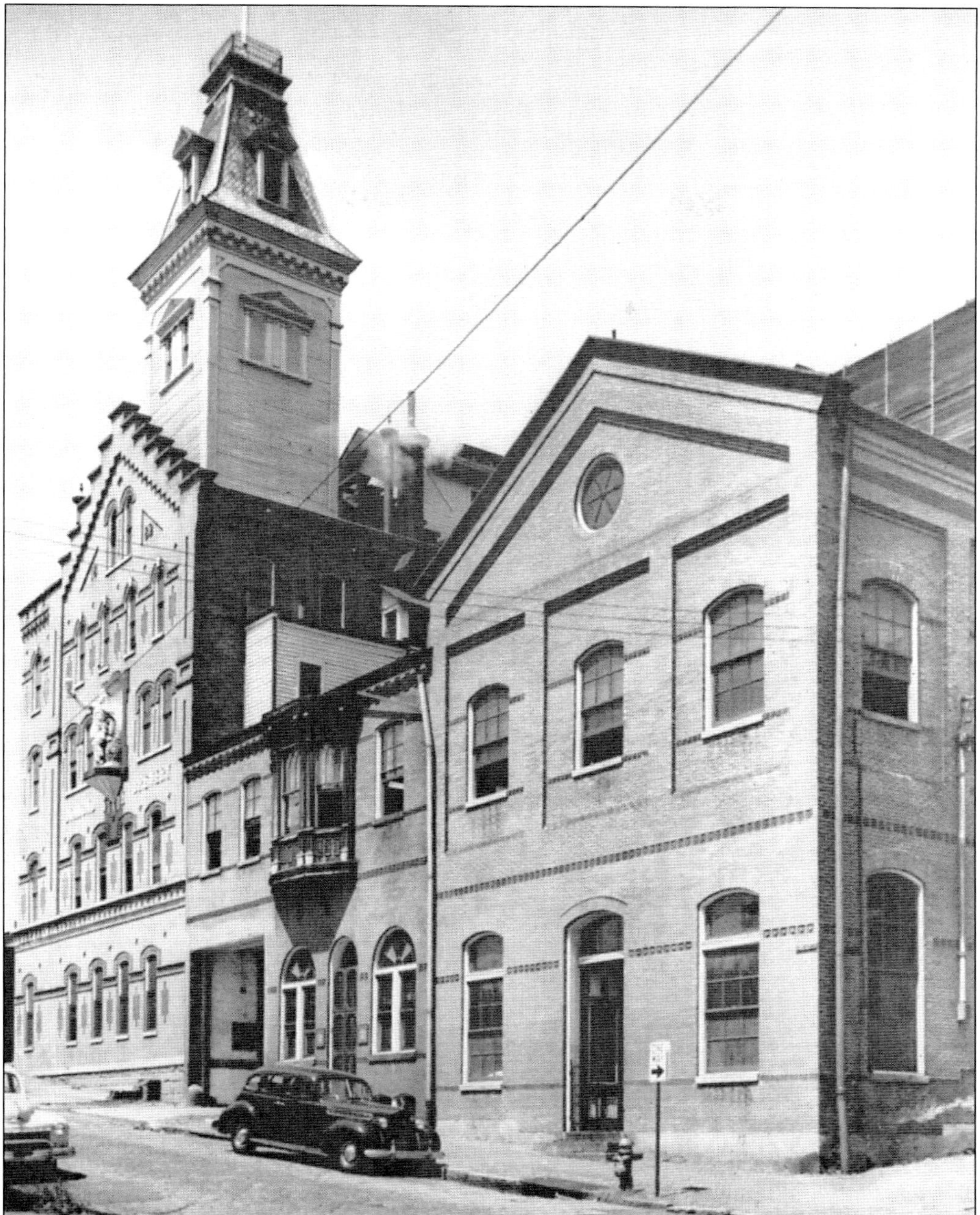

DIAMOND STATE BREWERY, C. 1947. Unfortunately, Diamond State was embroiled in several lawsuits from investors in its first few years of operation. The brewery was never able to meet the production and sales levels originally planned and barely managed to keep afloat through its first five years. Although World War II rationing of grain and other materials restricted the company's ability to get its product to market, Diamond State managed to gain market share. Though not substantial, the company finally turned a profit in 1942 and again in 1943. (Author's collection.)

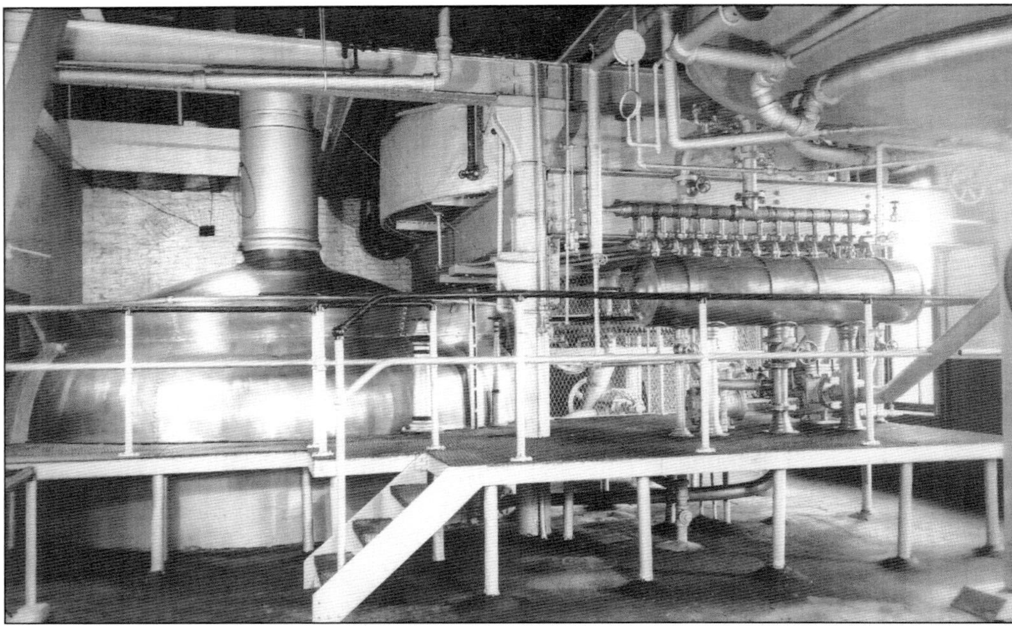

INSIDE THE BREWHOUSE AT THE DIAMOND STATE BREWERY, C. 1936. In its first several years of operation, the Diamond State Brewery produced other beers aside from its flagship Pure Grain Beer, including a cream ale, a bock, a lager known as Gem beer, and Pink Lady, a Berliner weiss beer flavored with raspberry. They also brewed a nonalcoholic malt beverage, Malta Castillo, for a short time, which was targeted to Delaware's Latino population. (DHS.)

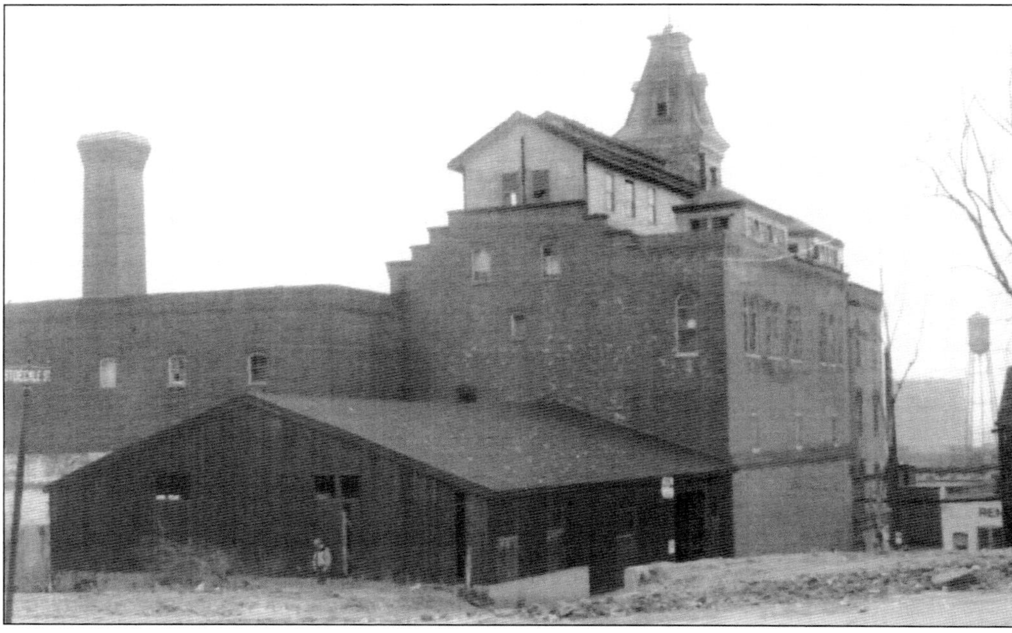

BACK OF THE DIAMOND STATE BREWERY, C. 1955. This photograph, taken from Sixth and Stoeckle Streets, is a rare view of the back of the Diamond State Brewery. One of the brewery's storage houses is located in the immediate foreground. The two-story brick building to the left is a keg cold-storage house. In the background, the five-story brick building with stepped gables and a cupola served as the brewhouse. (Norman Buckalew.)

DIAMOND STATE BREWERY, OCTOBER 1, 1955. This photograph, taken by Delaware Photo Club member Cameron F. Jones, provides a view of the brewery complex on the north side of Fifth Street near Jackson Street looking east toward Adams Street. The building housing the horse stables and the bottling and canning works is in the foreground to the right. (DHS.)

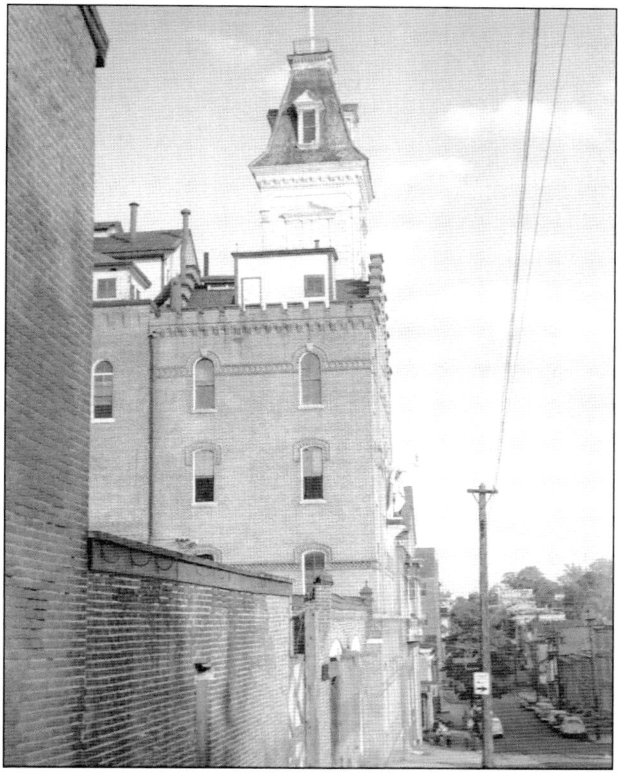

DIAMOND STATE BREWERY, VIEW FROM JACKSON STREET, 1955. Gambrinus is seen toasting the city of Wilmington from his perch above the brewhouse building. The arched lettering spelling out Joseph Stoeckle's name overtop the king's statue was removed when brewery reopened in 1936. (NBM.)

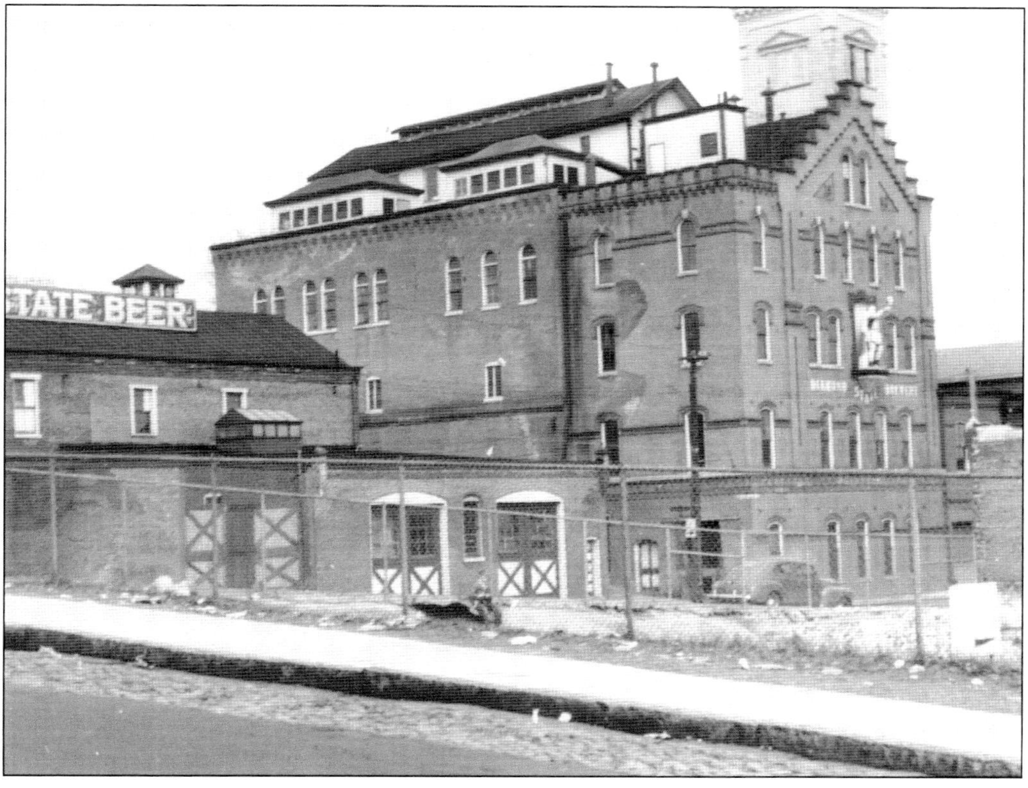

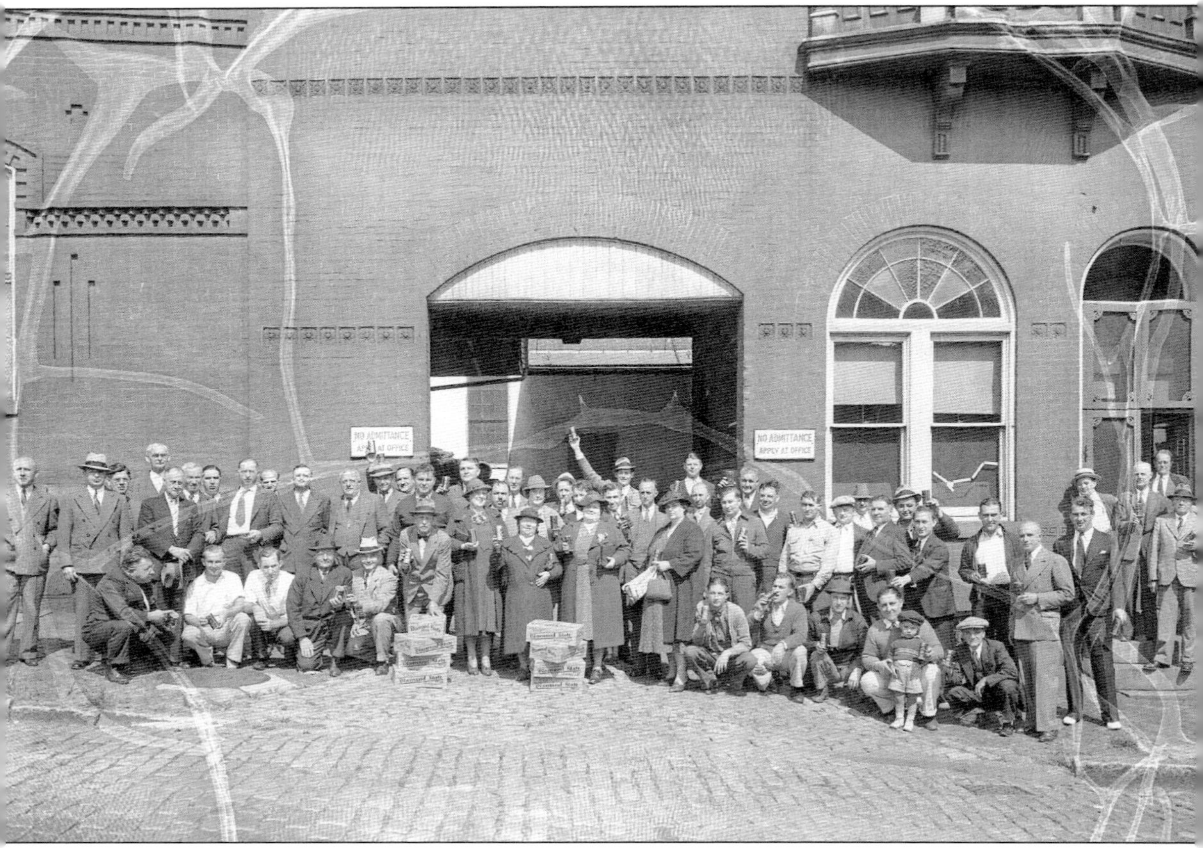

STAFF AND FRIENDS IN FRONT OF THE DIAMOND STATE BREWERY, FEBRUARY 15, 1943. A group poses with Diamond State Beer cans and cases in front of the courtyard entrance along the north side of Fifth Street. Chairman of the board, general manager, and vice president of the brewery Harry Wachtel is standing at the very far left. Standing in the second row, fifth from the left, is Floyd Mummert, the brewery's chief engineer. Pres. Adolph Dangel stands just to the left of Mummert. Directly in front of Dangel, kneeling and wearing a white hat, is Samuel Wachtel, Harry's brother, who was a company salesman. To the far right, standing on the bottom step of the office, is William Wolf, the Diamond State Brewery's office manager. (DHS.)

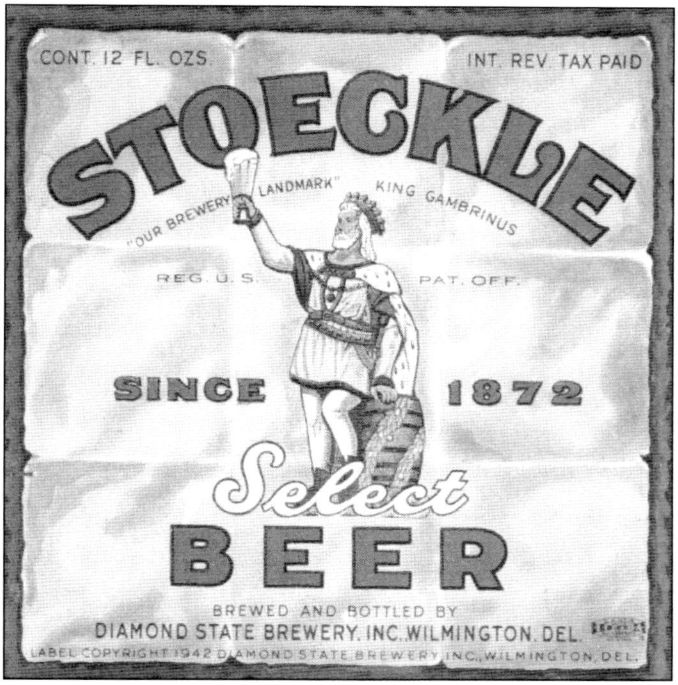

Stoeckle Select Label, 1943. In February 1943, Diamond State introduced Stoeckle Select lager and Select ale, the former of which was based on the original Stoeckle recipe. The beer's jingle, "A Famous Brew Since '72," harkened back to the brewery's glory days, as did the iconic image of the Gambrinus statue adorning Stoeckle cans and bottle labels. (Author's collection.)

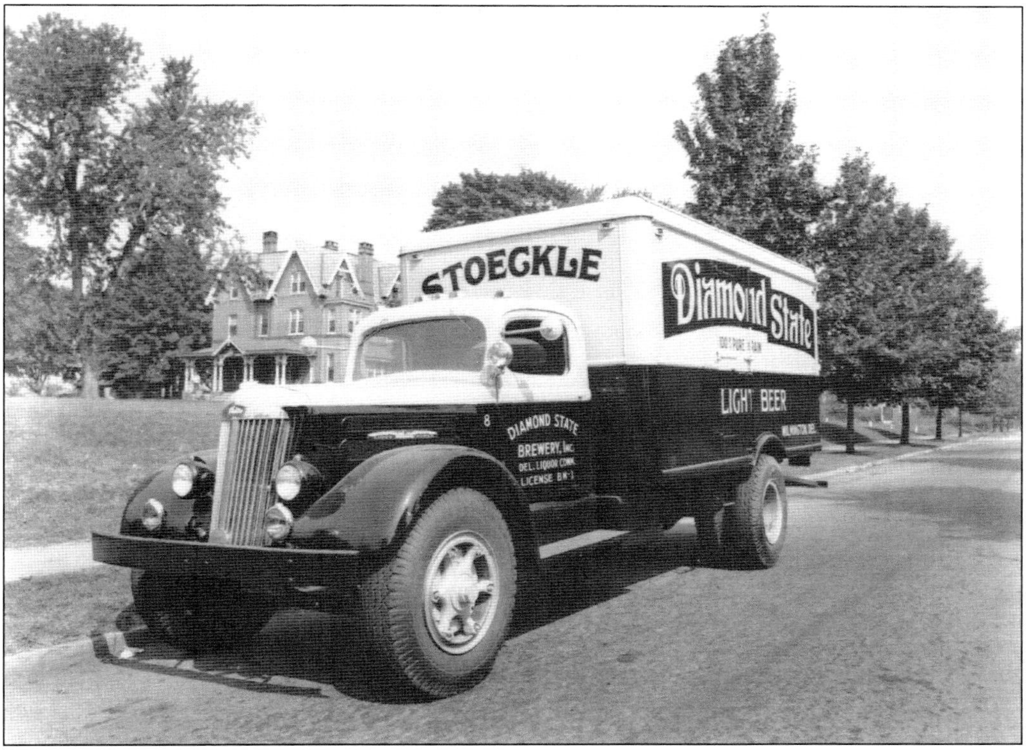

Diamond State Brewery White "Super Power" Delivery Truck, c. 1945. The brewery owned three White beer-delivery trucks and a single REO open-bed wagon, the latter of which was used for loading and hauling malt. The White trucks had gas-powered six-cylinder flathead engines. (DHS.)

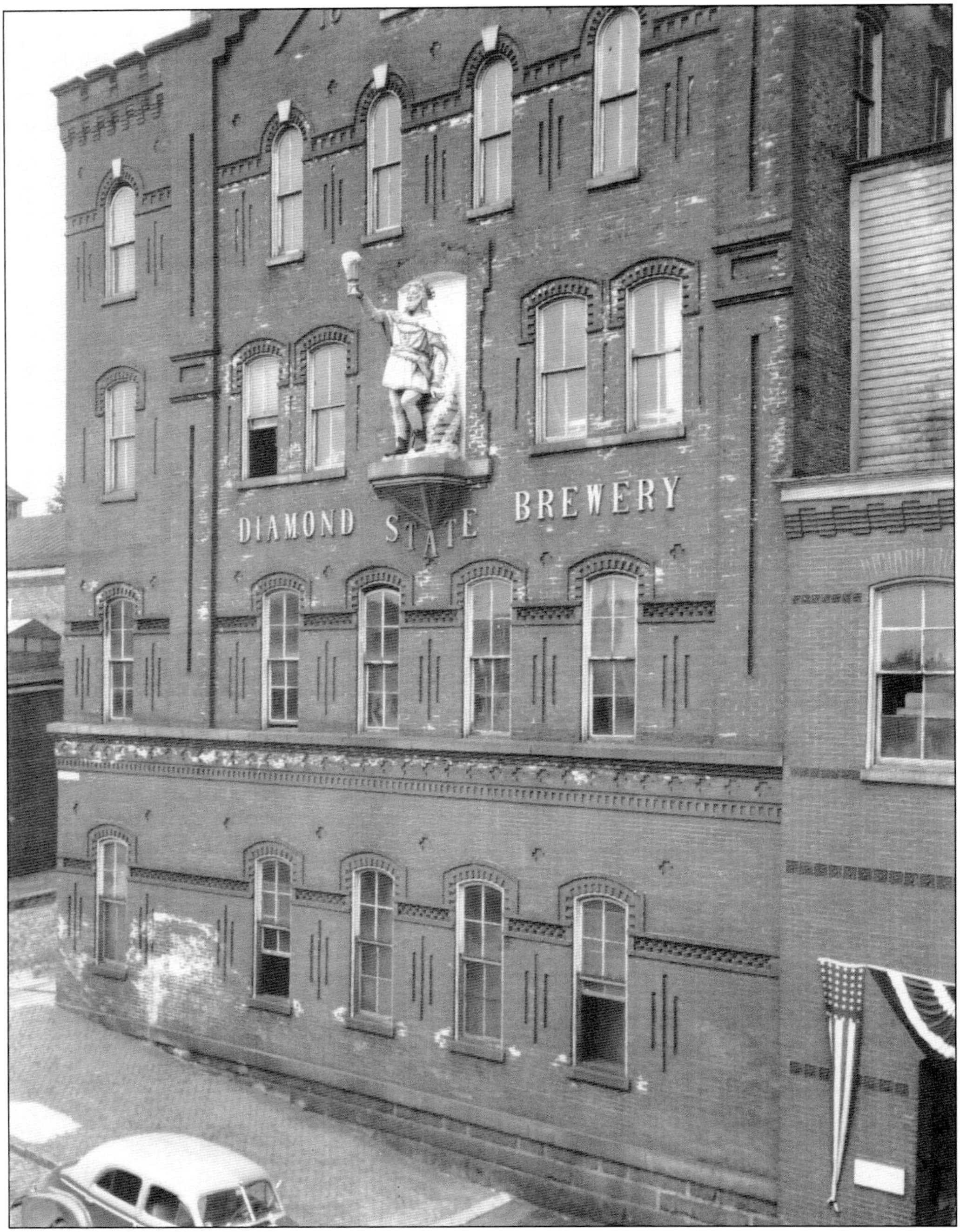

VIEW OF THE DIAMOND STATE BREWHOUSE, C. 1945. Business was very good for Diamond State in 1944 and the immediate postwar years. The company installed 18 glass-lined storage and pressure tanks in the lagering facility two stories beneath the brewery in 1947, boosting its annual capacity to 130,000 barrels. The following year, a new $150,000 three-story bottling plant with new machinery was added. The brewery experienced steady sales and profits through 1947. With depots in Vineland, New Jersey, and Philadelphia, Diamond State attempted to expand distribution beyond Delaware and increase sales in competitive markets in Maryland, southeastern Pennsylvania, and southern New Jersey. (DHS.)

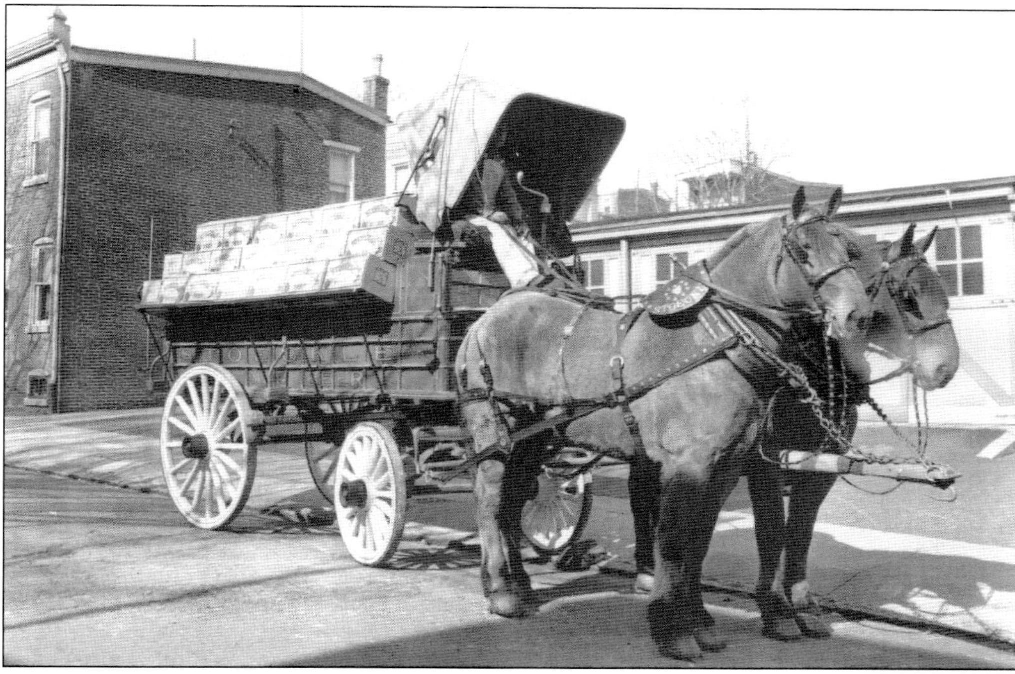

Diamond State Beer Wagon, 1943. The brewery purchased an old beer dray and had it renovated and repainted to market its Stoeckle Select products. The horses and carriage were used for promotional appearances in parades and at other special events around Wilmington in the 1940s and 1950s. Horses Andy (left) and Amos (right) are seen here pulling the wagon along Fifth Street, just west of Jackson Street. (DHS.)

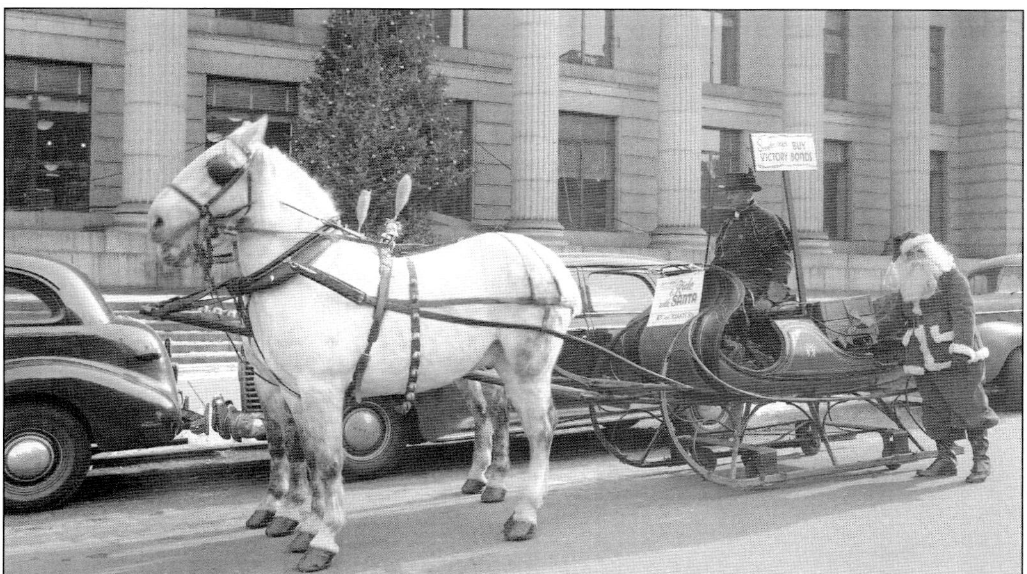

Diamond State Sleigh at Rodney Square, Wilmington, c. 1944. Diamond State's horse-drawn sleigh was often used in Wilmington's Thanksgiving parade and during war-bond drives. Pictured here are Arthur Johnson, driver and caretaker of Diamond State's horses, and, dressed as Santa Claus, brewery head Harry Wachtel. Brewery horses Charles (foreground) and Bob (background) pull the sleigh on wheels along King Street in front of the courthouse. (DHS.)

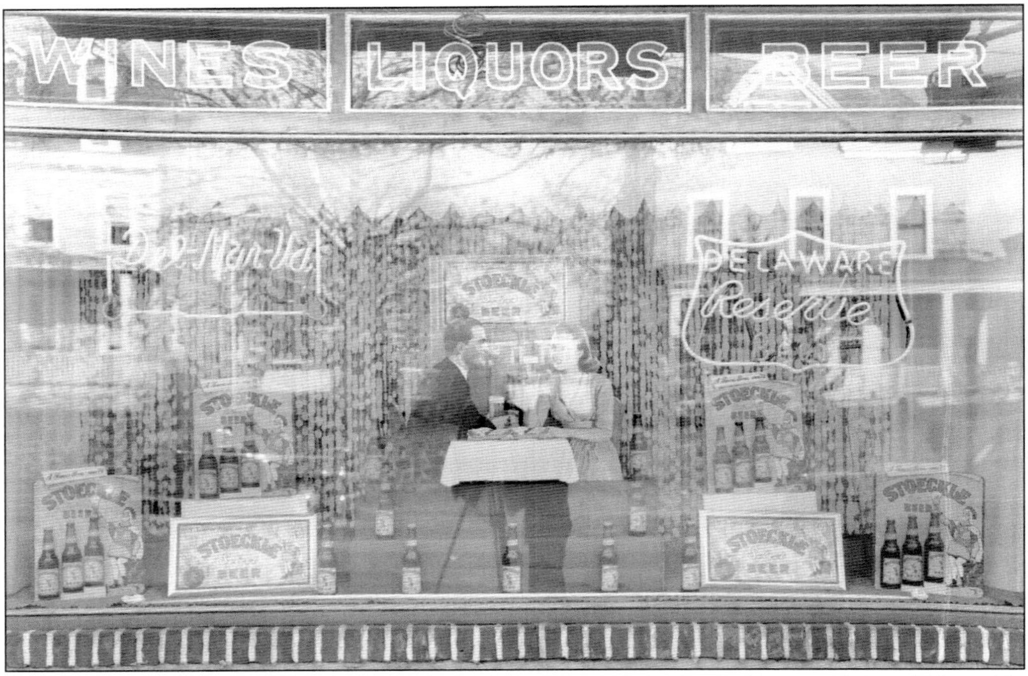

Retail Liquor Store Display, Wilmington, November 12, 1943. Diamond State's Stoeckle Select beer and Delmarva's Delaware Reserve beer are advertised here in an unidentified storefront. In the post-Prohibition era, advancements in packaging, transportation, and shipping and wider opportunities for breweries to advertise and market their products led to a greater reliance on retail sales. (DHS.)

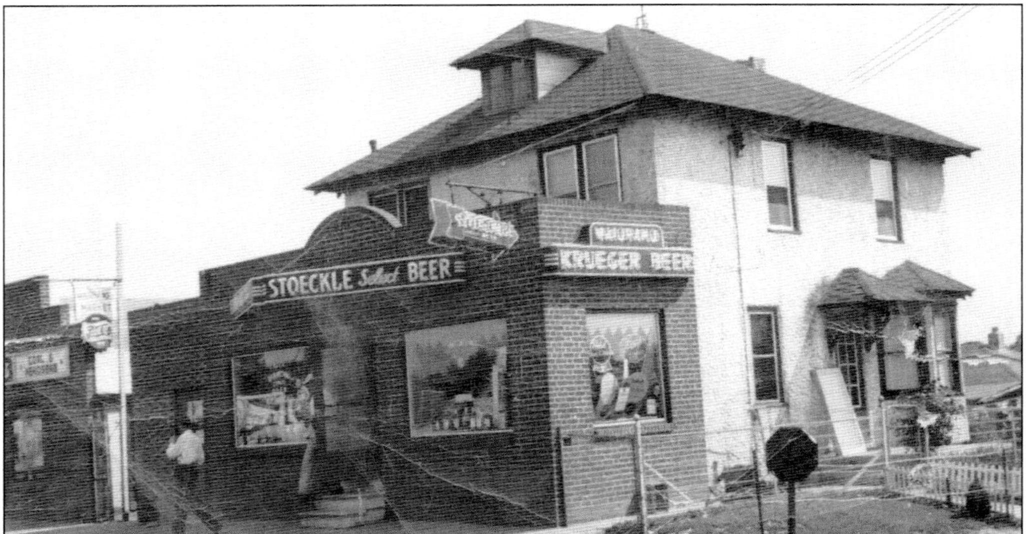

Maiorano's Liquors, Belvedere, c. 1945. Giovanni "John" Maiorano originally sold beer and other liquors in his grocery store along Newport-Gap Pike, near Clyde Street; however, repeal-era liquor regulations required him to build a dedicated package store. He converted the front porch of his home next door into a storefront and opened Maiorano's Liquors. In this photograph, the store displays Krueger and Stoeckle neon signs. The package store remained in the family until it closed in 1996. (Sonny Maiorano.)

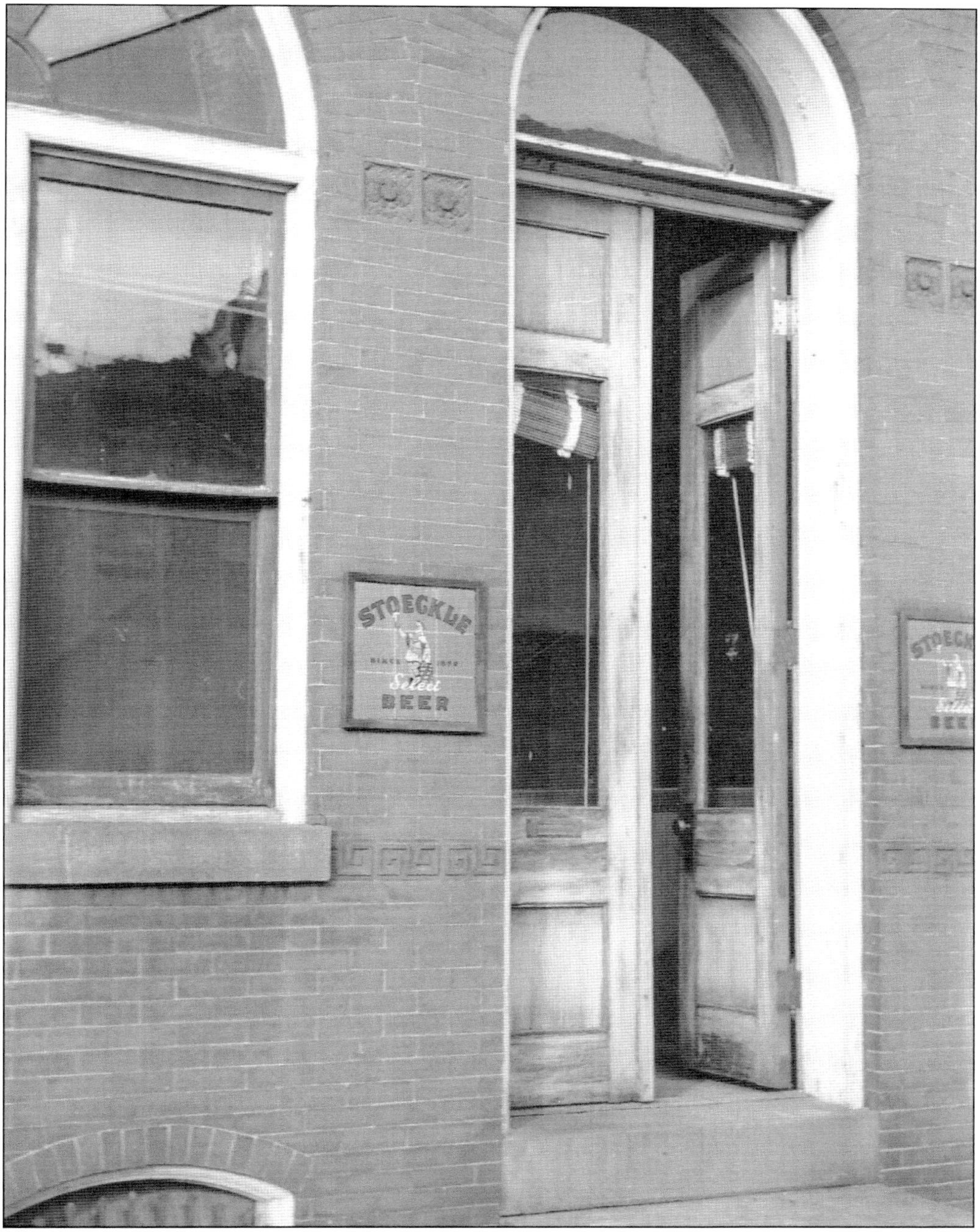

DIAMOND STATE BREWERY OFFICE DOOR AJAR, OCTOBER 1, 1955. Diamond State's finances started a sharp downward trend in 1948 as the result of competition from Philadelphia breweries and national brands, which had begun advertising and distributing in Delaware. In 1949, Adolph Dangel stepped aside as president in favor of Harry Watchel. Karl Heigenmooser, who left the Krueger Brewery across town when it closed, joined Diamond State as its vice president. Despite the organizational changes, Diamond State continued to experience less than desired sales through the early 1950s. In December 1950, the state highway department issued a report to the public showing the potential route of a new arterial highway through the city of Wilmington. The brewery was directly in its path. (DHS.)

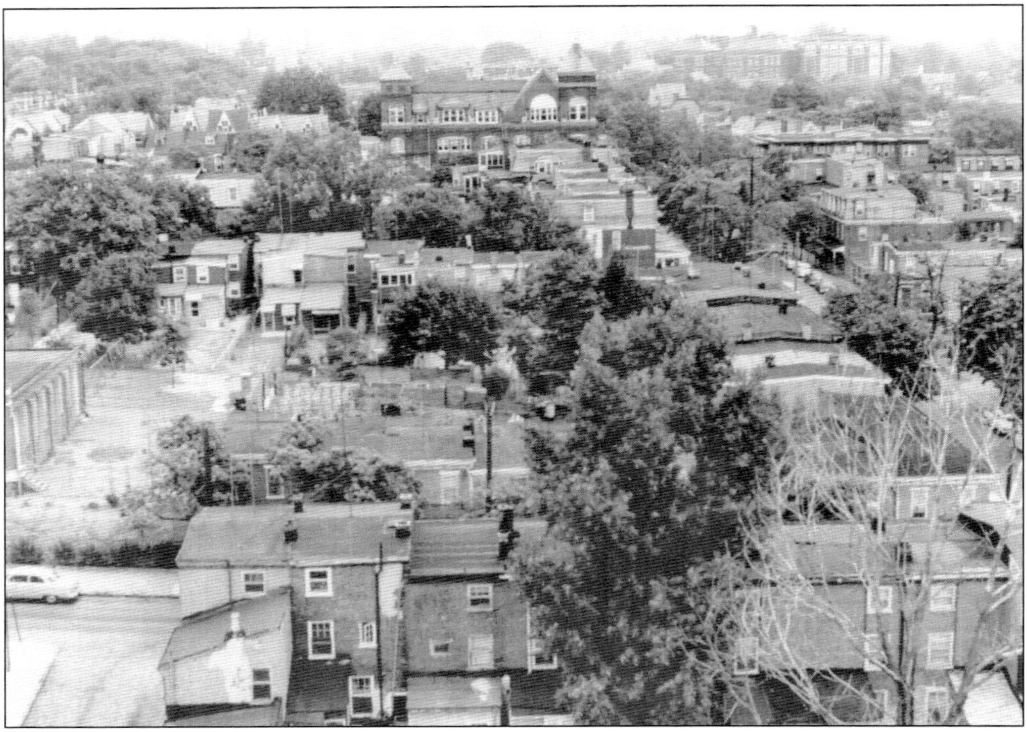

View of the Adams-Jackson Street Corridor Looking North from the Diamond State Brewery, August 9, 1957. With the future of the Wilmington's only remaining brewery less than certain due to the proposed highway, Wachtel resorted to a contingency plan. He placed a bid on the old Bavarian Brewery property, recently abandoned by the Krueger Brewing Company, but was unsuccessful. Diamond State's debt continued to mount through 1953 and 1954. (DPA.)

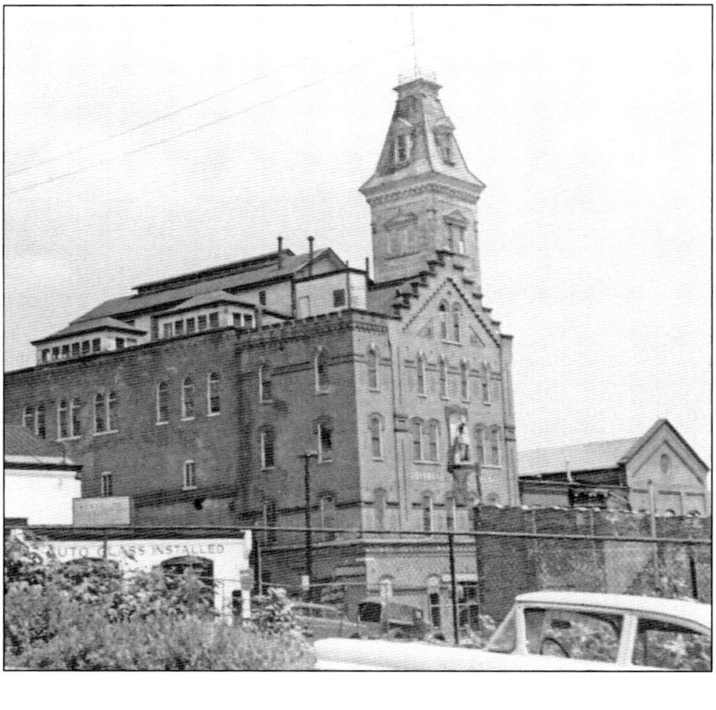

View From Jackson Street, c. 1958. In early 1955, with no other options available, the Diamond State Brewery declared bankruptcy and closed for good. The complex was sold three times within a year and a half, eventually coming under the ownership of Cohen Brothers Furniture Store. They used part of the brewery as a warehouse and rented a few of the remaining buildings to other businesses. (NBM.)

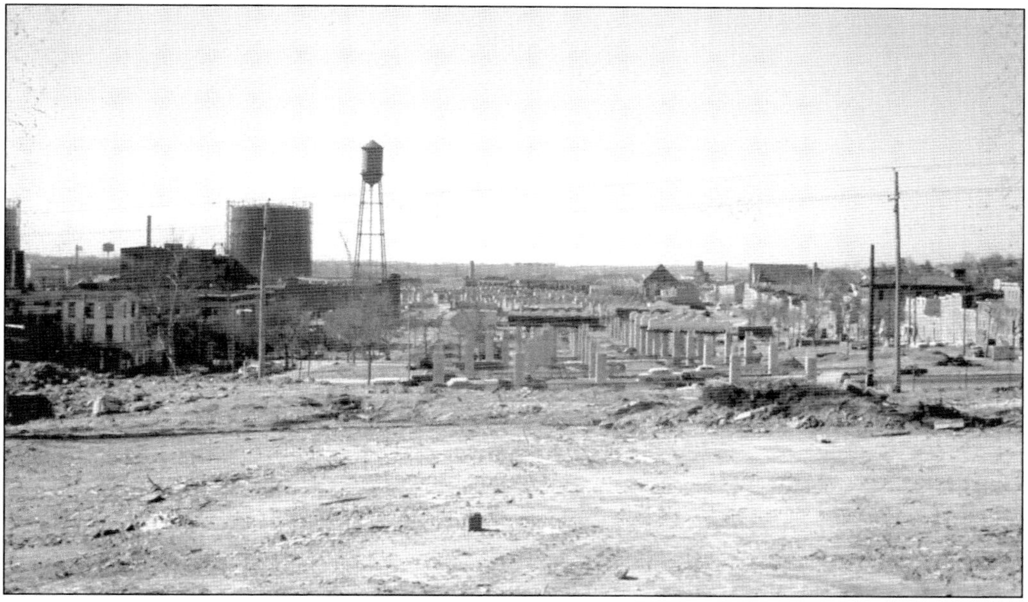

Former Diamond State Brewery Site, Looking Southward, 1965. A final decision was made on the path of the highway through Wilmington in 1959. The old Diamond State Brewery and hundreds of other structures in the Adams-Jackson corridor from Second Street north to Delaware Avenue would have to be removed. In 1962, the brewery, which had stood at that location for more than a century, was demolished. (Harry Rogerson.)

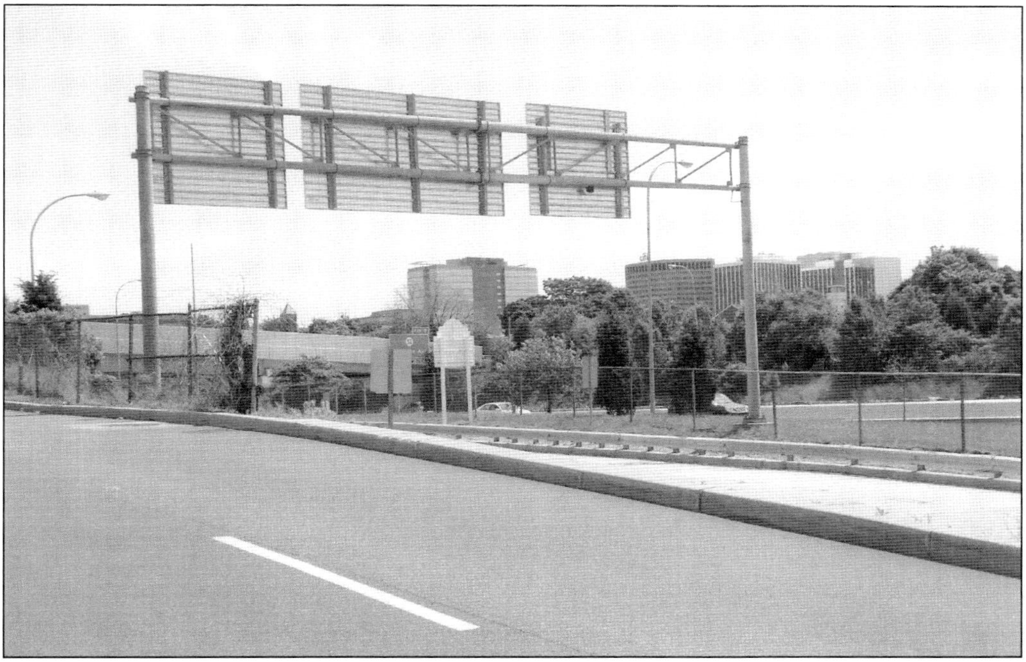

View of the Former Diamond State Brewery Location, 2014. The arterial highway through the city was incorporated into Interstate 95. Today, motorists traveling north on I-95 through Wilmington at Fifth Street pass through the spot where Diamond State's brewhouse was located. Travelers going southbound on I-95 at Fifth Street pass through the former location of the brewery's stables and bottling house. (Author's collection.)

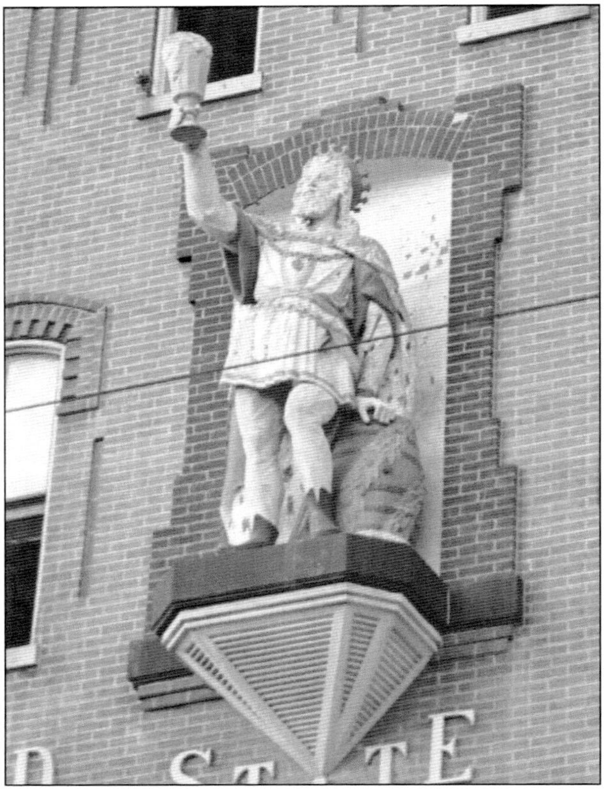

King Gambrinus Statue, Diamond State Brewery, October 1, 1955. The Gambrinus statue, cast by Michael Gebelt and Brothers of Brooklyn, New York, in 1882, has had a remarkable existence since being removed from the brewery in 1962. It was displayed for a short time at the Cohen Brothers Furniture store on Madison Street in Wilmington. Francis Corridori purchased Gambrinus in 1963 and prominently displayed that statue outside of his King's Inn restaurant in suburban Wilmington. (DHS.)

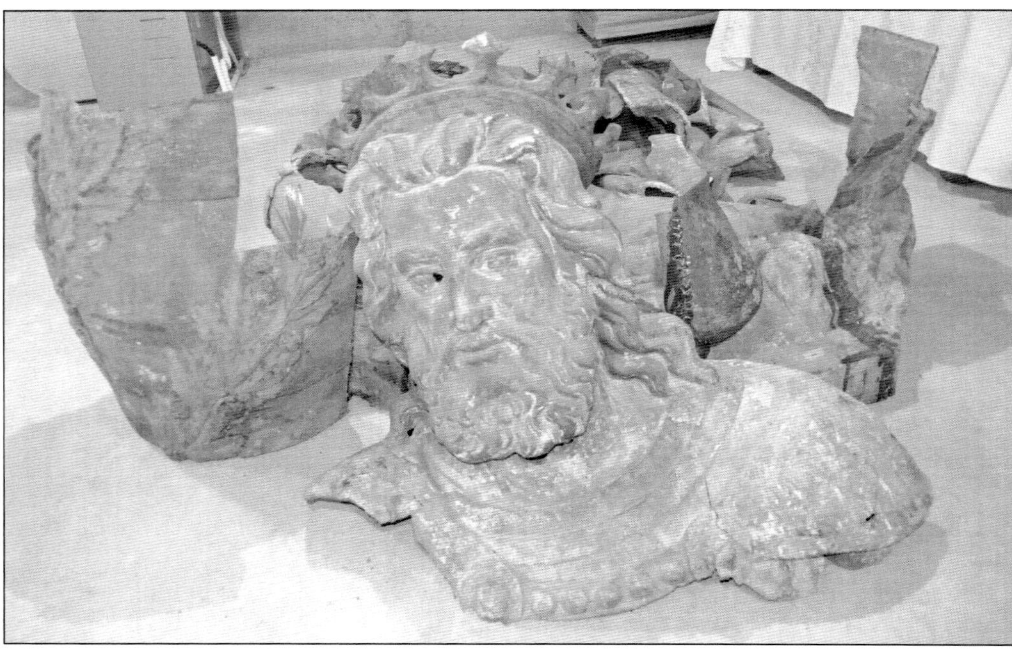

King Gambrinus Statue, 2015. When the King's Inn closed in the early 1970s, the Gambrinus statue was placed in storage. The statue was inadvertently dropped while being moved in 1978 and shattered into dozens of pieces. Currently, the statue is in possession of the author, who intends to have it restored and donated to a museum for permanent public display. (Author's collection.)

Four

Craft Beer Revolution 1990–Present

Consolidation of the brewing industry picked up steam through the late 1950s and early 1960s, as many regional brewing companies went bankrupt or sold their brands to larger national firms. Given the existing business environment and lower consumer demand, there was little chance for a new company to start up in Delaware. However, the Miller Brewing Company did purchase land in Newark in 1970 with the intent of constructing an enormous facility to serve as its Eastern production and distribution branch. Miller was purchased shortly thereafter by Philip Morris, the Newark plans were abandoned, and the land was sold.

The industry continued to consolidate through the 1960s and 1970s, as old beer styles and regional brands disappeared. By 1991, five brewing companies in the United States produced nearly 93 percent of the beer. The monolithic styles perfected by the large brewing companies—a cheaply made pale-yellow American pilsner and its reduced calorie counterpart—were expertly marketed and sold nationwide at the exclusion of other traditional beer styles.

The genesis of the craft-beer revolution began in 1978 with passage of the national regulation permitting homebrewing. Beer lovers who could not easily purchase the styles they sought to drink began making their own. Although homebrewing would not officially become legal in Delaware until 1998, many, including those who would later become professional brewers and brewery owners, were doing so a decade or more before.

Since 1990, the United States has experienced a resurgence in its brewing culture, led by the widespread proliferation of small-production breweries and brewpubs. Indeed, Delaware has been one of the most fortunate benefactors of the craft-beer revolution. By the end of 2013, the state had 10 craft breweries and ranked fourth in the nation in gallons of craft brew produced per adult. Dogfish Head Craft Brewing and Iron Hill Brewery are recognized nationally as production and brewpub industry leaders, and several of the state's other breweries have won medals in national and international competitions. With even more breweries being planned, there is no greater affirmation that a new golden age of brewing has arrived in Delaware.

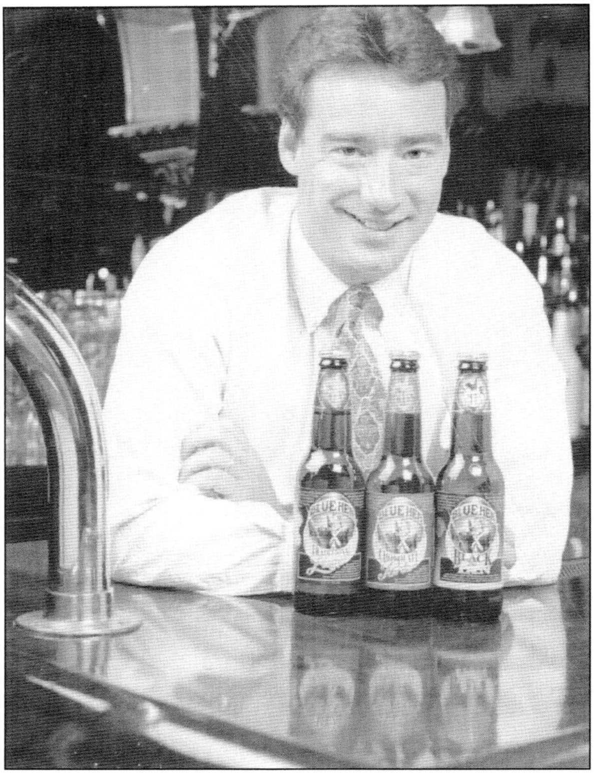

Blue Hen Beer President Jeff Johnson, 1996. As founder and president of the first beer company to operate in Delaware in four decades, Blue Hen Beer Company's Jeff Johnson faced significant challenges. He realized that he did not have the capital needed to start a production brewery, and brewpubs were not yet legal in Delaware. Instead, Johnson created the Blue Hen brand, based on the Delaware state bird and Revolutionary War regiment, and contracted with the Lion Brewery in Wilkes-Barre, Pennsylvania, to brew and package his beer. (Jeffrey Johnson.)

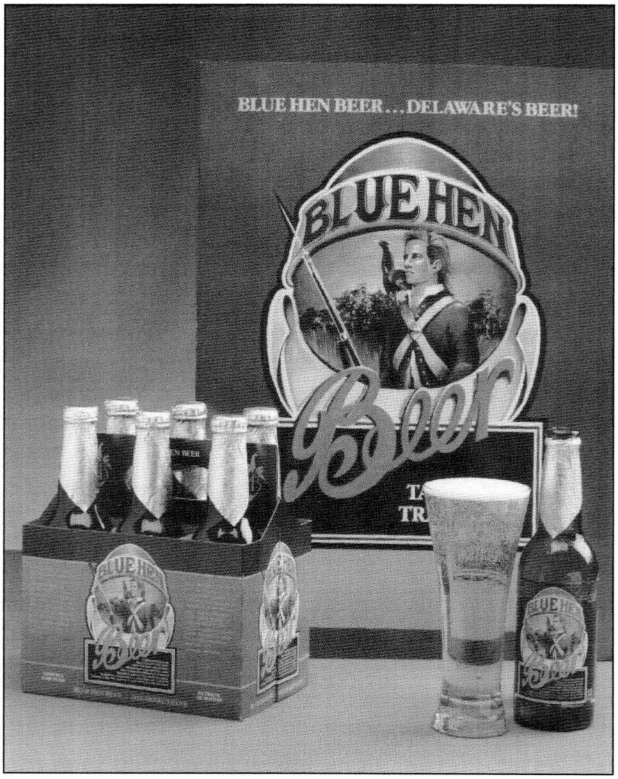

Blue Hen Beer Promotional, 1993. From 1990 until 1998, Blue Hen distributed its award-winning bottled Munich helles-style lager, chocolate porter, and black and tan throughout Delaware and into northern Maryland and southeastern Pennsylvania. Though sales were initially good, the downturn that began in 1993 eventually led Johnson to sell Blue Hen to Independence Brewing Company of Philadelphia in 1998. They produced the Blue Hen line for two years before meeting a similar fate. (Jeffrey Johnson.)

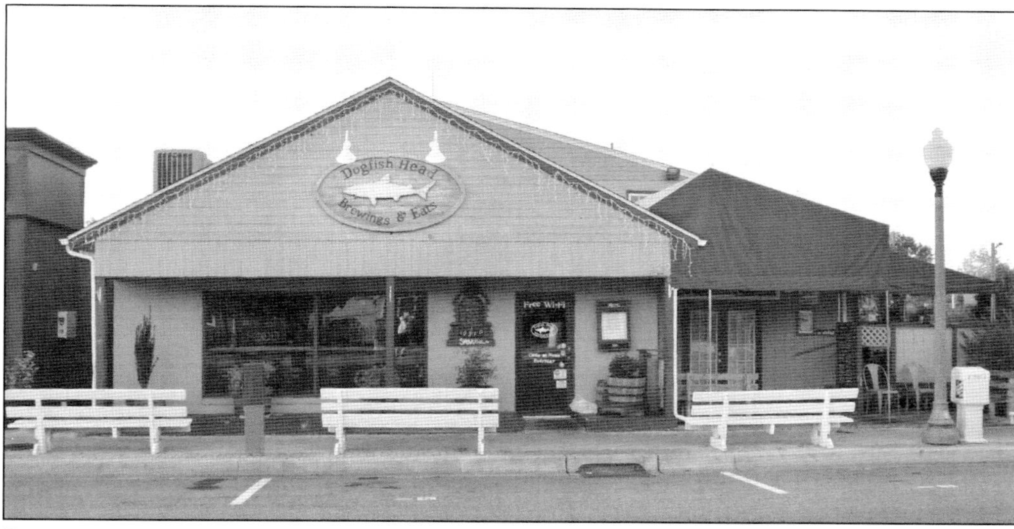

Dogfish Head Brewings and Eats, Rehoboth Beach, 2014. The Dogfish Head Craft Brewery empire began in this humble building in June 1995, shortly after Delaware passed legislation allowing brewpubs to operate in the state. Founder, president, and, at the time, head brewer, Sam Calagione started brewing 10-gallon batches of his handcrafted beer in the back of the pub. Only 15 months after opening, the pub was kegging and bottling its beer for distribution. (Author's collection.)

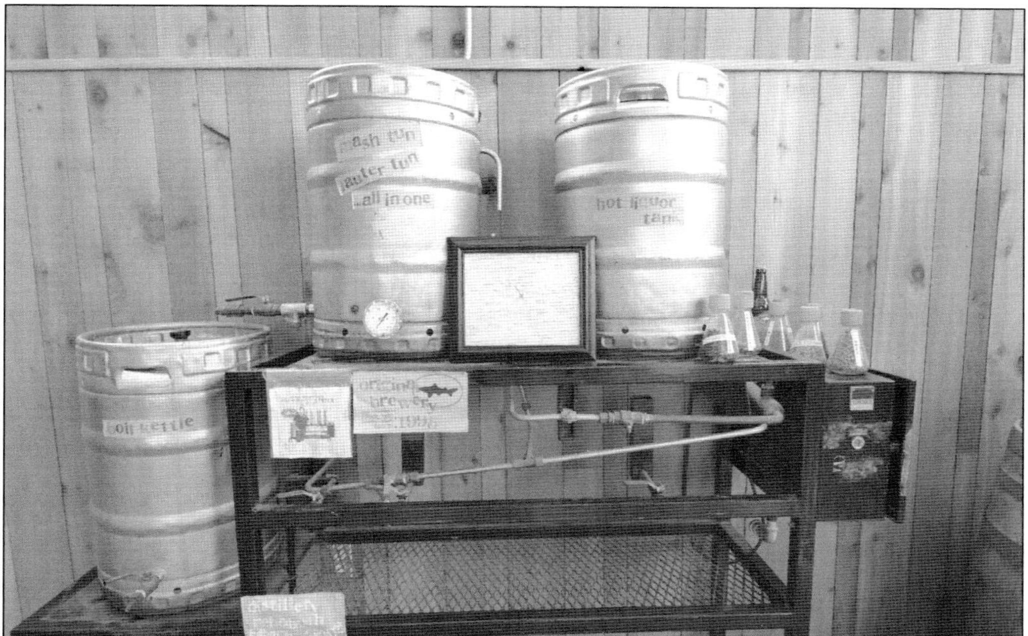

Dogfish Head's Original Half-Barrel Brewery, 2014. In June 1997, Calagione separated the brewing production from the pub by establishing Dogfish Head Craft Brewery. Brewing moved to a new 30-barrel brewhouse five miles north to Nassau. The facility was assembled using an assortment of used equipment, including fermenters from a yogurt company, a bottle-filling machine from a soda plant, a 1950s-era brewery keg-filling system, and other equipment from defunct local canning and dairy businesses. (FB.)

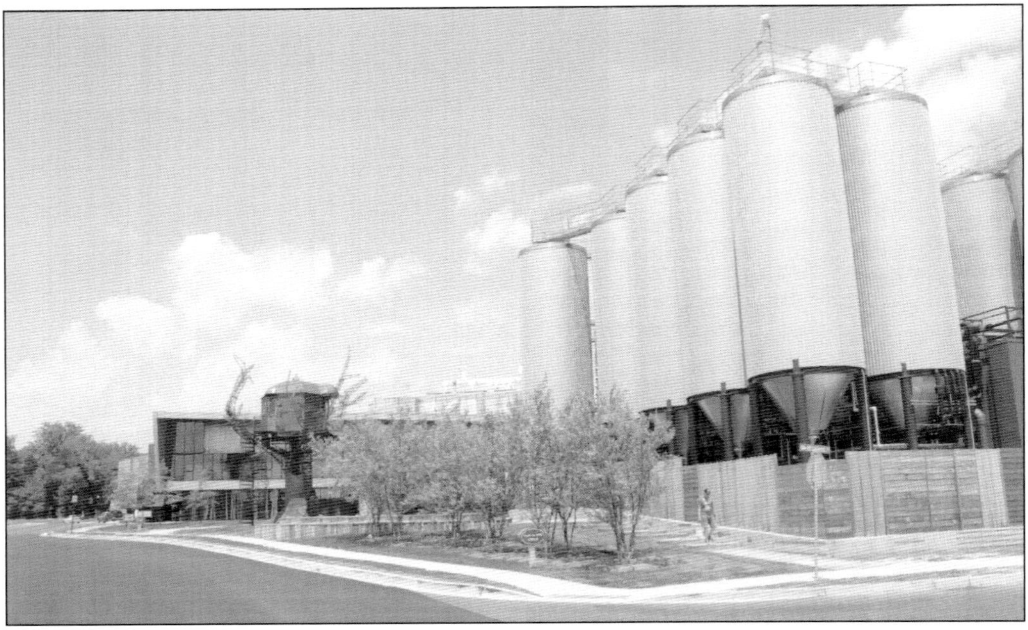

Dogfish Head Craft Brewery, Milton, 2014. Over the next five years, Dogfish Head's "off-centered ales" repertoire expanded from its original three offerings, Shelter pale ale, chicory stout, and Immort Ale, to include several other unique, award-winning styles. Expansion of its production facilities became a necessity, as the brewery's sales dramatically increased, its market expanded, and its products gained national acclaim. In June 2002, the company greatly expanded operations by moving to a 100,000-square-foot former canning warehouse in Milton. (FB.)

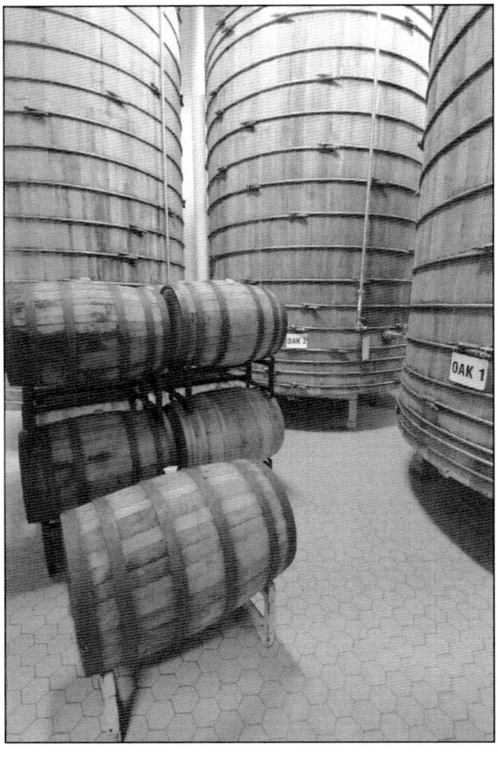

Wood Fermenting Vessels, Dogfish Head Brewery, 2014. In 2008, Dogfish Head installed the largest wooden brewing vessels made in America since before Prohibition. Wood from the 10,000-gallon tanks, one made of Paraguayan palo santo and the others of oak, contribute vanilla and spicy flavors during the fermentation process to select Dogfish Head beers. The brewery also uses smaller casks for a few other brews. (FB.)

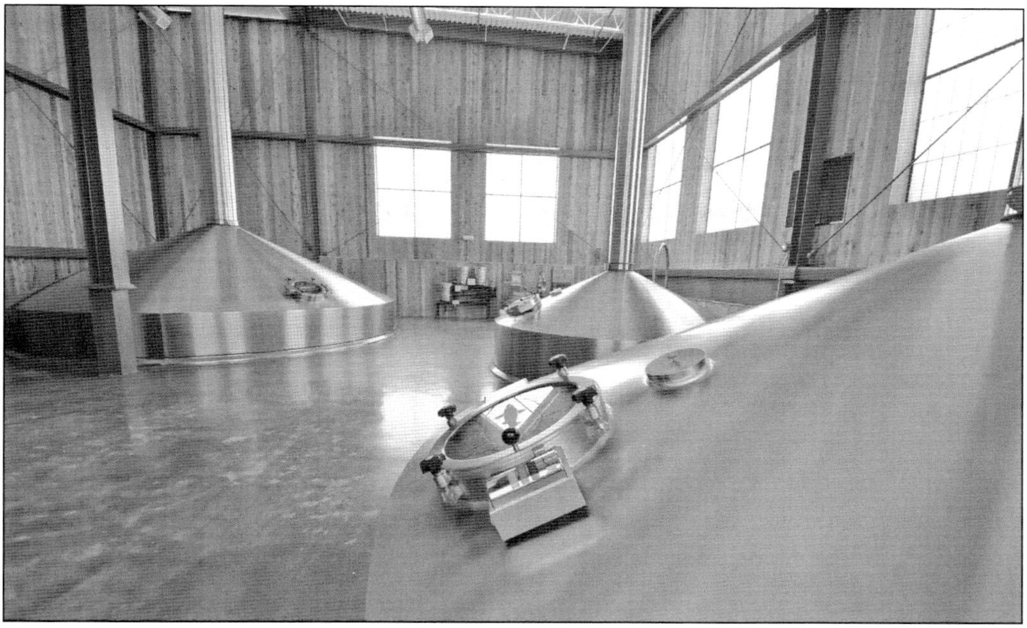

Dogfish Head Brewhouse, 2014. Dogfish Head doubled the size of its brewery footprint in 2013 when they added a 75,000-foot facility containing a 200-barrel brewhouse, packaging facility, and storage warehouse. The company now employs nearly 200 workers and has become an important driver of the Sussex County economy. (FB.)

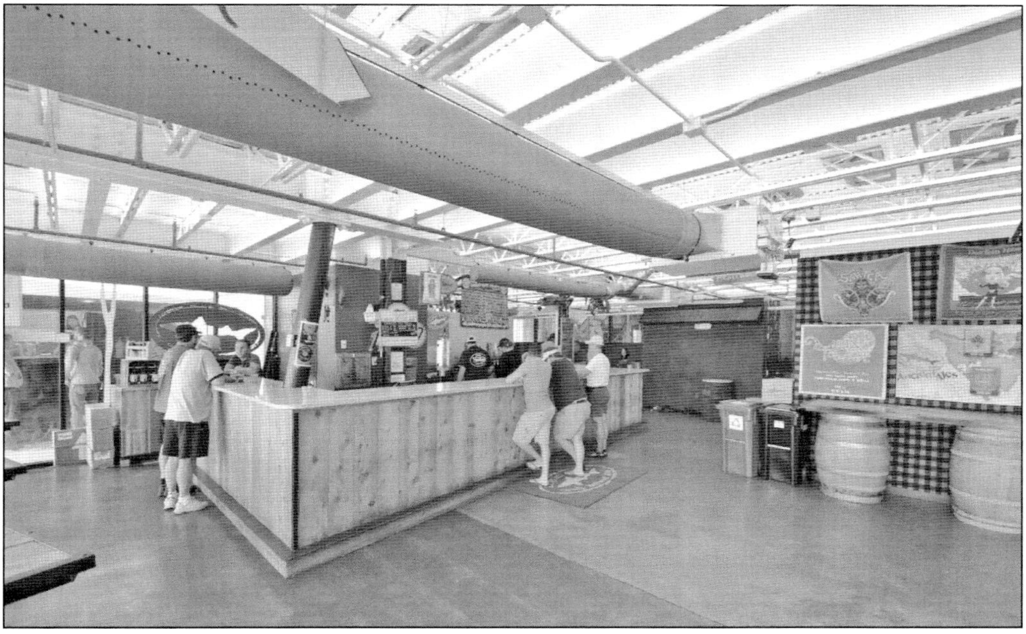

Dogfish Head Hospitality Room, 2014. Dogfish Head's production grew to over 175,000 barrels in 2013, which made it the 20th-largest producer in the United States and largest ever in Delaware. The brewery's "extreme beers," including its award-winning IPAs and ancient ales, have gained worldwide notoriety and are currently shipped to over 30 states across the country. The Milton brewery has become a tourist attraction, drawing more than 1,000 visitors a week for tours. (FB.)

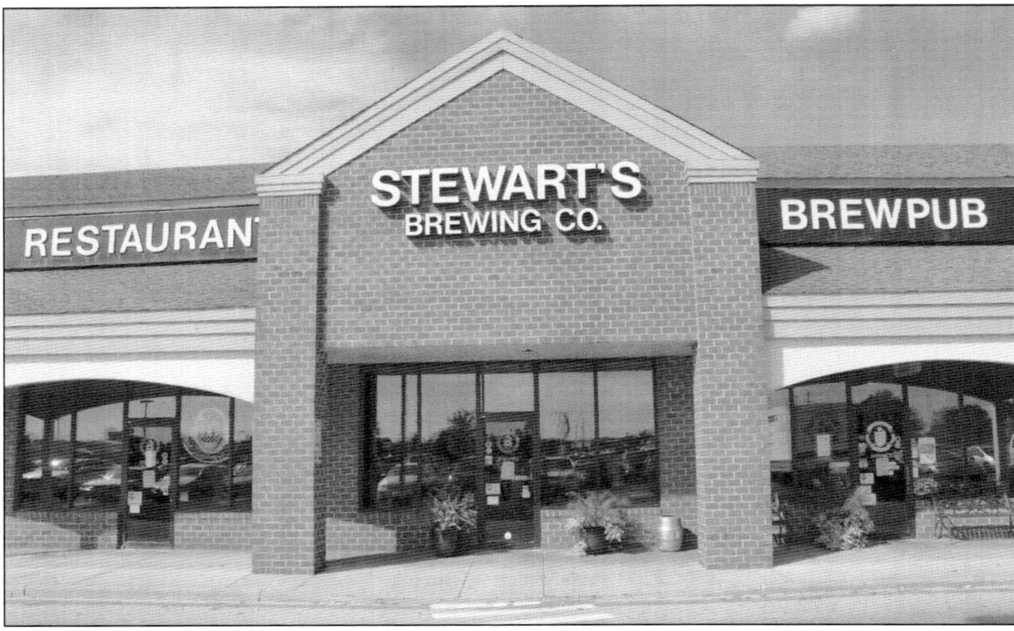

STEWART'S BREWING COMPANY, BEAR, 2014. On the heels of Dogfish Head, Al and Greg Stewart opened their eponymous brewpub in Governor's Square Shopping Center on July 27, 1995. Stewart's Brewing Company became the first bar in New Castle County to produce its own beer since Wilmington's lager beer brewing saloonkeepers of the 1870s. (FB.)

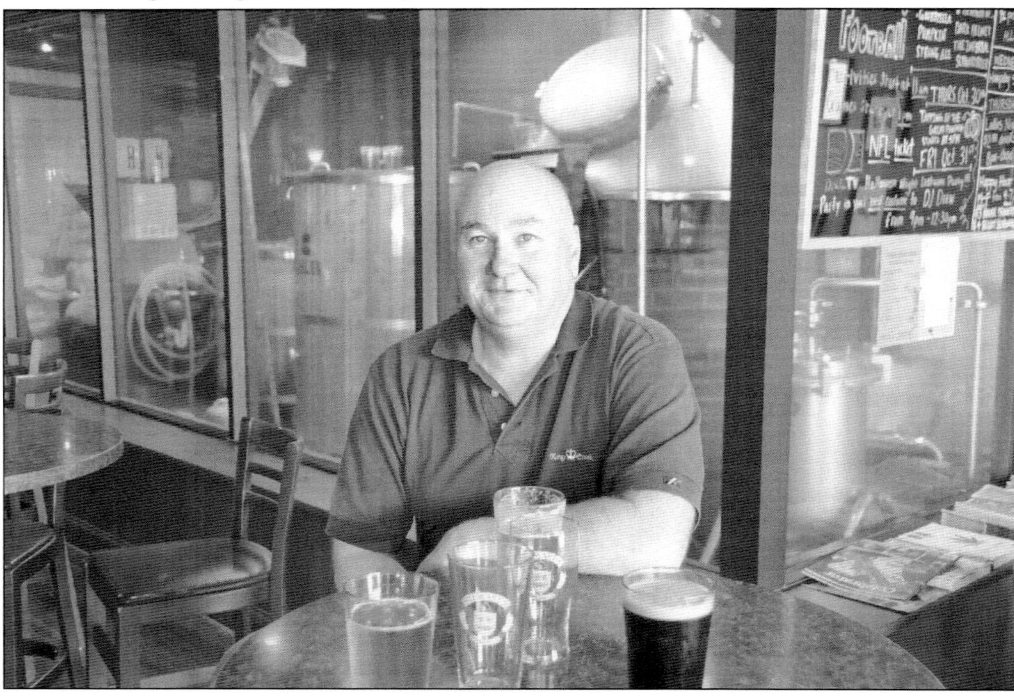

STEWART'S FOUNDER AND PRESIDENT AL STEWART, 2014. Stewart's original seven-barrel Peter Austin brewhouse has stood the test of time and is still in use. The brewery has produced over 60 styles of beer, most of them seasonal brews, along with its stable of five tried-and-true house brews. (FB.)

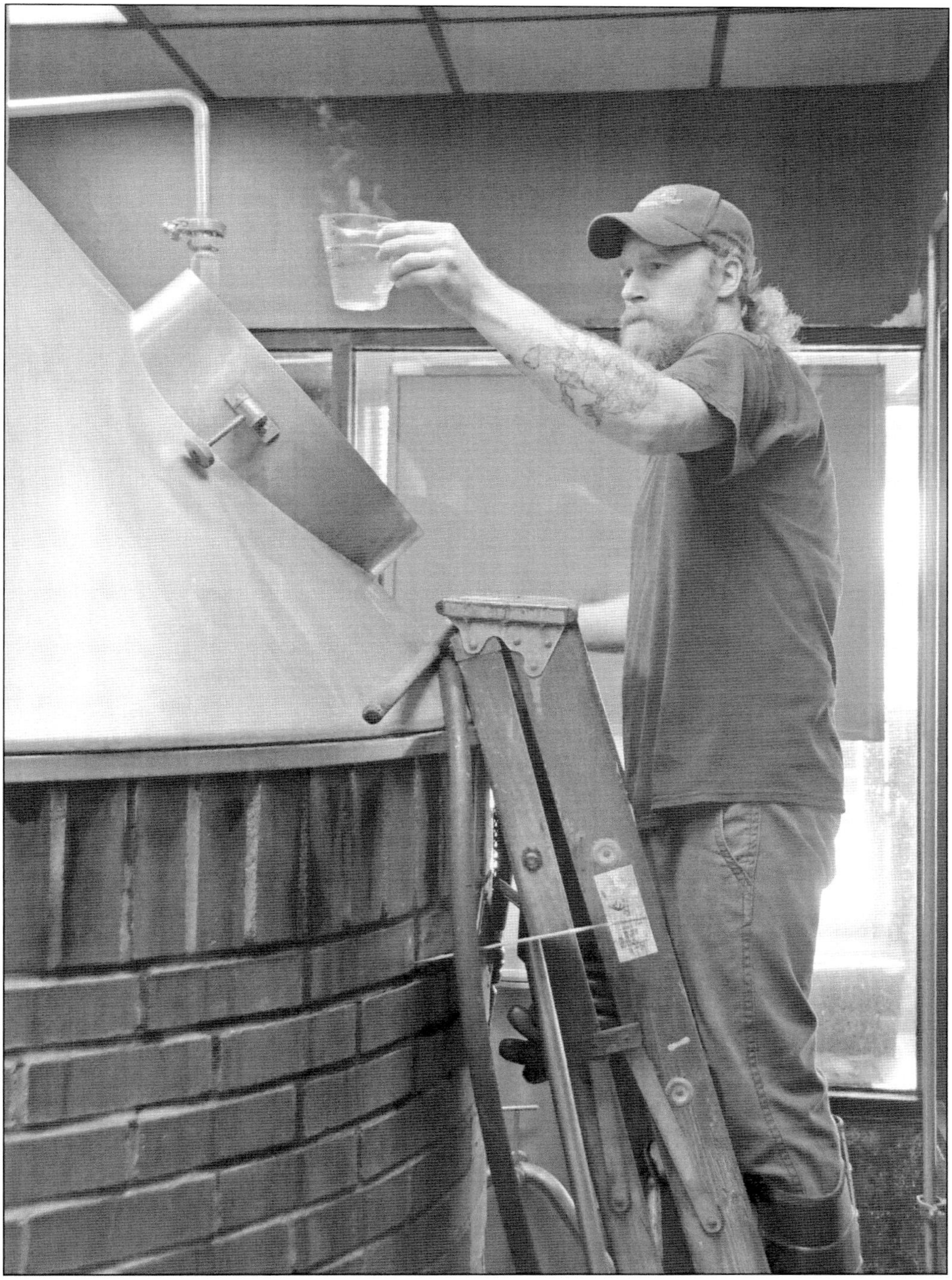

Stewart's Assistant Brewer Eric Boice, 2014. When Ric Hoffman was promoted from assistant brewer to head brewer in 2000, Stewart's began garnering national recognition for its quality ales and lagers. The creativity of Hoffman and assistant brewer Eric Boice remains the key ingredient in Stewart's continued success. To date, Stewart's has accumulated 10 Great American Beer Festival medals and four World Beer Cup awards. The brewpub has developed a loyal following and has not had to expand to survive in a competitive environment. (FB.)

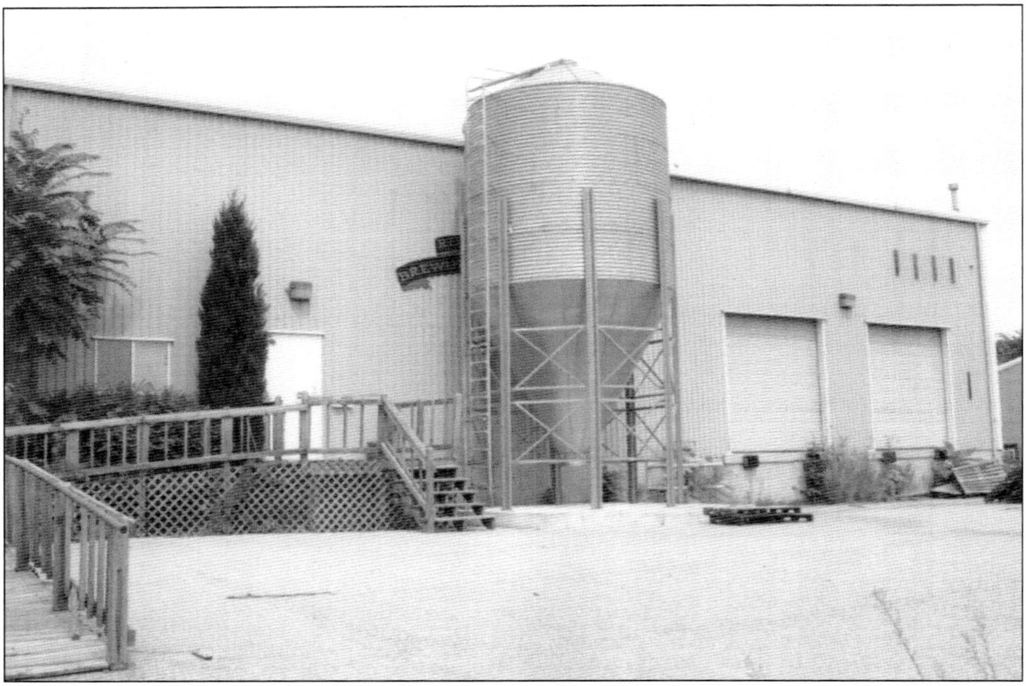

Rockford Brewing Company, Wilmington, 1998. When it opened for business on June 1, 1995, Marty Haugh's Rockford Brewing Company became the first brewery to operate in Delaware since the Diamond State Brewery closed 40 years earlier. Rockford's production brewery, located on St. James Court in Wilmington, utilized a 25-barrel Criveller brewing system. Aside from being a longtime homebrewer, Haugh was a former mechanical contractor and designed the brewery's piping and system controls. (Author's collection.)

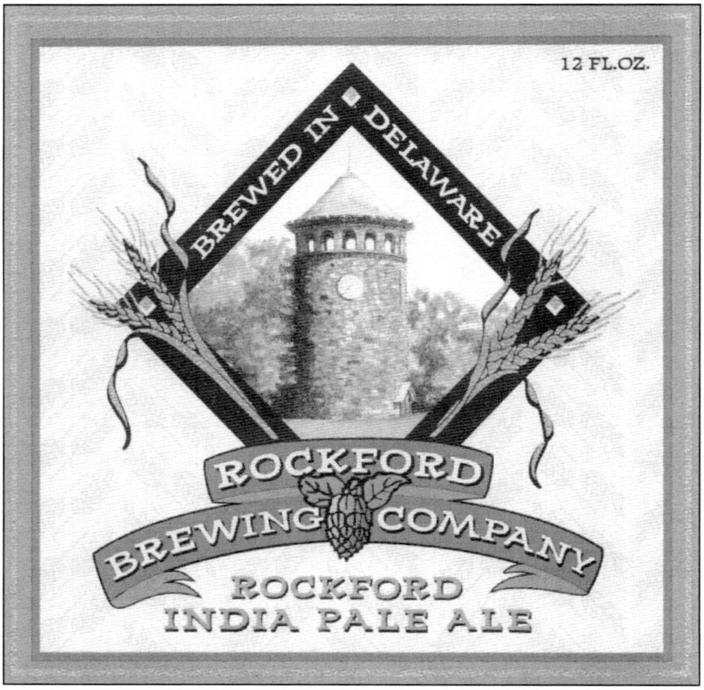

Rockford India Pale Ale Label, 1998. The company's first beers included its bottled and kegged Czech-style pilsner, golden lager, and a red ale, which were distributed in Delaware, Pennsylvania, Maryland, and Washington, DC. An IPA was later offered. Rockford was immediately forced into a market where shelf space was dominated by the largest breweries and microbreweries. Beleagured by production and distribution issues, Rockford was forced to close in June 1998. (Author's collection.)

BRANDYWINE BREWING COMPANY FOUNDER DAVID DIETZ, GREENVILLE, C. 1995. One month after Stewart's opened its doors, David Dietz unveiled his new brewpub, Brandywine Brewing Company, in Greenville. The company employed an 8.5-barrel Newlands brewing system and produced about 1,000 barrels a year. Though Dietz's Greenville brewpub remained popular, he closed Brandywine Brewing Company in December 2004 after his lease expired. (David Dietz.)

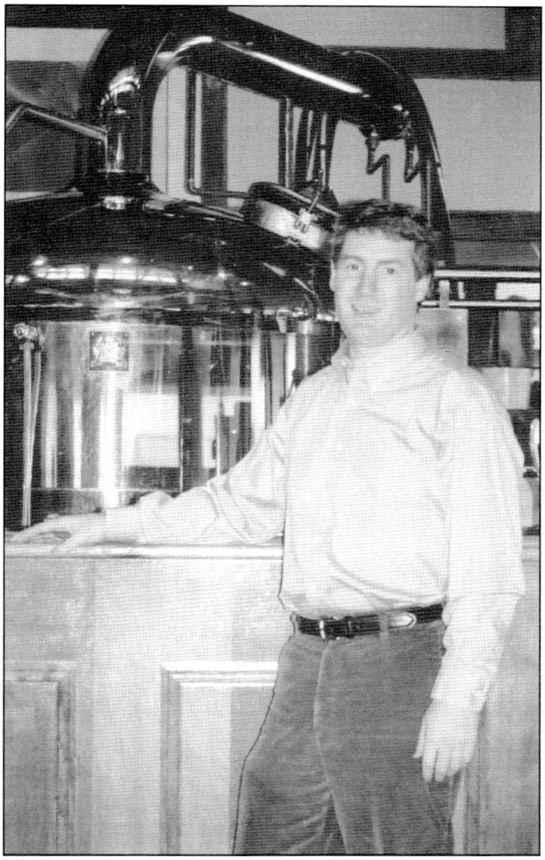

BRANDYWINE BREWING COMPANY TAVERN, WILMINGTON, 2005. The initial popularity of Dietz's Greenville brewpub inspired him to open a second location on the northeast corner of Ninth and Orange Streets in September 2000. The restaurant, which had its beer delivered from the Greenville location, was poorly received and went out of business within six months of opening. Dietz currently runs the successful BBC Tavern and Grill, just down Kennett Pike from where his original brewpub once stood. (Author's collection.)

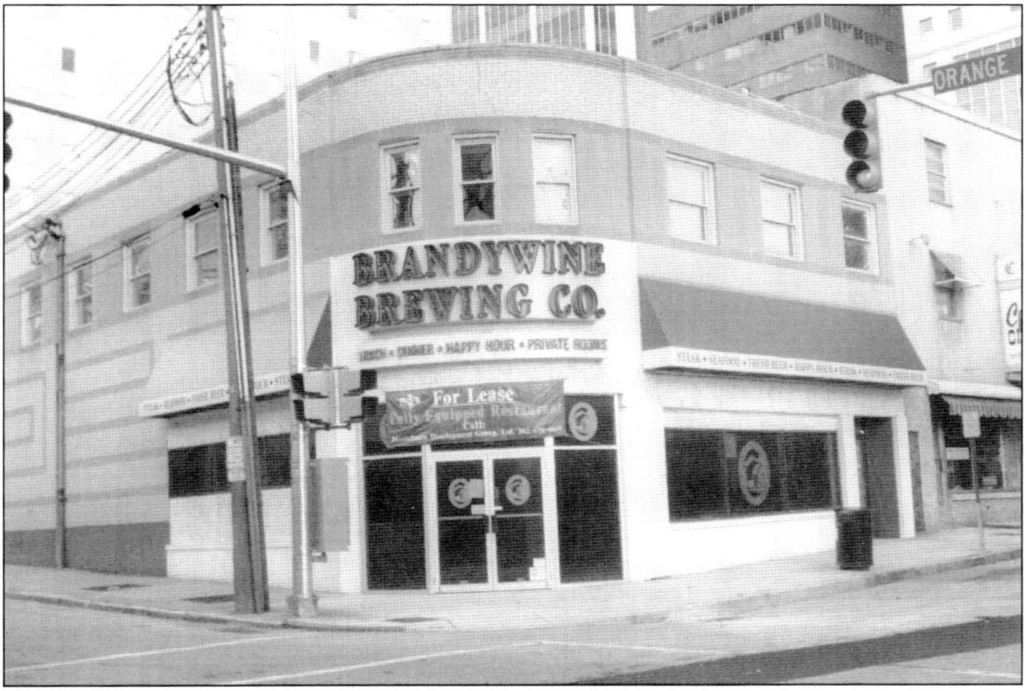

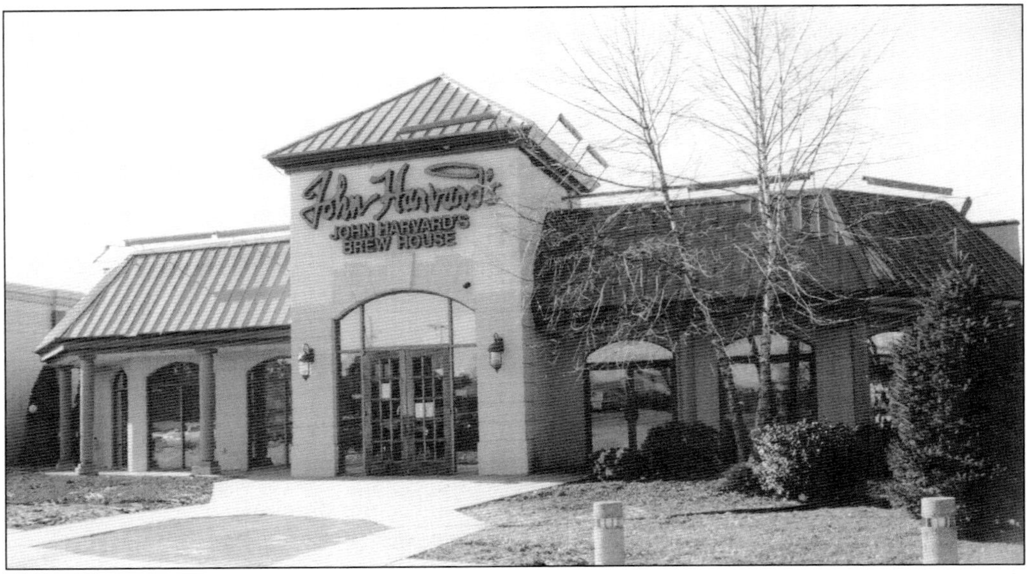

JOHN HARVARD'S BREWHOUSE, WILMINGTON, 2005. When it opened at 303 Rocky Run in March 1998, John Harvard's suburban Wilmington location became the 14th owned by the New England-based brewpub chain. The 8,401-square-foot restaurant and brewery produced exceptional beers and was popular during its 7.5-year run. Sales did not meet the corporation's expectations, and the location closed in September 2005. (Author's collection.)

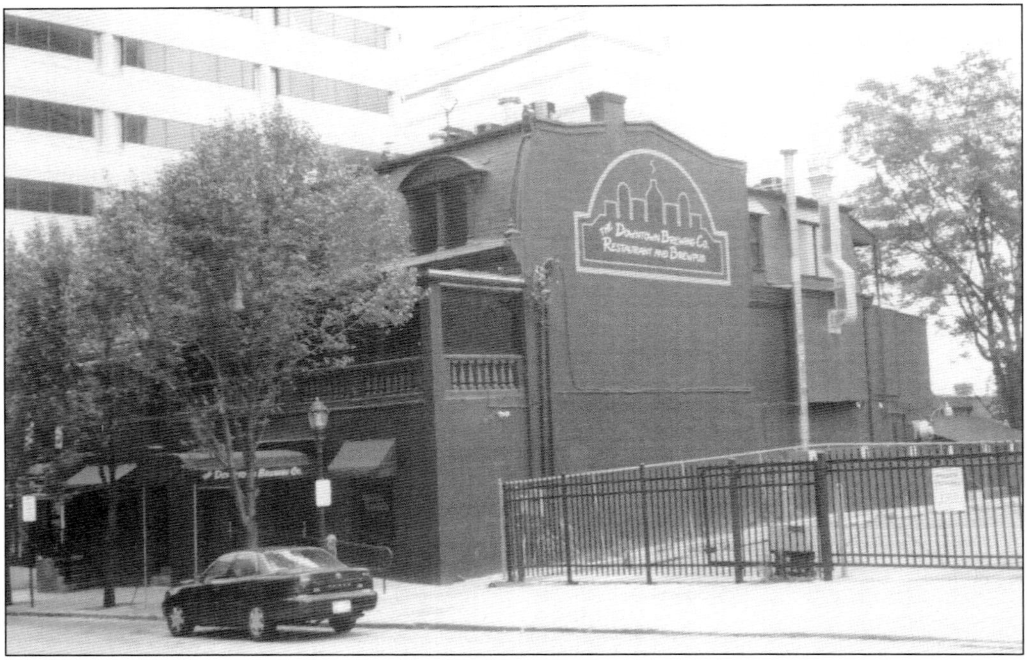

DOWNTOWN BREWING COMPANY, WILMINGTON, 2003. Impressed by the momentum of downtown revitalization in Wilmington, Greg Stewart sold his interest in Stewart's Brewing Company to his brother Al. In July 2000, Greg opened a brewpub of his own in a complex of former 19th-century homes at 1210 Market Street. The Downtown Brewing Company produced a variety of traditional English ales and German lagers. Unfortunately, after-hours business alone could not sustain the pub, forcing its closure in December 2003. (Author's collection.)

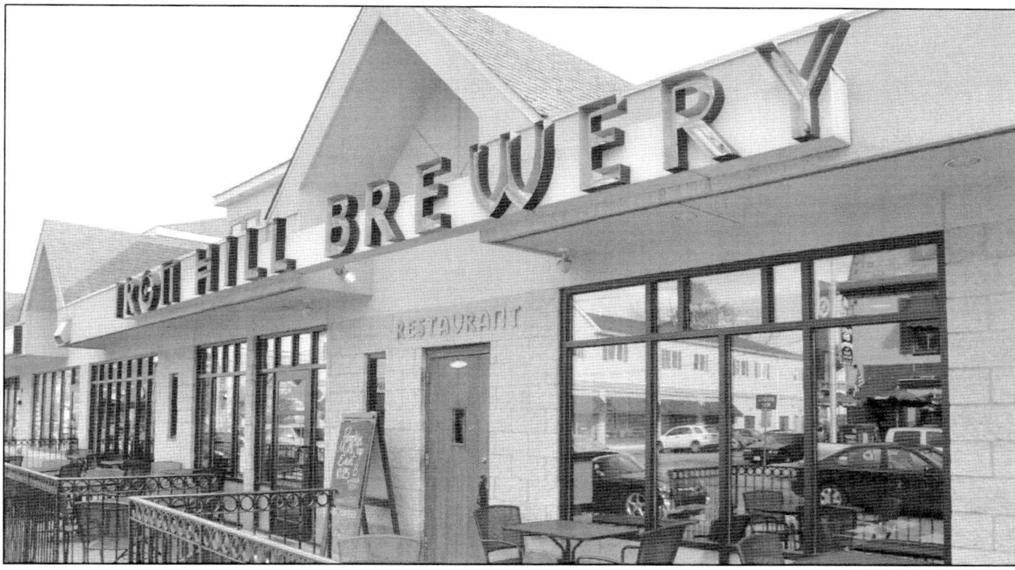

IRON HILL BREWERY, NEWARK, 2014. Founded by homebrewers Kevin Finn and Mark Edelson and restaurateur Kevin Davies, Iron Hill Brewery opened at 147 East Main Street in Newark on November 14, 1996. The brewery took its name from the tallest hill in Delaware, Iron Hill, located one mile south of Newark. Iron Hill remains the first and only brewery to operate in the city of Newark. (FB.)

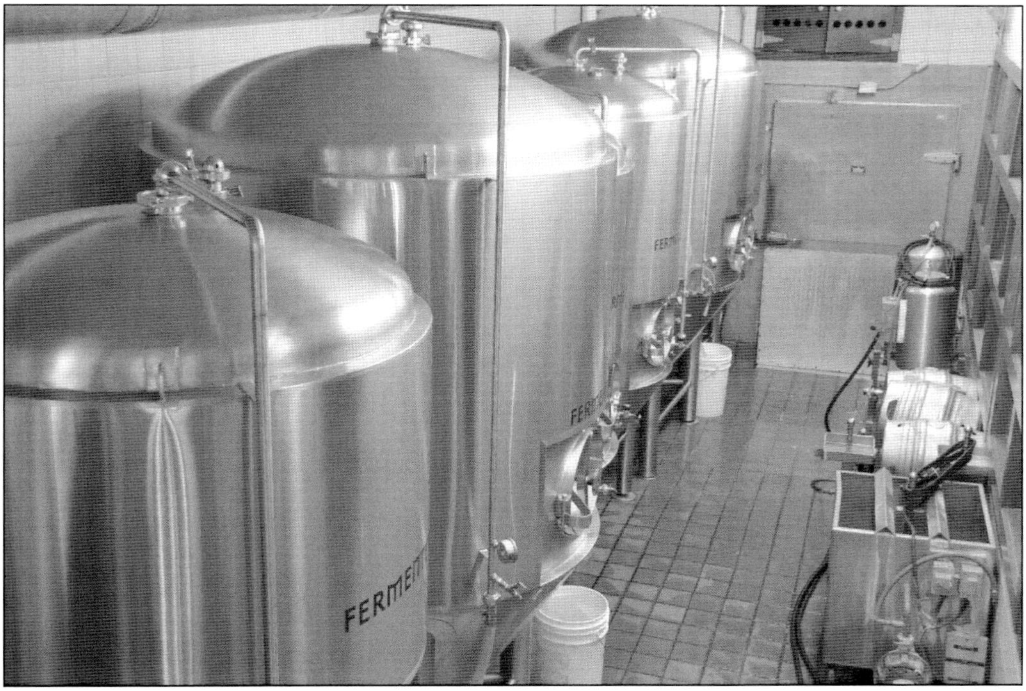

FERMENTERS INSIDE THE NEWARK BREWHOUSE, 2014. Iron Hill's Newark brewhouse utilizes a 10-barrel direct-fire brew kettle and contains six fermenters producing roughly 1,000 barrels of beer a year. The brewpub's upscale food menu and rotating variety of handcrafted ales and lagers proved enormously successful from the start. The brewery also attained immediate national recognition by earning a gold medal at the Great American Beer Festival in 1997. (FB.)

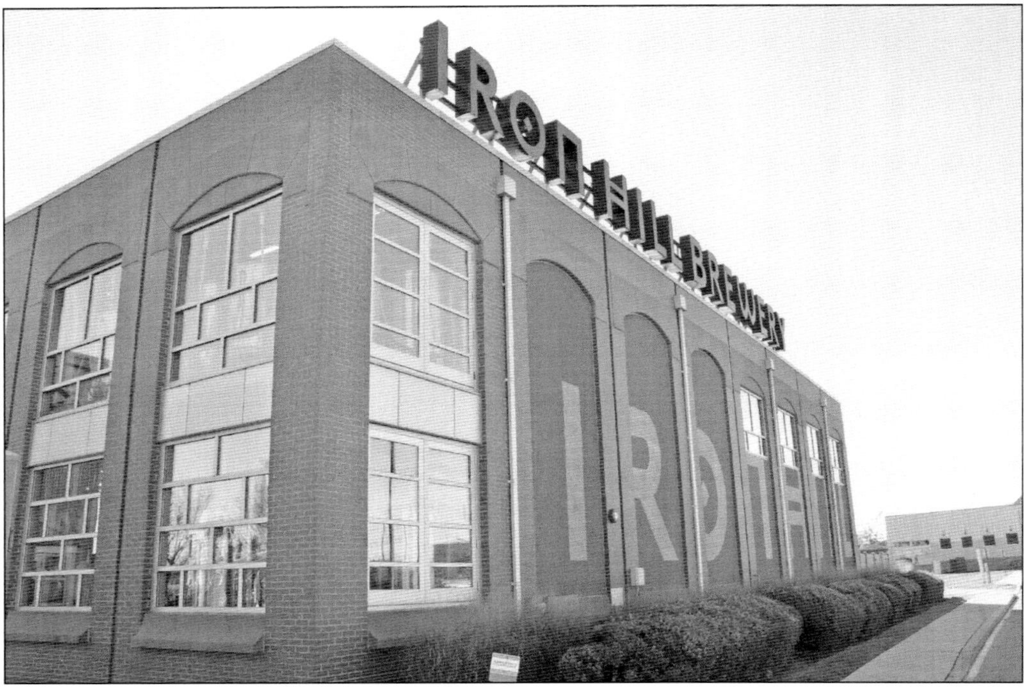

IRON HILL BREWERY, WILMINGTON, 2014. Encouraged by the success of their Newark operation, the Iron Hill partners formed the Wilmington-based Chesapeake and Delaware Brewing Company in 1997 with expansion in mind. The company opened two additional brewpubs in nearby Pennsylvania before opening the largest brewpub in Delaware on September 24, 2003, along the Wilmington riverfront. (FB.)

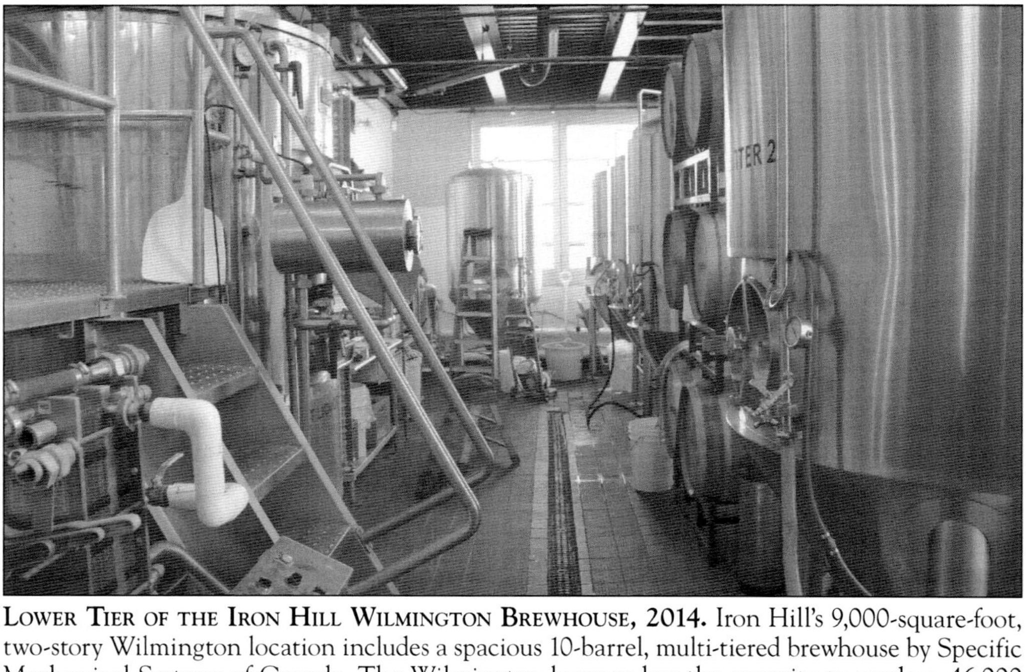

LOWER TIER OF THE IRON HILL WILMINGTON BREWHOUSE, 2014. Iron Hill's 9,000-square-foot, two-story Wilmington location includes a spacious 10-barrel, multi-tiered brewhouse by Specific Mechanical Systems of Canada. The Wilmington brewery has the capacity to produce 46,000 gallons of beer per year. (FB.)

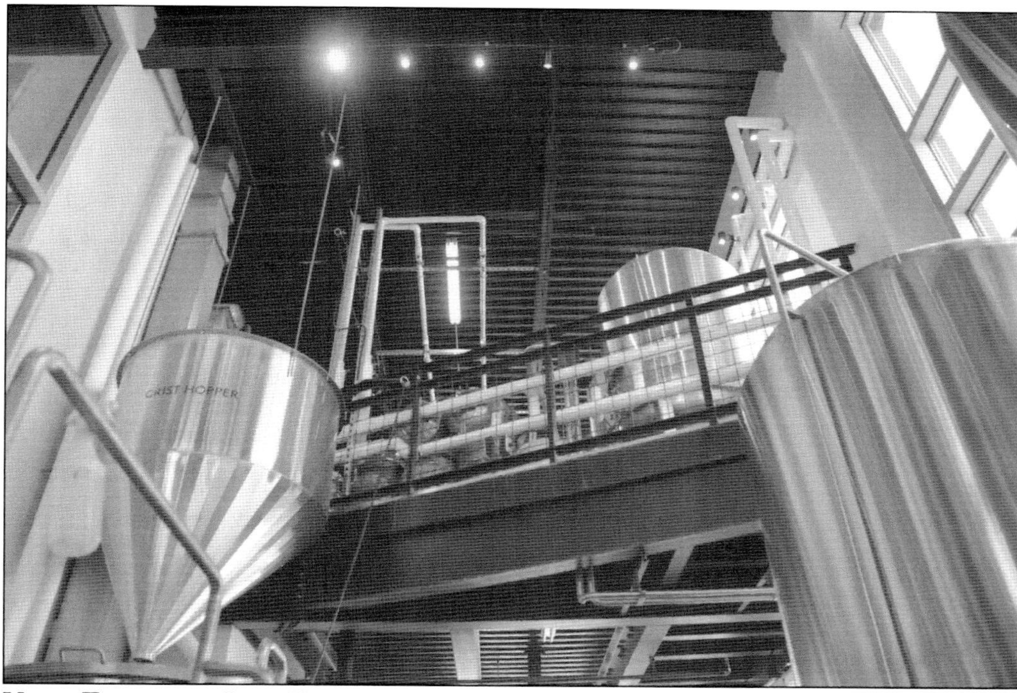

Upper Tier of the Iron Hill Wilmington Brewhouse, 2014. In addition to the dozens of house ales and lagers brewed at each of its locations, Iron Hill also offers beers from its bottle reserve series, which may be taken home or consumed on premises. In July 2014, the brewery also canned its first beer for purchase at the pubs. (FB.)

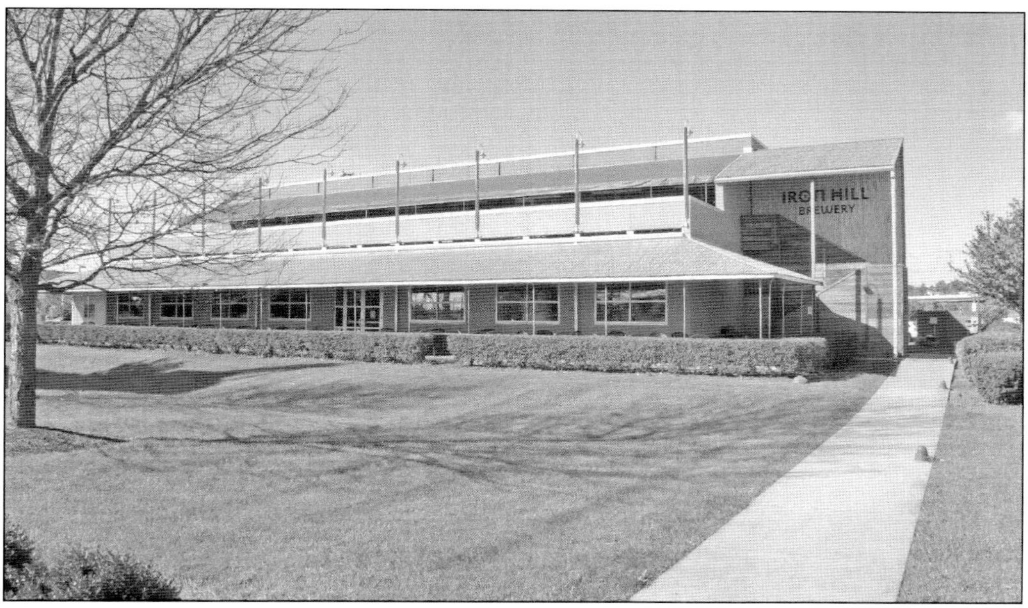

Rear of Iron Hill Brewery, Wilmington, 2014. Aside from the two Delaware pubs, Iron Hill also operates nine other locations in Pennsylvania and New Jersey. The chain has received unparalleled recognition since its founding, having won 22 World Beer Cup medals and 42 medals in an 18 consecutive-year period at the Great American Beer Festival. Additionally, Iron Hill was honored at the 2010 World Beer Cup with the prestigious Large Brewpub of the Year. (FB.)

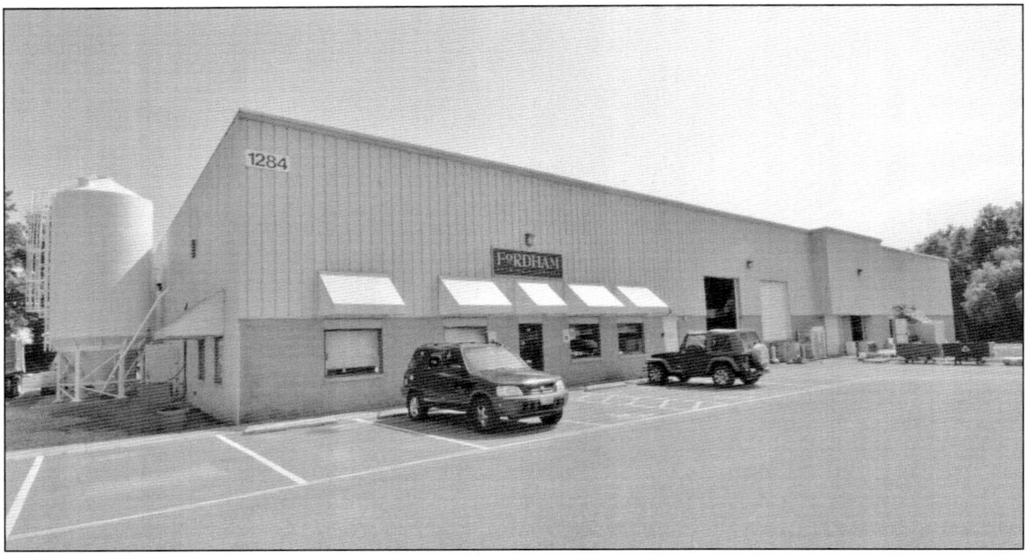

Fordham & Dominion Brewing Company, Dover, 2014. In late 1996, Bill Muehlhauser's Fordham Brewing Company sought to expand production by moving its brewing operations from the Rams Head Tavern in Annapolis, Maryland, where it had operated for a year. A deal that would have placed the brewery in Middletown, Delaware, ultimately fell through. Muehlhauser was eventually successful in moving Fordham to the First State when the company relocated to this 15,000-square-foot warehouse in Dover in November 2003. (FB.)

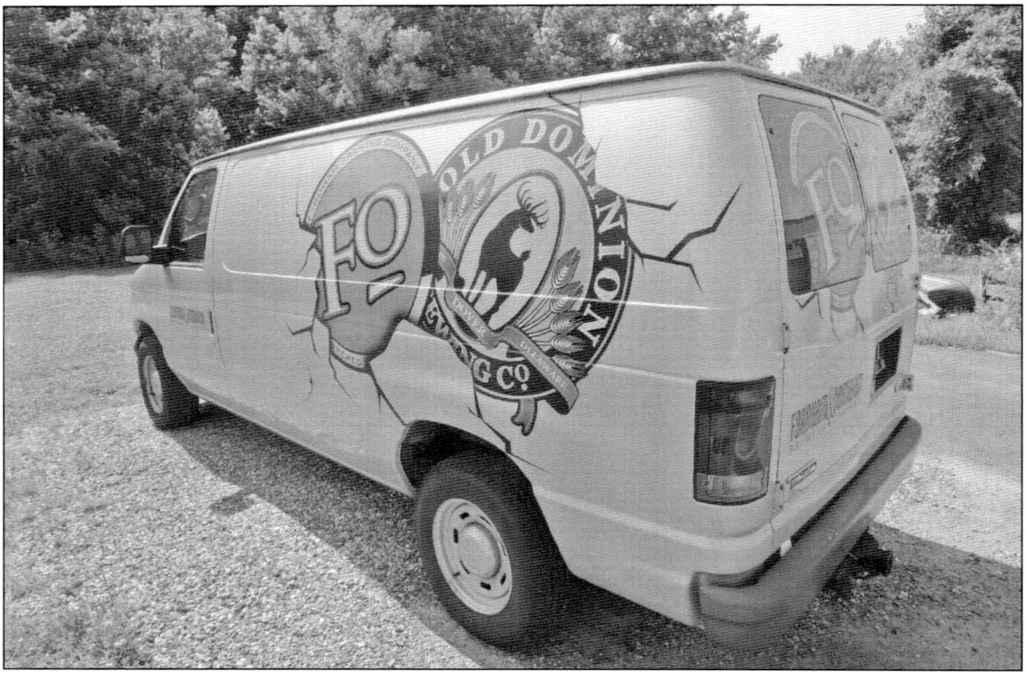

Fordham & Dominion Van, 2014. Jerry Bailey's Old Dominion Brewing Company began its run as an Ashburn, Virginia, brewpub in 1989. The company's beer and craft root beer became so popular that they opened a production brewery. In March 2007, Bailey sold his company to Coastal Brewing Company, a partnership between Fordham and Anheuser-Busch. The new company began trading as the Fordham & Dominion Brewing Company. (FB.)

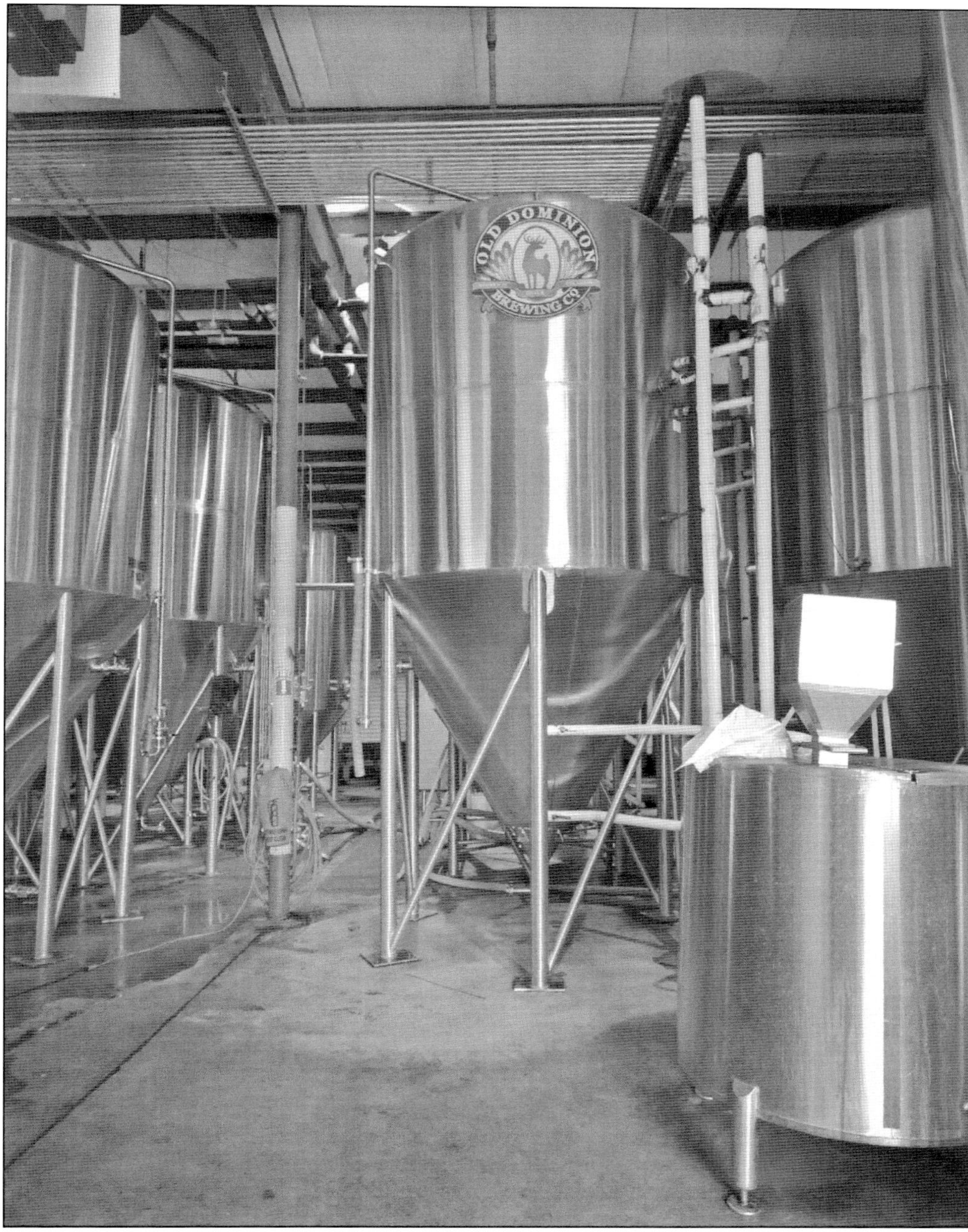

Fordham & Dominion Bright Tanks, 2014. All production of Old Dominion's line of products was consolidated with Fordham's and moved to the 25,000-barrel Dover brewery in May 2009. Jim Lutz became president of Coastal Brewing in January 2011, and since that time, Fordham & Dominion has continued to refine its separate Fordham and Dominion brands as well as its Old Dominion soft-drink line. Fordham's identity has not strayed far from its roots, as the current offerings are still mainly session ales and traditional lagers. The Dominion brand has become the brewery's line of bolder, higher-gravity beers. The brewery won its first World Beer Cup medal in 2014, taking home a gold medal for its Candi Belgian Tripel. Fordham & Dominion distributes its beers and sodas in Delaware, Maryland, Virginia, and other areas along the East Coast. (FB.)

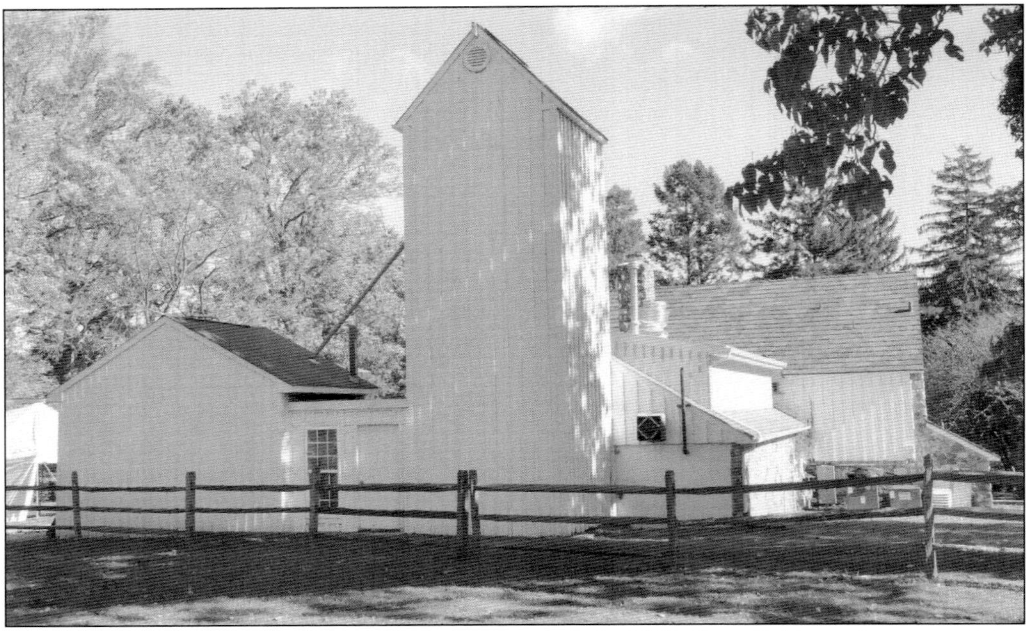

Twin Lakes Brewing Company, Greenville, 2014. In 2002, Sam Hobbs and partners Matt Day and Jack Wick began planning a small brewery to be located in a renovated tractor barn and art studio on Hobbs's Greenville estate. The dream became a reality in April 2006, when Twin Lakes Brewing Company opened for business. The brewery takes its name from a pair of landmark ponds fronting the historic 252-acre farm along the Kennett Pike. (FB.)

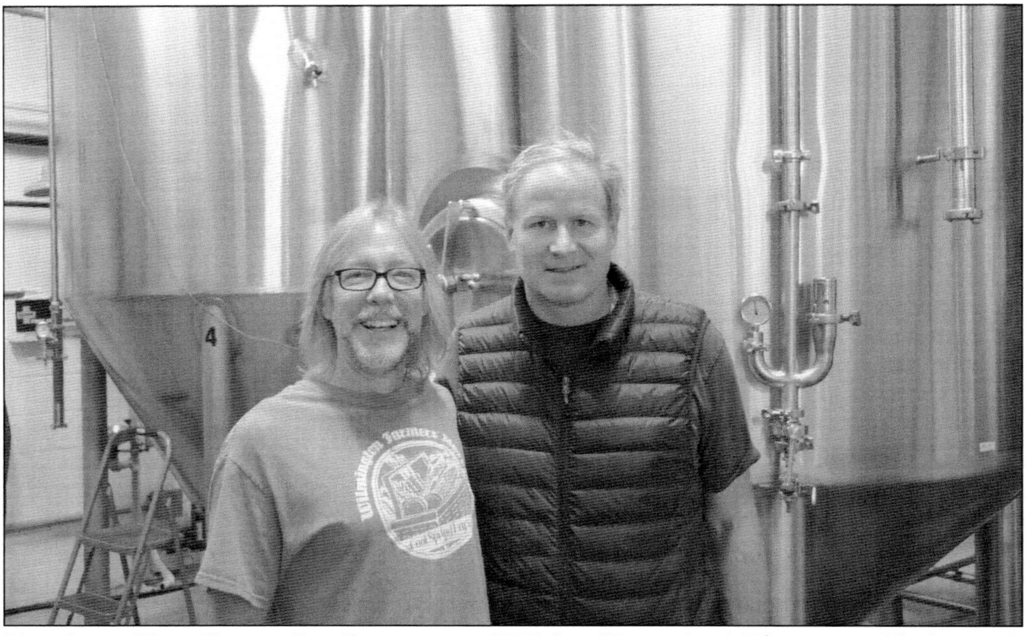

Twin Lakes Head Brewer Rob Pfeiffer and CEO Sam Hobbs, 2014. The source of the brewery's "Fresh, Local, Delicious" ales and lagers is a deep rock aquifer located on the farm. Twin Lakes operates a steam-fired, 25-barrel, gravity-fed brewhouse, which includes five fermenting vessels. The brewery is overseen by Rob Pfeiffer, who began at Twin Lakes as an assistant brewer in 2006 and became head brewer two years later. (FB.)

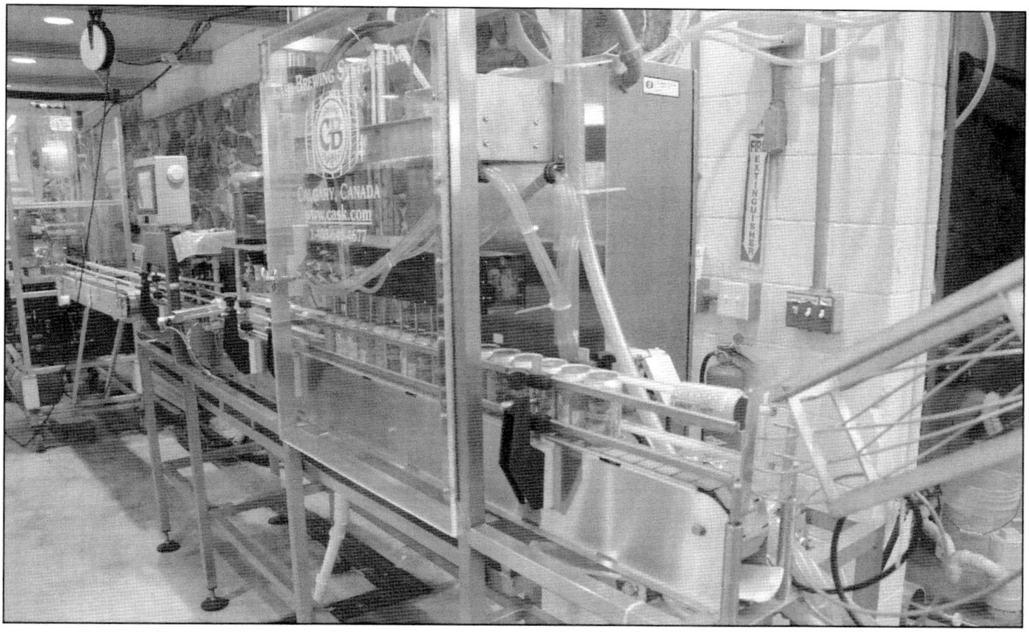

Twin Lakes Canning Line, 2014. During the first five years of operation, Twin Lakes' products were only available on draft in taverns and in growlers at the brewery. That changed in 2011 when they added a canning line and began making its most popular beer, Greenville pale ale, available to consumers in cans. The brewery continues to produce all of its locally and historically named beers on draft. (FB.)

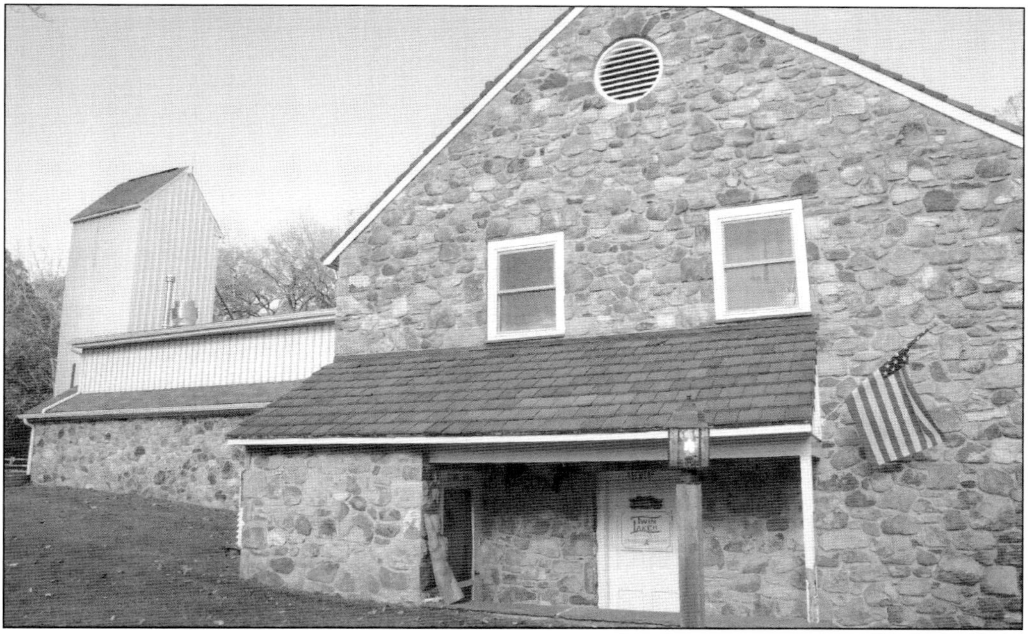

Twin Lakes Tasting Room and Brewery Entrances, 2014. In addition to Greenville pale ale, Twin Lakes' regular draft beer lineup includes Route 52 pilsner, Tweeds Tavern stout, Winterthur wheat, and Caesar Rodney golden ale. As with Delaware's other breweries, Twin Lakes offers regular tours of its brewery and ample hospitality. The tasting room is where the tours begin, and beer is available for sampling or purchase. (FB.)

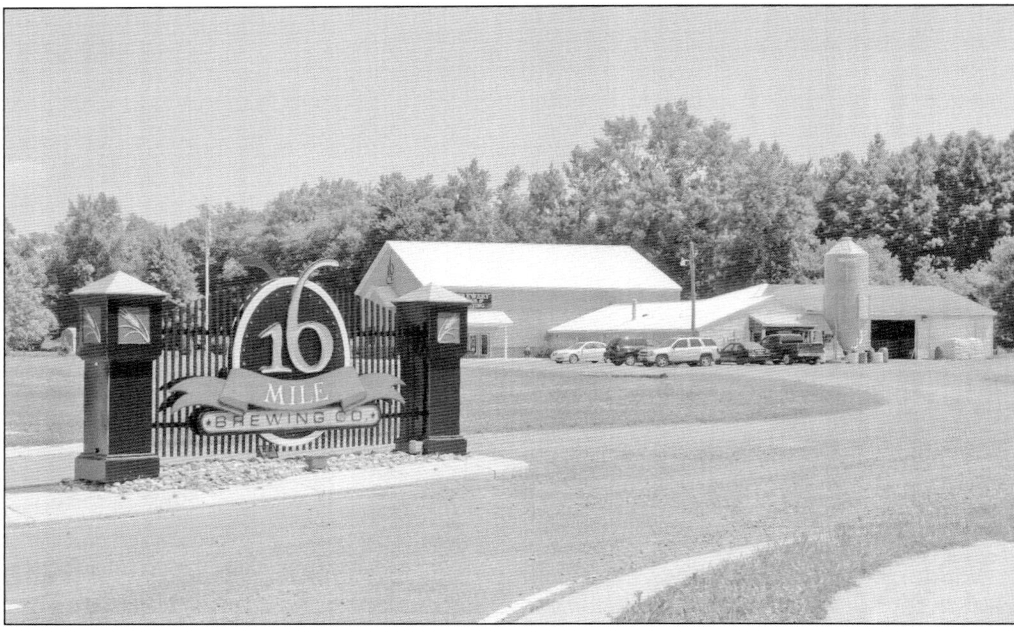

16 Mile Brewing Company, Georgetown, 2014. The local adage is that Georgetown is 16 miles from anywhere, and the name was adopted by native sons Brett McCrae and Chad Campbell when they opened 16 Mile Brewing Company at the edge of the town in August 2009. Like its northern counterpart Twin Lakes, 16 Mile also established residency in a former farm building. (FB.)

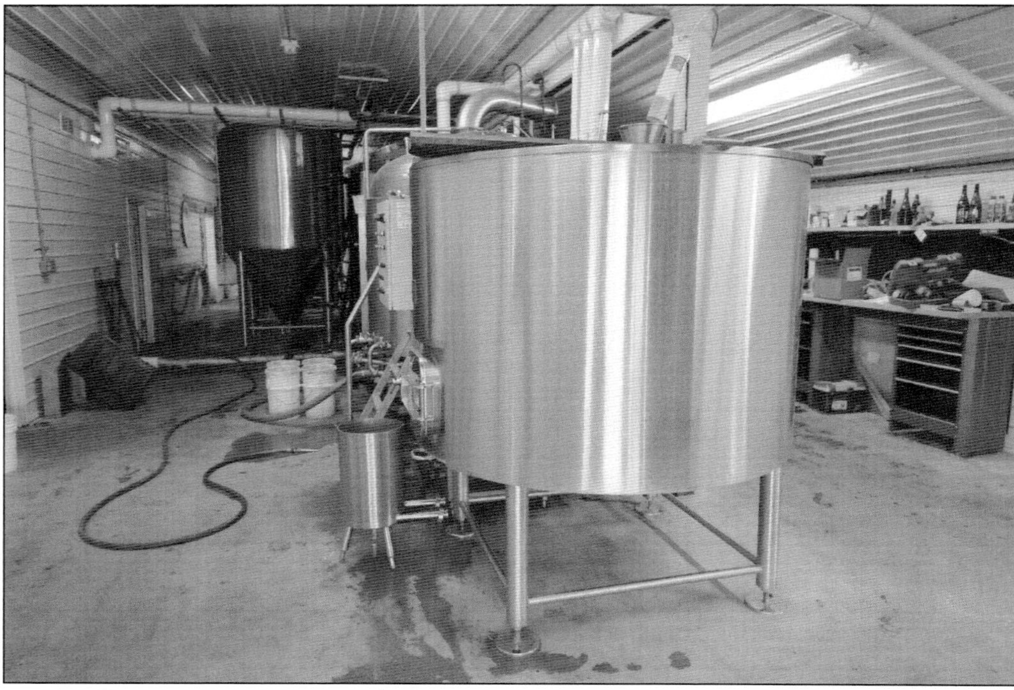

16 Mile Brewhouse, 2014. From the beginning, 16 Mile has produced its fine English-style ales utilizing its custom-designed 15-barrel Newlands Systems brewhouse. The company initially offered its Amber Sun, Blues' Golden, and Old Court ales on draft and in unique, beautifully decorated 22-ounce aluminum bottles. Initial production was about 3,000 barrels a year. (FB.)

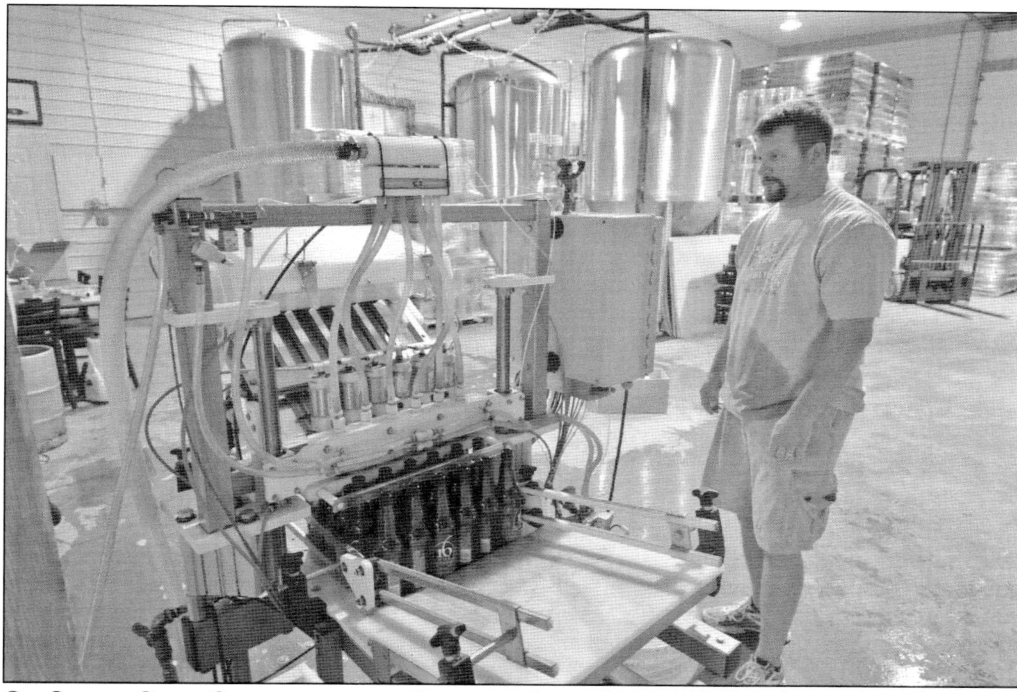

CO-OWNER CHAD CAMPBELL ON THE BOTTLING LINE, 2014. 16 Mile's slow and steady growth paid off, and in 2011 the company launched an expansion plan to increase its output to 10,000 barrels to better serve Delaware and the rest of the Delmarva Peninsula. As part of the plan, the brewery increased storage capacity and switched to packaging an expanded selection of its beers in standard 12-ounce glass bottles. (FB.)

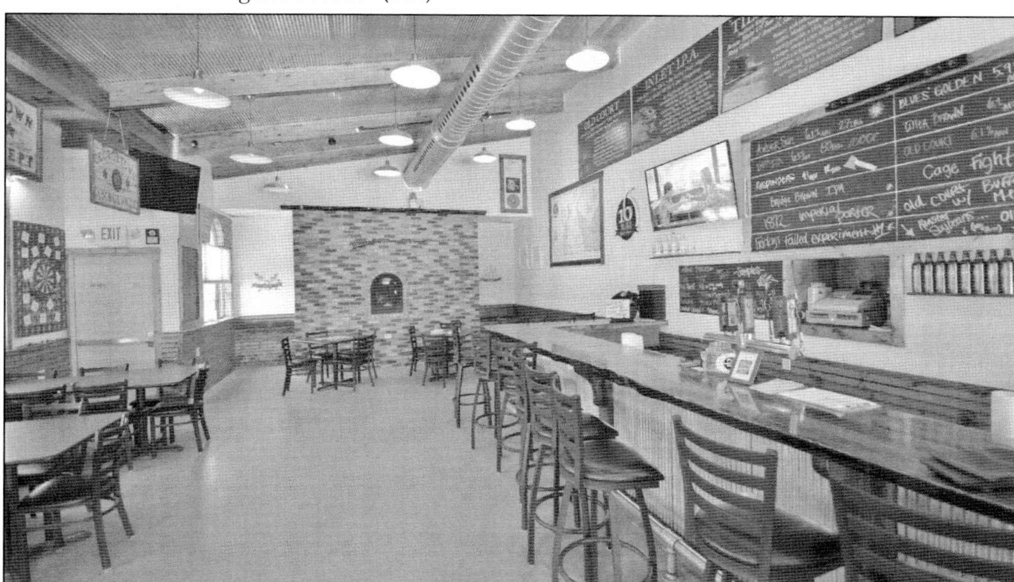

16 MILE TAVERN, 2014. This well-appointed taproom was also added as part of the brewery's 2011 expansion. The 16 Mile Tavern features a cozy bar offering a half dozen or more house brews and a small stage for musical performances. The brewery remains committed to producing quality ales for its market within a 100-mile radius of Georgetown. (FB.)

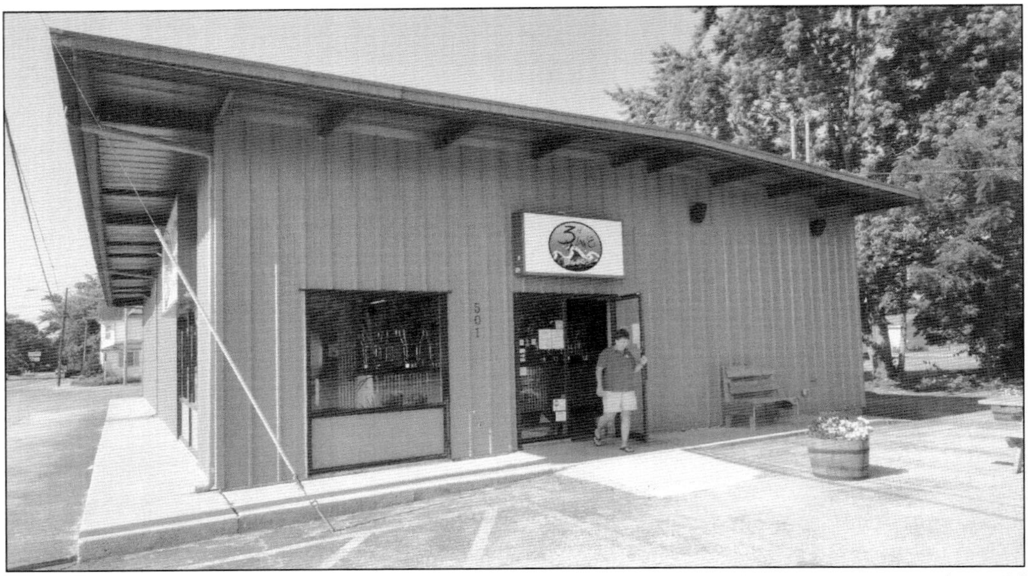

3RD WAVE BREWING COMPANY, DELMAR, 2014. Brothers Tom and John Knorr renovated an old Delmar grocery store on Bi-State Boulevard and opened Evolution Craft Brewery Company in April 2009. True to its name, the company quickly evolved into one of the region's most popular brands. In February 2012, the Knorrs relocated the business to a much larger facility in Salisbury, Maryland. Lori Clough and Suellen Vickers purchased the completely outfitted brewery within months of Evolution's departure. In September 2012, 3rd Wave Brewing Company opened for business. (FB.)

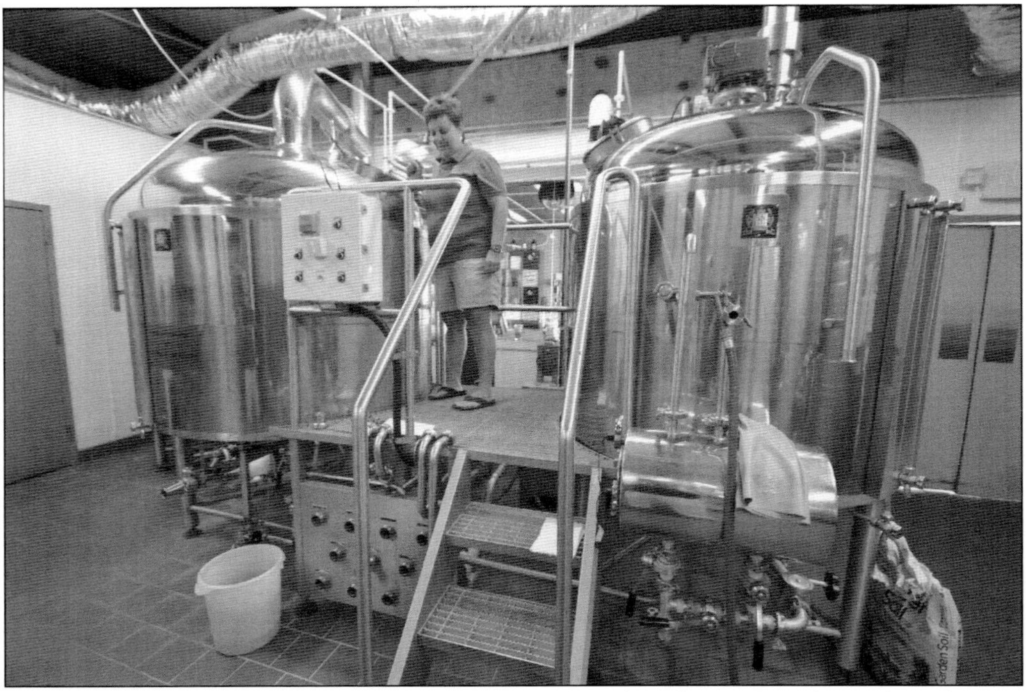

3RD WAVE'S BREWHOUSE, 2014. Lori Clough (pictured) and Suellen Vickers, former homebrewers and surfing aficionados, named their brewery for the third wave in a set, which is said to be the best one to surf. (FB.)

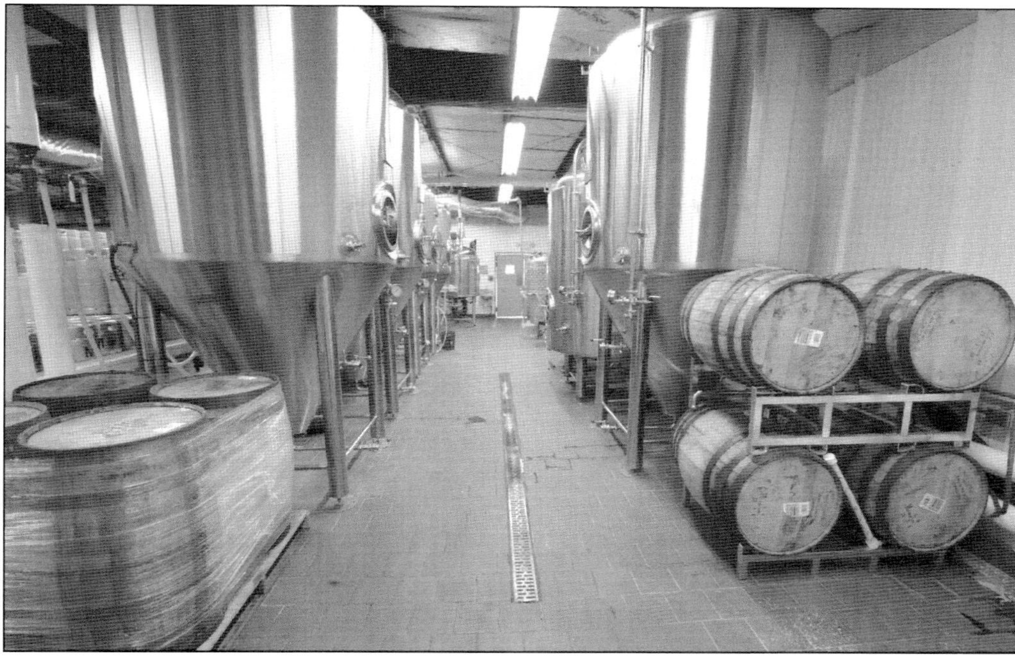

3rd Wave Brewery Fermentation Area. 3rd Wave's 10-barrel Newlands Systems brewhouse specializes in the production of IPAs, Belgian-style ales, and wheat beers, along with a variety of other handcrafted ales. While the brewery's main area of distribution is Delaware and Maryland, 3rd Wave continues to make a name for itself in the wider Mid-Atlantic region. (FB.)

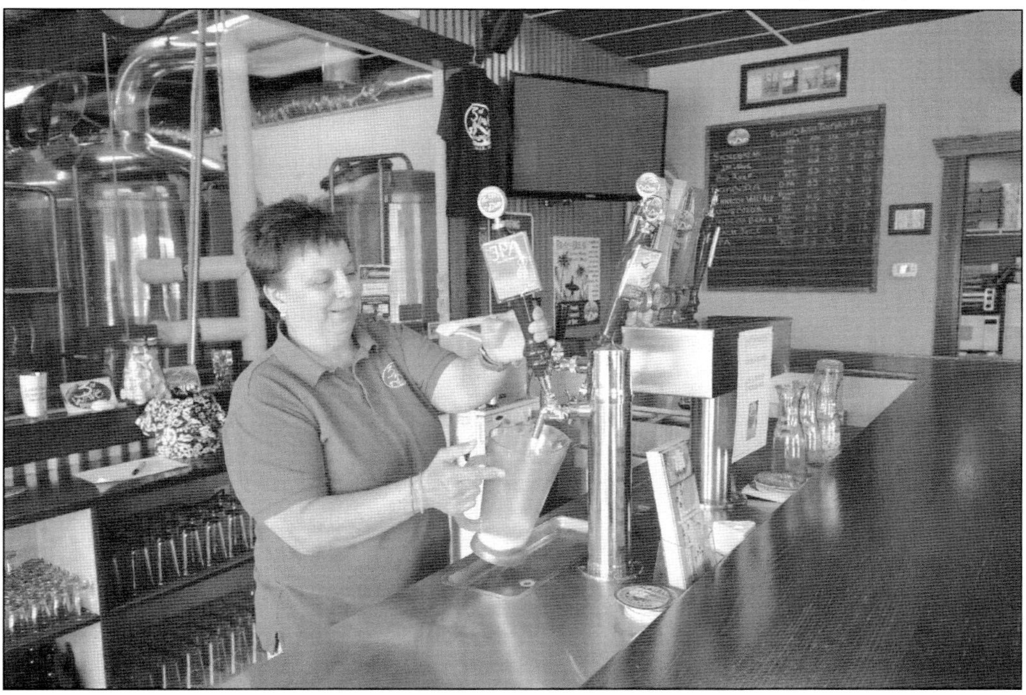

Lori Clough in the 3rd Wave Tasting Room, 2014. Locals and those farther afoot visit the 3rd Wave Tasting Room for fresh beer poured 10 feet from where it is made. The brewery also has an outdoor patio, which features live music during warmer months. (FB.)

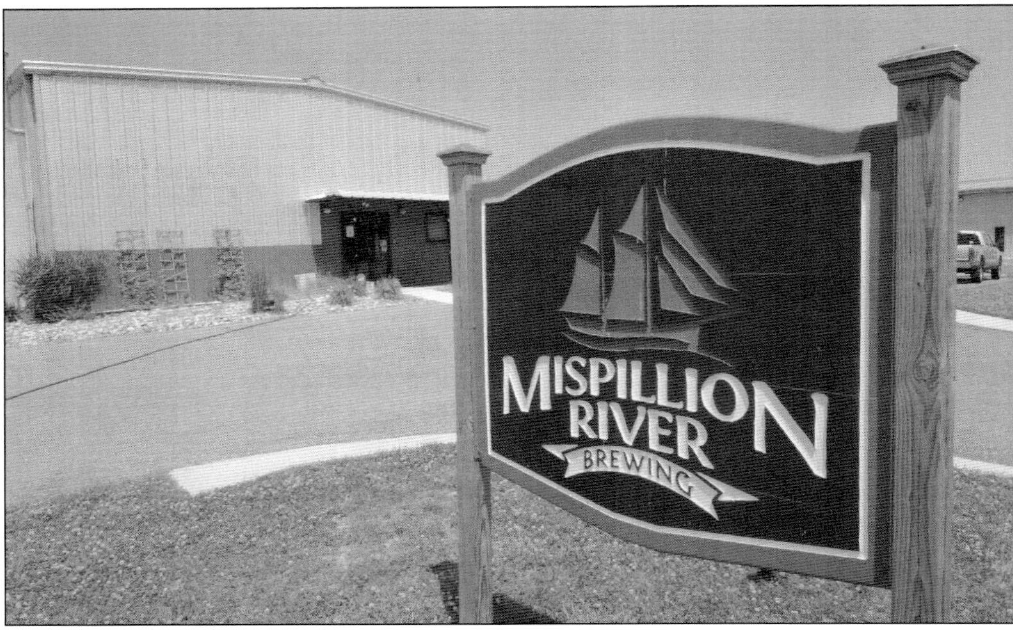

Mispillion River Brewing Company, Milford, 2014. When Milford's first-ever brewery opened at 255 Mullett Run Street in November 2013, Mispillion River Brewing Company owners Eric and Megan Williams did not imagine that their brewery would be at full capacity within its first year of operation. (FB.)

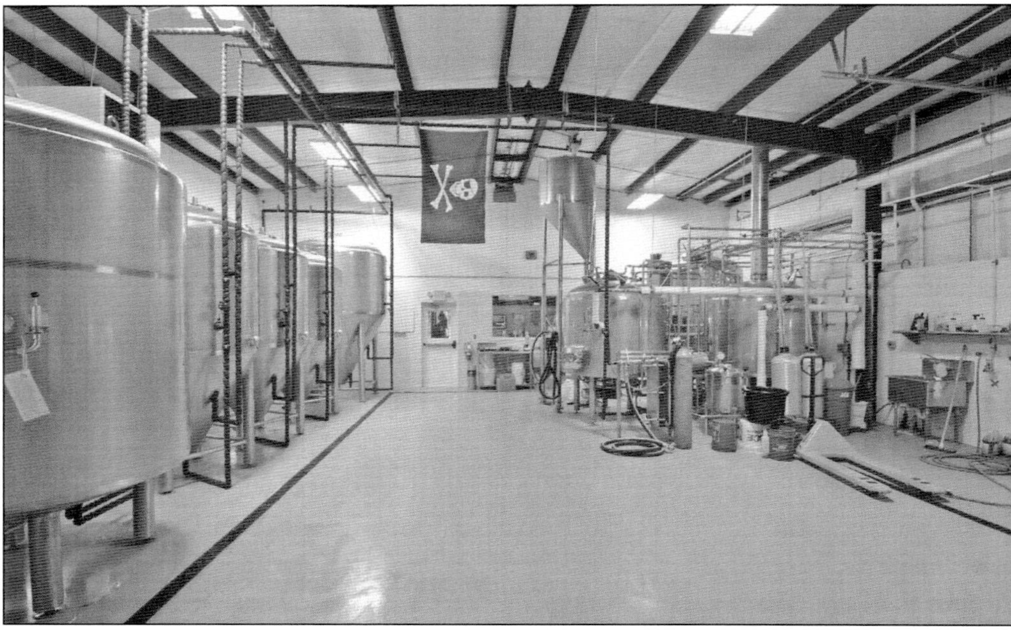

Mispillion River Brewhouse. Mispillion River has made phenomenal strides in a short time, producing over 1,000 barrels of beer and more than 100 different varieties. Remarkably, the brewery even won a silver medal at the 2014 World Beer Cup. The heart of the plant is Mispillion River's 15-barrel stainless-steel brewhouse supplied by Minnetonka Brewing and Equipment. A single 30-barrel fermenter, three additional 15-barrel fermenters, and a 30-barrel bright tank complete the works. (FB.)

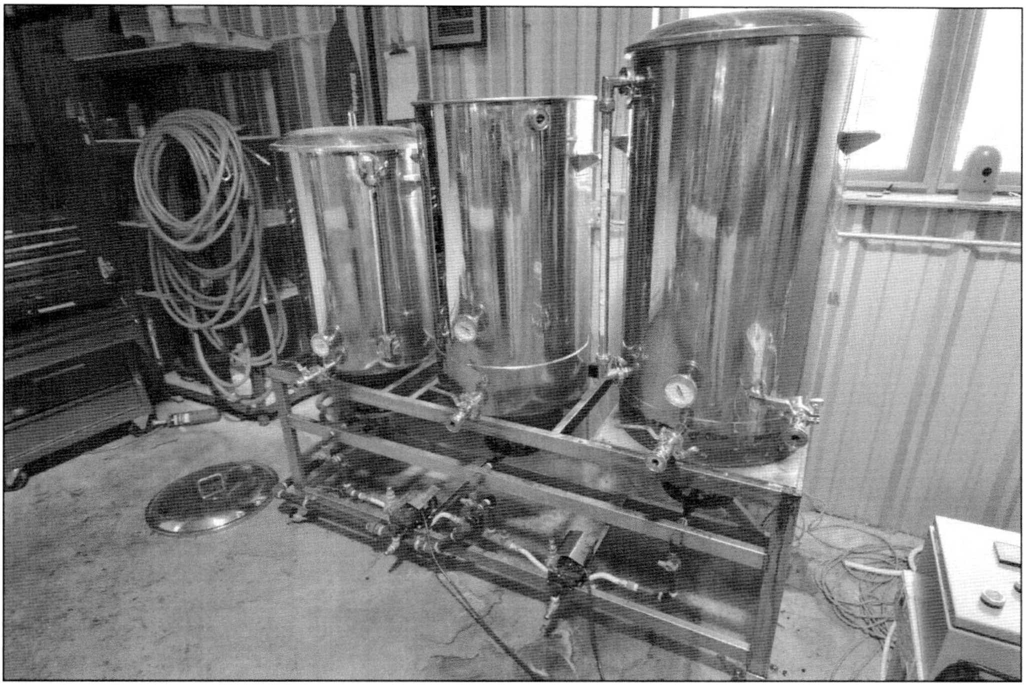

Mispillion River's Pilot System. A single-barrel pilot brewing system complements Mispillion River's larger main system. The miniature system allows for greater creativity and the production of a wide array of small-batch brews. In 2014, the brewery began canning its Reach Around IPA and the award-winning Beach Bum Joe Belgian ale for distribution throughout Delaware. (FB.)

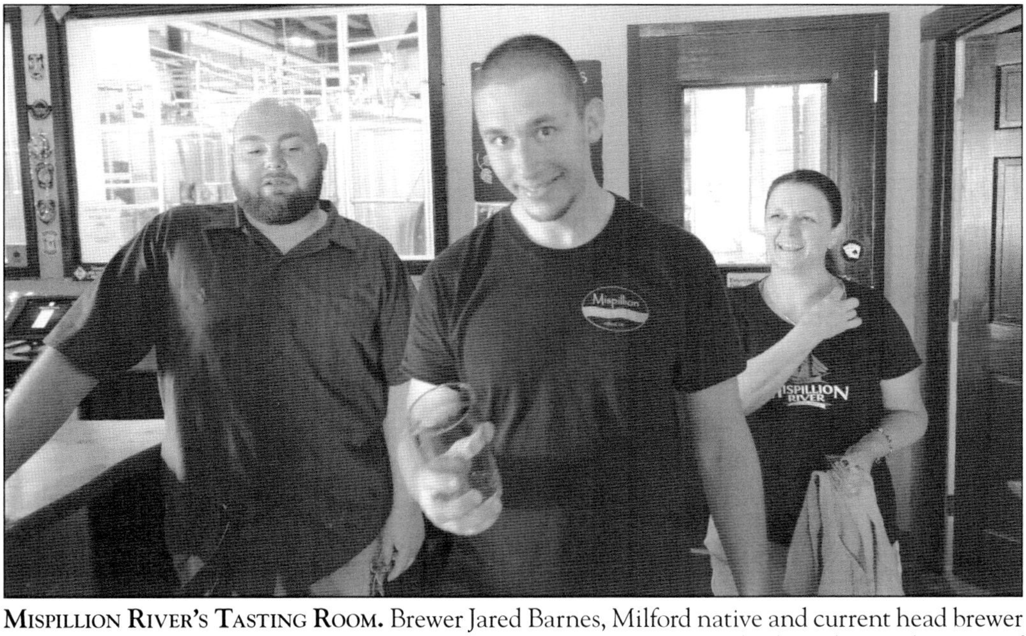

Mispillion River's Tasting Room. Brewer Jared Barnes, Milford native and current head brewer Ryan Maloney, and tasting room manager and co-owner Tammy Perlot have been a big part of Mispillion River's early success. The tasting room, featuring a rotating selection of 10 taps, has quickly become a popular community gathering spot in Milford for those in search of unique craft beer and weekend music. (FB.)

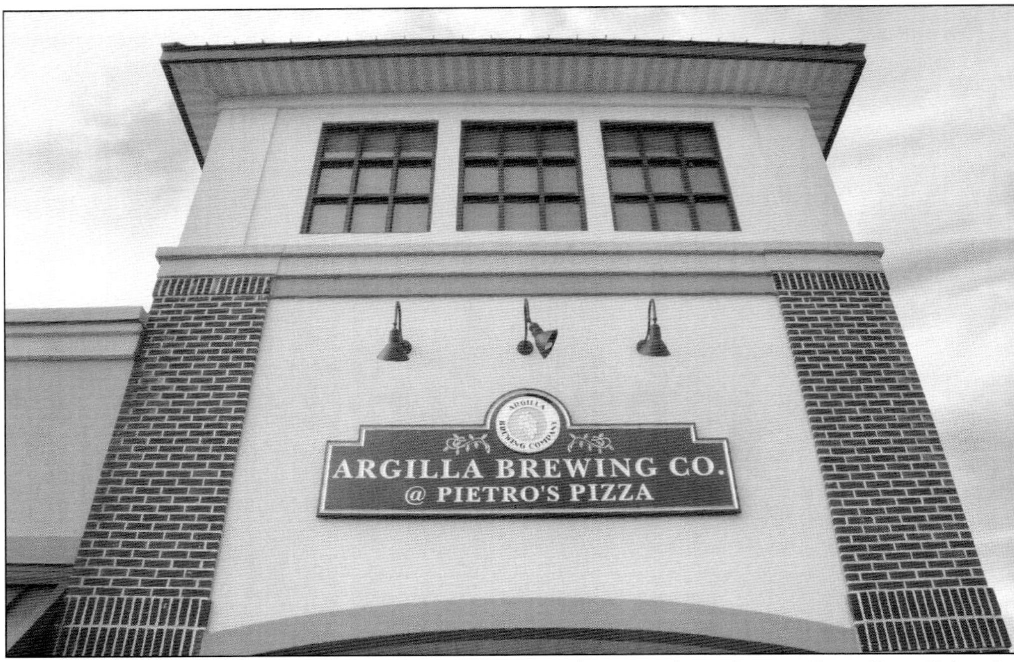

ARGILLA BREWING COMPANY, NEWARK, 2014. In 2011, longtime homebrewer Steve Powell decided to consolidate his popular Pietro's Pizza restaurant with a new nanobrewery. The name Clayton Brewing Company had already been taken, so Powell settled on Argilla, the Italian word for clay, which was close enough to the name Clayton. Argilla Brewing Company at Pietro's Pizza moved into suburban Newark's Meadowood Shopping Center in March 2012. (FB.)

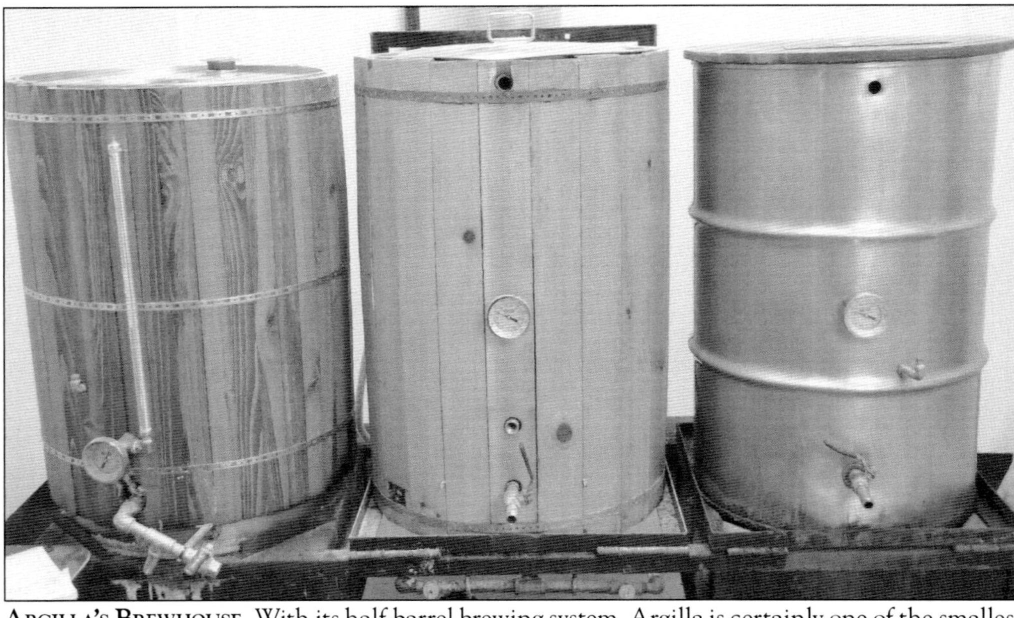

ARGILLA'S BREWHOUSE. With its half-barrel brewing system, Argilla is certainly one of the smallest breweries in Delaware. Argilla typically has four house beers on draft, along with a small selection of rotating guest beers from Delaware and regional breweries. The small size of Argilla's brewery is certainly no indication of the excellent quality of the ales produced by Powell and brewer Bryan Taylor. (FB.)

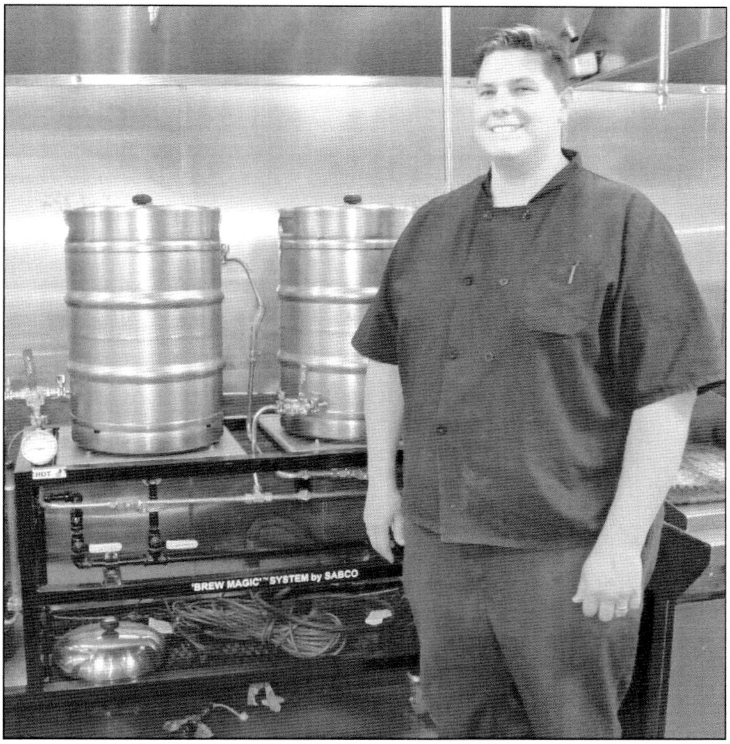

Paul Egnor, Pizza by Elizabeths, Greenville, 2015. Pizza by Elizabeths executive chef Paul Egnor, a veteran homebrewer, pitched the idea of starting on-site brewing to Betsy LeRoy, owner of the popular restaurant. In April 2014, Egnor began creating his unique ales in what is currently Delaware's smallest brewery. Using a 15-gallon Sabco Brew Master system, Egnor and assistant brewer Steve Lewis produce approximately 60 gallons of draft beer per week. (Author's collection.)

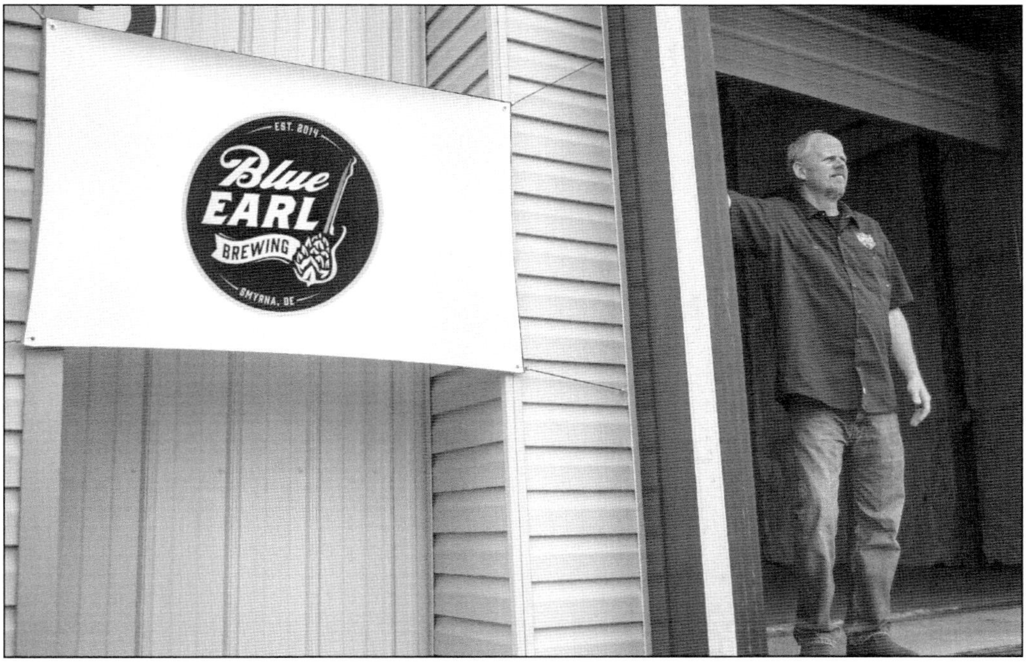

Owner Ron Price, Blue Earl Brewing Company, Smyrna, 2014. The newest entry in the ever-growing bevy of Delaware breweries, Blue Earl, opened on May 16, 2015. Price, a longtime homebrewer, anticipates that his 15-barrel production brewery will produce more than 500 barrels during its first year of operation. Blue Earl's kegged and prepackaged beer will be available throughout Delaware. (Jordan Dougherty.)

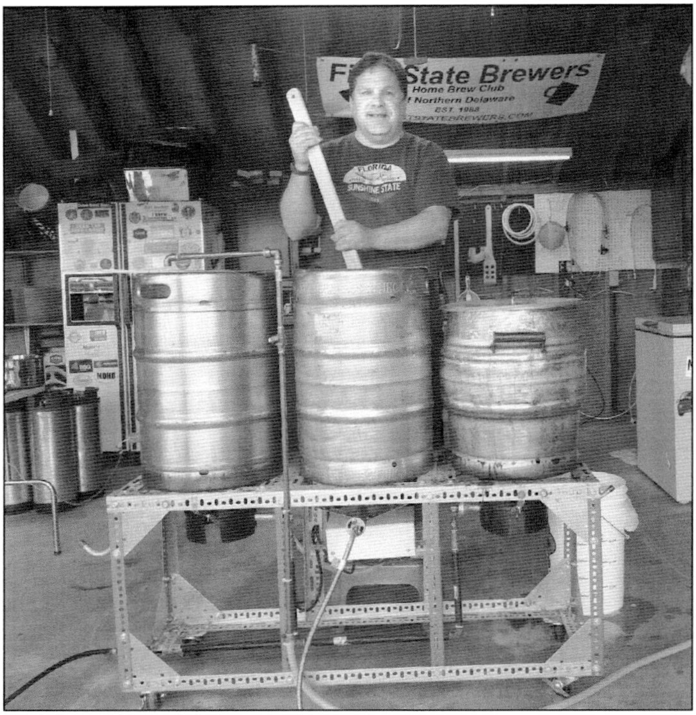

Scott Bieber's Home Brewery, Middletown, 2013. The First State Home Brewers, Delaware's first club officially sanctioned by the American Homebrewers Association, got its start in New Castle County in 1988. Bieber has been a club member since 1990 and served for a number of years as club president. First State Home Brewers members meet once a month to share brewing experiences, recipes, and homebrewed beer. (Scott Bieber.)

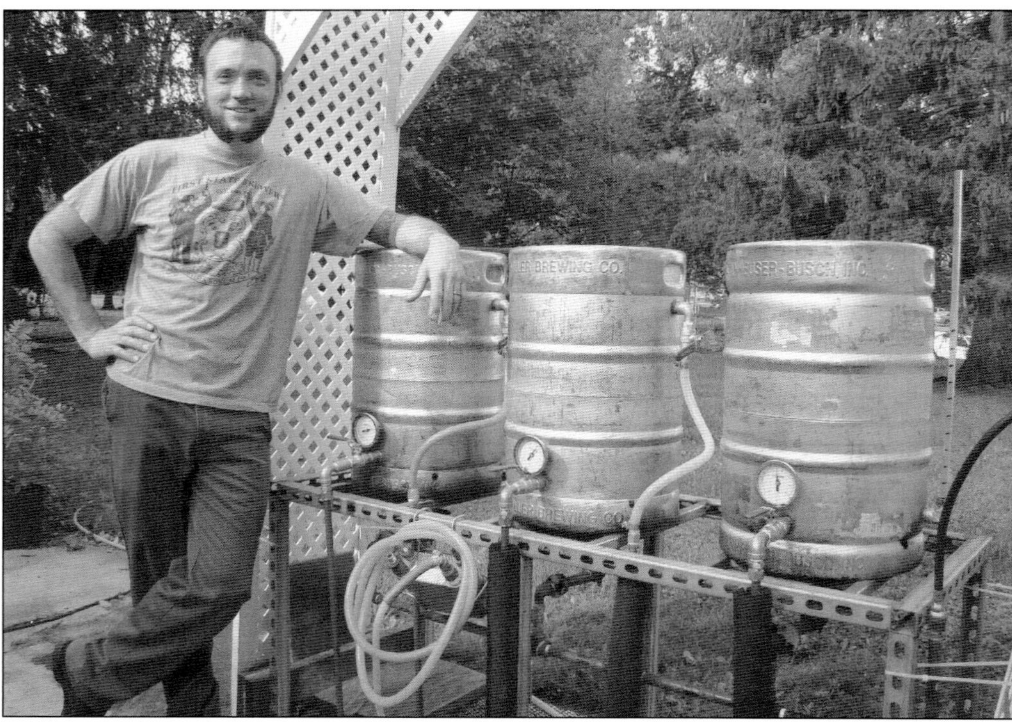

Joebob Jacobs's Home Brewery, Newark, 2014. Jacobs began homebrewing in 2007 and eventually joined the First State Home Brewers club. In 2014, he entered a partnership with Craig Wensell and Keith Hughes with the intention of starting the Bellefonte Brewing Company, a production brewery in the works to be located in North Wilmington. (Joebob Jacobs.)

About the Organizations

The author's proceeds from the sale of this book are being donated to the Delaware Historical Society and the Friends of Historic Riverview Cemetery. Please consider contributing directly to these two fine community organizations.

For more than 150 years, the nonprofit Delaware Historical Society has served as the statewide organization that preserves, explores, shares, and promotes Delaware history, heritage, and culture to strengthen the community.

Delaware Historical Society
505 North Market Street
Wilmington, Delaware 19801
www.dehistory.org

Friends of Historic Riverview Cemetery supports the restoration and preservation of Wilmington's most culturally diverse nonprofit public cemetery. Spread across 42 acres, Riverview serves as the final resting place for more than 36,000 people, including many who worked in the brewing and allied industries in the 19th and early 20th centuries. The cemetery was placed in the National Register of Historic Places by the US Department of the Interior on July 3, 2012.

Friends of Historic Riverview Cemetery
P.O. Box 2173
Wilmington, Delaware 19899
www.riverviewcem.com